M000307509

The Creation of Value by Living Labour

A Normative and Empirical Study

VOL. II

Canut International Publishers

Berlin London Istanbul Santiago

Cheng Enfu   Wang Guijin   Zhu Kui

The Creation of Value by Living Labour
A Normative and Empirical Study

VOL. II

Translating Editor Alan Freeman   Sun Yexia

"B&R Book Program"
The Creation of Value by Living Labour: A Normative and Empirical Study
Volume II
by Cheng Enfu, Wang Guijin and Zhu Kui
Liu Hui and Sun Yexia, translators
Alan Freeman and Sun Yexia, translating editors
Originally published (in Chinese) by Shanghai University of Finance and
Economics Press
Original Chinese Copyright © 2005
1st Chinese Edition (ISBN: 978-7-81098-525-3)

Canut International Publishers
Canut Turkey, Batı Mh. Karanfil Sk.. 10, Istanbul, Turkey
Canut Germany, Heerstr. 266, D-47053, Duisburg, Germany
Canut UK, 12a Guernsay Road, London E11 4BJ, England
Tel: +49-216-499-75-09
www.canutbooks.com / info@canutbooks.com

Copyright © 2019 of the 1st English Edition
All rights reserved. No part of this book may be used or reproduced in any
manner whatsoever without the written permission of the publisher.

Paperback Edition
ISBN: 978-605-7693-04-4

About the Authors

Cheng Enfu, born in July 1950, is the Director of the Academy of Marxist Philosophy, director of the Western Economic Studies Center of CASS, and the President of WAPE (World Association of Political Economy). Cheng Enfu is also the chief editor of the journals *International Critical Thought* and *World Review of Political Economics* (World Association of Political Economics) published by Routledge and Pluto Press, respectively. His academic expertise is in theoretical economics. His other works include:

Enfu Cheng, Xin Xiangyang. "Fundamental elements of the China model", *International Critical Thought*. Volume 1, 2011 - Issue 1;

Enfu Cheng, "Four Theoretical Hypotheses of Modern Marxist Political Economy", *Social Sciences in China*, Autumn 2007, 3-17;

Enfu Cheng, Xiaoqin Ding. "A Theory of China's 'Miracle': Eight Principles of Contemporary Chinese Political Economy", *Monthly Review*, Jan 01, 2017;

Enfu Cheng, Yexia Sun. "Israeli Kibbutz: A Successful Example of Collective Economy", *World Review of Political Economy*, Vol. 6, No. 2 (Summer 2015), pp. 160-175;

Enfu Cheng, Jiankun Gao. "Comments on and Prospects for China's Current Macroeconomic Development: Ten Measures to Guide the Economic New Normal", *World Review of Political Economy*, 2016, 7;

Enfu Cheng, Zhongbao Wang. "Enriching and Developing Marxism in the Twenty-First Century in Various Aspects: Six Definitions of Marxism", *International Critical Thought*, 2018, 2;

Enfu Cheng. "Marxism and Its Sinicized Theory as the Guidance of the Chinese Model: The 'Two Economic Miracles' of the New China", *World Review of Political Economy*, Vol. 9, No. 3, Fall 2018;

Enfu Cheng. "La interdependencia económica y comercial como posible amortiguador del conflicto", *Vanguardia Dossier,* Vol.70, No. 4, 2018.

Wang Guijin, born in 1965, Doctor of economics, Shanghai University of Finance and Economics, currently works in the finance bureau of Huangshan city, Anhui Province.

Zhu Kui, born in 1974, Doctor of economics, is a tutor in Huazhong Agricultural University.

Contents

Explanatory note

The research findings of this book are based on key research projects of the Ministries of Education of China and Shanghai led by Professor Cheng Enfu, president of the Academy of Marxist Philosophy and director of Western Economic Studies Center of CASS.

This is the second of two volumes, containing the last 7 of 18 chapters.

Professor Cheng was responsible for designing the structure and framework of this book. He also helped finalize the ideas in the first part of this book and made final revisions for the whole book. Professor Cheng contributed the first chapter. Wang Guijin, Professor Cheng's doctoral student, contributed Chapters 3–11. Zhu Kui, another doctoral student of Prof Cheng, contributed Chapters 3–8 of this volume. Prof. Qi Guangying contributed Chapter 2.

The English translation was edited by Alan Freeman with the diligent aid of Sun Yexia.

Considering the complexity of the research projects, the authors of this book welcome criticisms should any inappropriateness occurs. The authors of this book may be reached at 65344718@vip.163.com.

A note on the translation

Translation of a technical work in a specialist field is never an easy matter. This work was originally translated into English by Chinese mother-tongue speakers; I then rendered this into colloquial English, taking care as far as possible to ensure that both the sense of the text, and the mathematical formulae and tables, were as true to the original as possible. In this I was enormously helped by Sun Yexia who fielded an endless stream of queries over the years that the translation took up, and without whose assistance and knowledge, the translation would have been impossible.

Translation always involves the difficult choice between faithful accuracy to the language of the original, and communication in the idioms to which the reader is accustomed. The choice is all the more difficult when technical terms are involved, which may have acquired, in the literature of the two languages, nuances of meaning which differ. We opted to render the text in the most comprehensible terms employing wherever possible the technical language that is in general use in the English literature on Marx's value theory, on the grounds that Marx's own language follows recognized conventions by the official translations of his and Engels' works, and the meaning of any variations in usage is better established from the context than from an exact rendering.

An example that can clarify this point is the so-called 'two equalities', which have dogged the post-Marx literature on transformation, being first that the total price of production of outputs is equal to their total value, and second that total surplus value is equal to total profit. This expression is the most common in the English literature but there are variants: Seton for example refers to 'invariant postulates'. The authors, perhaps more correctly, employed a term most accurately translated as 'invariances' or 'invariant equations'. For the most part we have employed the term 'equalities' but the reader should be aware that the three terms 'equalities', 'invariance postulates' and 'invariant equations' are interchangeable. For this, and some other terms, we have been guided by context, and have steered clear of forced uniformity.

A second vexed issue is that of citation. The Chinese authors have generally worked from the Chinese versions of cited texts where these were available, which leads to problems if the English is 'retranslated' from the Chinese, since this will not correspond to the English original. We have made every effort to locate the original English text of cited works but in some cases this has not been possible. In these cases, the citations given refer to the Chinese text that the authors used.

In naming cited authors, where possible we have used the full Chinese name, in the normal Chinese order (family name first).

Alan Freeman
Geopolitical Economy Research Group, University of Manitoba

Acronyms used in the text

GDP	gross domestic product
GNP	gross national product
MELT	monetary expression of labor time
OCC	organic composition of capital
R&D	research and development
S&T	science and technology/scientific and technological

1
Introduction

This is the second of two volumes comprising *The Creation of Value by Living Labour: A Normative and Empirical Study*. The first opened with a review of the literature on labor's role in production, laying the ground, as the work's title suggests, for a detailed empirical study of creative, scientific, and management labour in China, conceived of as an economy with mixed forms of property.

Its central concern was how best to maximize the social and economic benefits of these highly productive forms of labour, extending these benefits to the whole of society by preventing their monopolization and misuse by property-owners.

The present volume underpins that analysis with a detailed discussion of the Marxist literature on the relation between labor, value and price. This may come as a surprise to both neoclassical scholars and to Marxist and other heterodox scholars. Why do Chinese economists consider a Victorian 'minor post-Ricardian', as Samuelson (1957, 911) derisively labelled Marx, relevant to the economy of the modern powerhouse that is China? And why should Westerners pay any attention to Chinese discussions of obscure sixty-year-old debates, riddled with mathematical subtleties and apparently confined to the ivory towers?

To answer this question, it is necessary to turn it upside down. It has come to the attention of the world that China's economic successes, for a long time overlooked or dismissed by Western writers, are without precedent. No country has sustained a growth rate so large for so long, or raised so many people out of extreme poverty in a mere thirty years. No nation of any size except South Korea has achieved Chinese levels of development since the epoch of high imperialism. Even were China's growth to stop tomorrow,

1

its economic achievements to date would be unparalleled in the history of capitalism.

These achievements are, first and foremost, the result of the policies China has adopted, and these are, in turn, profoundly influenced by China's revolutionary origins, by the role of the Communist Party of China and its leadership within the Chinese state, and consequently by the influence of Marx's ideas. These thus have a direct bearing on one of the most economically successful experiments in world history.

This is not to assert Marx's ideas alone are responsible for China's success, nor that their application is some kind of guarantee of further success, nor even that China has correctly understood or applied them. China's economic policies are a unique blend of carefully considered judgements, pragmatic experimentation, and the important capacity to absorb and apply ideas from a wide range of sources. It would be entirely wrong to think of Chinese intellectual life, as Western critics are inclined to do, as a dogmatically organized monolith in which Marxism serves only to whip dissenters into line. Indeed, within Chinese University economics departments, neoclassical ideas predominate, which can hardly be squared with the fairytale of doctrinaire dominance.

What *is* the case is that Marx's ideas play a role. His influence is ubiquitous. Almost every University has a school of Marxism. The Marxism section of the Chinese Academy of Social Sciences, which played a substantial role in the present volume, is a respected and influential organization. Xi Jinping's speech,[1] on the 200th anniversary of Marx's birth, went beyond a formal eulogy: it was a statement of intent. When Xi states 'Marxism is a theory of practice that directs the people to change the world' these are not empty words but a commitment to take practical measures, strengthening and funding Marxist research and study, re-enforcing the influence of Marxist theory and developing it in ways that can guide Chinese policy. Within the CPC, the leading organ of the state, Marx's theories continue to be widely studied and referred to.

---

1   'Marx's theory still shines with truth' http://www.china.org.cn/china/2018-05/04/content_51113925.htm, accessed 23 June 2019

The esteem in which Marx's ideas are held is a result of China's revolutionary origins and its impact on China's wide-ranging and passionate discussions on economic and foreign policy. China's liberation and the foundation of its modern state, in a monumental war led by Communists against both a murderous occupier and the intense and militarized resistance of its landlord and other pro-imperialist classes, is not a remote historical event. It lives in the immediate family memory of every Chinese citizen.

Communist and Marxist ideas do not occupy, in Chinese thinking, the same mental space as in late Soviet society, in which they fell victim to a kind of universal cynicism, percolating downwards from leaders who had effectively given up on the doctrine they preached and decided to become capitalists.[2] That historically unique state of affairs was a reaction to a seventy-year siege of the world's first Communist-led state, and to the immense sacrifices which saved the world from Hitler. These harsh experiences fueled a deep-seated urge to end isolation by any means. Coupled to the historical pro-Europeanism of Russian society, arising from its origins in the dissolution of the world-spanning Mongol Empire, this expressed itself in the widespread idea, still entertained in Russian intellectual circles despite a welcome recent revival of anti-neoliberal ideas, that 'Marxism failed' in the Soviet experiment.

Things are very much otherwise in China. The view that 'Marx was wrong' or that 'Marx's time is past' is of course widespread, like anywhere in the world, but the defeatism with which these ideas are expressed in the West, and in Russia, is absent. China is a society as confident of its past as of it future; it knows that notwithstanding the ancient civilization it sprang from, of which is justly proud, it would not, in its present form, exist, without Marx's contribution.

Not least (as can be inferred from Xi's speech) in the thinking of the left wing of Chinese society, understanding and developing Marx's ideas is not of mere academic interest but is a practical matter. In the first volume, when the authors argue that society should reward capitalist owners not in proportion to their capital but in proportion to their labour – albeit recognizing the high value-producing and value-production-enabling quality of the

2   See for example Kotz and Weir (1997), Dzarasov (2013)

managerial and scientific skills that the entrepreneur contributes – they are discussing a central issue in China's contemporary class struggles, which with good reason they consider decisive for China's future.

Chart 1: Average Annual growth of GDP per capita of the Industrialised countries

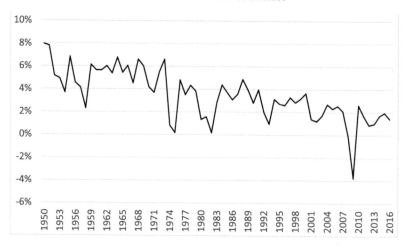

Notes: See Freeman (2019a) for detailed description of sources.
The graph exhibits the population-weighted average of the annual growth rate of GDP in constant local currencies of 2010.

In summary, to deny the potential economic importance of Marx's ideas, or their connection to China's successes, is simply to fly in the face of the facts. These ideas do not manifest a romantic attachment to a long-dead thinker but constitute a live force in what is probably the most important economic development in the world today.

Now let us turn the spotlight around. If Western commentators permit themselves to judge 'Marxism' by the performance of the Soviet economy, shouldn't they also judge their own pet theories by the performance of their own economies? How does the performance of the rest of the world stand up to the claim that 'neoliberalism' works – or indeed, the wider claim that neoclassical economics as a whole is superior to Marxism?

As Chart 1 shows, the annual growth rate of the industrialized or 'Global North' countries – those the IMF designates 'advanced' – declined systematically throughout the postwar era, and during the period of China's rise, fell from its highest point in the neoliberal era in 1986 at 5% to the catastrophic low of –4% following the 2008 crash. Since then it has not risen above 2%, a quarter of its highest postwar level and a third of its consistent average in the 1960s.

Chart 2: Gap between the annual growth of GDP per capita of China and that of the Advanced ('Global North') countries

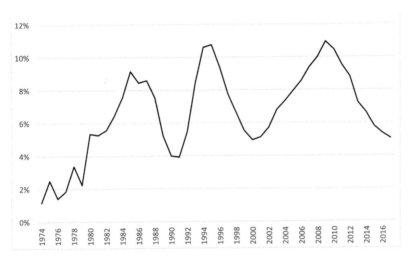

Notes: Source data from Freeman (2019b) and author calculations. Base data is measured in constant 2010 local currencies. For the Global North annual growth is weighted by population as for Chart 1 before subtracting it from China's annual growth. The chart shows a moving average exhibited at the end of a four-year period so that, for example, the 11% peak of 2009 refers to the years 2005-2009 and thus includes the financial crash of 2008.

Moreover, neoliberalism alone cannot be held responsible. The decline definitively started with the pre-neoliberal 1974 slump, which ushered in a decade of low growth from which neoliberalism provided only a temporary respite.

Are there then no grounds for concluding, by the identical reasoning of the critics of 'Marxism', that 'Western Economics' has failed?

5

A comparison of the two growth rates, shown in Chart 2, is particularly striking. China's average growth rate, since 1980, has never been less than 4% higher than the North's. Moreover, the gap has a counter-cyclical component, tending to rise during the slumps of the capitalist world and decrease during its booms. China's growth, this suggests, has a major autonomous component, 'de-linking' it from the increasingly traumatic crises afflicting the North.[3] Both facts belie any simplistic explanation for China's success, such as the superficial idea that it is somehow a simple consequence of 'embracing capitalism'. The rest of the world has 'embraced capitalism' for at least a hundred and fifty years but shows scant signs of emulating China's achievements.

This judgement calls for no extreme or even contested assertions. We have not claimed China is perfect, or socialist, because we do not need to, in order to recognize that, by the standards of the neoclassical mainstream itself, China's *economic* achievements are systematically superior to those countries that embrace mainstream theory. As a simple empirical test of whether Marxism is worth paying attention to, our comparison is as legitimate as it is salutary.

Neither need we argue that this success is inevitable, or will continue forever. Of course, new factors are coming into play. Trumpism – a backhanded compliment to China's success – is only one signal of a new stage in what Desai (2013) designates the 'geopolitical economy' of the multipolar world order. The Silk Belt and Road initiative, the growing economic co-operation between China, Russia, and a wider group of countries centered on the Shanghai Cooperation Organization, the growing tensions among the NATO powers, their headlong drive towards war, and the inexorable if painful demise of the dollar, are all game-changers, and it would be foolish to project past trends into this new period without taking these new developments into account.

Yet even if China's growth stopped tomorrow – which commentators agree is highly unlikely – the past forty years alone raise a big question mark over the twin tropes that Marxism is an economic failure, and neoclassical economics is a success. This is a primary reason for the present volume's interest; however its importance goes beyond this simple fact, as we shall see.

---

3   See Freeman (2019a, 2019b) and the important factual website Ross (n.d.)

A landmark encounter

This volume may superficially appear, especially to readers skeptical of Marx's contribution, as yet another scholastic debate about how many Marxist angels can dance on the head of a Ricardian pin: a fruitless hagiological discussion in place of looking at practical reality. Even Marxists may question the need for yet another book on the 'transformation problem'. Has the subject not been done to death?

Actually, such a reaction would be entirely misplaced because this book is no such enterprise. The authors set out to assess a *theory*, not a man: this they designate the Labor Theory of Value (LTV).[4] It consists of a scrupulous discussion of a problem within that theory, namely how, if labor is the source of all value, and if value ultimately determines the magnitude of price, can goods sell at other than their values?' Can we account for the deviations of price from labor-time values so as to lay bare what is really happening in a capitalist economy? And can we do so without abandoning the foundational postulate shared by Smith, Ricardo and Marx, that the magnitude of value is determined by the time of labor? This is the much-vaunted 'transformation problem', not really a problem at all but as the authors stress, a research field.

Second, the starting point is not just Marx's work but the whole way the LTV entered modern economics, starting in ancient Greece and arriving at present-day China by way of Petty, the Physiocrats, the classicals, Marx and modern Marxism. The volume then studies the modern history of that theory. It presents, and critiques, both Chinese and Western Marxists through the lens of the 'transformation problem'. It would however be mistaken to see it as simply a recapitulation of that issue. It should be read as a statement of how Chinese scholars understand debates on the LTV both in their own country and in the West.

4   The term 'labor theory of value' is Kautsky's, coined to counter Böhm-Bawerk's distinction between the (allegedly wrong) 'objective' value theories of Marx and the classics, and the 'subjective' theories of the marginalists. Marx uses the broader term '*The* Theory of Value'. This is a stronger usage than Kautsky's because Marx does not speak of a *variety* of theories of value, but says that in *any* rigorous formalization of value, its magnitude must be determined by the time of labor engaged in producing commodities. In this volume we use the authors' terminology, having expressed these reservations.

Third, as we have just shown, the implications of this discussion are supremely 'real-world' because they bear directly on the future of the Chinese and world economy. The attitude is that Marx is the most systematic exponent of a practical theory, which citizens and their government need to know about in order to make good policy judgements.

This is a quite different viewpoint from that of scholars in countries where Marxism has no influence on policy. It contrasts with Western scholarship, especially the recent developments covered in the final chapter, which has been obliged to focus on defending Marx, in the face of a determined onslaught unleashed at the turn of the last century, unrelentingly pursued through two wars and their aftermath by both right and left, and culminating in the wholesale renunciation of Marx's legacy by most of the Marxists themselves and the almost complete exclusion of the LTV from academia and intellectual life.

The book therefore constitutes a landmark encounter between two traditions, each arising from specific circumstances, which have come to remarkably similar conclusions. Its interest lies not just in the scholarship itself, but in the significant agreements that this registers, making it possible to identify a research agenda for a genuinely emancipatory economic science, in which all scholars can participate on the basis of mutual respect and understanding.

The position of Marx within debates on the theory of value

Since the topic of the book is a theory, not a man, why do the ideas of one particular man – Marx – count for so much within it, and more generally in Marxist discussions? We approach this from the basic propositions of Marx's formulation of the LTV, which can be summarized as follows:

Proposition 1: labour, engaged in the production of commodities, is the sole source of value;

Proposition 2: the owners of the means of production appropriate what remains of this value, after deducting the value consumed in producing it, and the value consumed by the labor that produced it.

From these he deduces a number of conclusions, including (in Volume III) for the case where commodities are sold at their price of production rather than their value, having however purchased the means to make these commodities at their values. These conclusions include, notably:

Conclusion 1: the total value of the commodities produced in any period is equal to the total price of production of the same commodities.

Conclusion 2: the total value appropriated by the owners of the means of production is unchanged.

These amount to the assertion, in mathematical terms, that value and profit are invariants of distribution, although Marx does not put it this way. In mathematical terms also they constitute a generalization of propositions 1-2, in that Marx shows propositions 1 and 2 still hold, when the restriction that they must be purchased and sold at their value is removed, for the most important and paradigmatic case when goods are sold in such a way as to equalize profits, though purchased at their value.

To this we may add a third, integral to Marx's theory because it forms the basis his theory of capital accumulation.[5]

Conclusion 3: the ratio between profit, and accumulated privately-owned value, decreases as long as accumulation proceeds.

The book focusses on the first two conclusions but it should be noted that the third is an essential component of Marx's LTV and a major target of Marx's critics, especially his Marxist critics. The charge that it is logically false forms a substantial part of the attempt to delegitimize his theory, to which we turn later.

The propositions and the conclusion constitute what logicians call a 'formalization' of the theory. This allows us to test the validity of theory with a combination of inductive and deductive evaluation, standard in other branches of science. Central to any such test is the basic criterion of induction: do the propositions and their conclusions correspond to what is observed in real life? But in order to apply inductive methods, we also need criteria of logic: on which propositions do the conclusions actually depend?

---

5   The law of accumulation covers many issues too numerous to list, but certainly includes the long-term development of capitalism, its crises and their resolutions. This includes trends such as the long-term decline of Chart 1, or the crash of 2008, which neoclassical theory failed to explain, foresee, or forestall. On these issues see Heinrich (2013) and the response from Kliman et al. (2017)

Given this standard procedure, why is the person of Marx relevant? Well, firstly, Marx has presented a more cogent and rigorous argument in support of this theory than anyone before or since. To study the LTV without reference to his writing would be akin to studying relativity without Einstein.

The second point concerns a profound but common misapprehension: paying attention to Marx is not the same as treating him as a doctrinal source of truth. This is pertinent because the latest phase of the Western scholarship, covered in Chapter 8, arises as noted from Western Marxist scholars' need to respond to the frontal attacks on Marx which dominate Western intellectual life. For this reason, scholars from the 'Temporal Single System Interpretation' (TSSI) of Marx, to which this writer belongs, pay special attention to the question 'what actually was Marx's theory?' This is often misunderstood, or even maligned, as a doctrinal or dogmatic quest. This criticism is clearly expressed by Laibman who writes (Freeman, Kliman and Wells 2007, 1)

> *The new orthodoxy in Marxist political economy goes beyond the mere affirmation of the foundation concepts of Marxism as the most fruitful basis for continuing development of critical and revolutionary social science. The new orthodox Marxists (NOMists) assert that Marx's formulations, in both the theory of value and the analysis of capitalist accumulation and crisis, are literally and completely correct; that Marx made no errors, bequeathing to us a system that is complete in all essentials; that Marx was far ahead of his time, and totally misunderstood in the hapless 20th century.*

In parenthesis, this claim is factually false: no TSSI scholar has ever claimed that Marx is literally correct or complete. But more importantly, it misses the point. TSSI scholarship does not address the question 'how can we learn truth from Marx's writings?' but 'how can we ascertain what Marx's theory actually is?' The reason is very straightforward: if we don't accurately interpret the theory, how can we verify whether it is wrong or right?

As mentioned, and as with any science, in order to judge whether a theory is valid, we have to assess how well it can explain reality, in comparison with the alternatives. We can devise and apply systematic procedures to this

10

end.[6] But as also mentioned, in order to conduct such an enquiry, we must know what any given theory *really* says, and what its presuppositions really are. Otherwise we are not actually testing that theory, but something else.

We can illustrate this with an example from the Keynesian literature. Keynes' theory is almost universally represented, especially in undergraduate textbooks, by the static ISLM diagrams proposed by Hicks (1937) in his famous 'Mr. Keynes and the "Classics"; a suggested interpretation'. Hicks's interpretation is widely contested,[7] especially stoutly by left Keynesians like Joan Robinson who coined the epithet 'Bastard Keynesianism' for this body of theory.

However, it is also frequently claimed, especially by neoliberal writers, that Keynes's theory was 'refuted' in the 1970s when repeated monetary and fiscal stimuli failed to forestall the slump of 1974, simply stoking inflationary pressures.

But was this a true test of Keynes' theory? If the full raft of his proposed policies had been adopted, not least the Chapter 19 proposal for the 'socialization of investment' and the 'euthanasia of the rentier', not to mention his proposed restructuring of the world banking system, roundly defeated by the Americans at Bretton Woods, would the result have been the same? In short, was it really Keynes' theory that was found wanting, or a bastard theory masquerading as his?

Nobody claims that the massive (and, frankly, turgid) literature on Keynes arises from a dogmatic belief that his ideas are "literally and completely correct". The point is to ensure, when evaluating economic propositions by observing the effect of an action, which theory the action really puts to the test, before designating it a 'proof' that the theory was wrong.

Why should the attempt to identify Marx's real theory be thought of otherwise?

---

6   These procedures include *pluralism* (Fullbrook 2013) which allows us to test different alternative explanations against each other. They also involve a different view of logic from that espoused by most heterodox critics of 'deductivism' following Dow (1987) who argues that axiomatic reasoning is a means of deriving doctrinal truths from unchallenged assumptions, and should be replaced, at least within economics, by a different type of logic. We argue that this is a misuse of formal logic and the solution is to use it properly: not as a means to prove conclusions from unchallenged propositions, but analytically, to identify hidden assumptions precisely in order to challenge them.

7   The Wikipedia entry https://en.wikipedia.org/wiki/Mr_Keynes_and_ the_%22Classics%22 presents this disagreement quite thoroughly, which suggests the Keynesians have put quite a lot of work into it..

The concept of theoretical counter-revolution

The issue at state is that of interpretation. We can make it especially clear by considering Marx's (1894, 165) well-known statement, cited in Chapter 6, on the cost-price of capitalist purchases:

> *It is necessary to remember this modified significance of the cost-price, and to bear in mind that there is always the possibility of an error if the cost-price of a commodity in any particular sphere is identified with the value of the means of production consumed by it.*

This issue to which Marx refers is this: in his exposition in Chapter 9 of Volume III, the outputs (before production starts, at the end of the period) are expressed in prices of production, and the inputs (before production starts, at the start of the period) are expressed in values.[8]

The statement above has two interpretations. Almost all the commentators discussed in the first seven chapters of this volume suppose that Marx admitted *he* had a problem and did not solve it, setting it aside for later analysis. The very idea that there is a 'transformation problem' rests on this reading.

But there is a much simpler interpretation: Marx was warning *others* of a possible mistake, which he regarded as relatively easy to correct. This is far more consistent with the text, not least the telling sentence that follows: 'Our present analysis does not necessitate a closer examination of this point.' It is hardly conceivable that a writer as scrupulous as Marx, on such a key issue, would seek to brush aside his *own* mistake with such a remark.

We can, furthermore, distinguish between the two interpretations on the basis of *evidence* taken from the text. This goes beyond merely selecting a quotation that confirms our prejudices or supports our case, which is the way most writers on Marx proceed. Kliman (2007,62) proposes the *Stigler* criterion, broadly accepted in textual interpretation and specifically endorsed by Barkai (1965, 1967) in a key debate with Stigler over the interpretation of

---

8   The terms 'inputs' and 'outputs' are not Marx's. but have become the preferred terms in the subsequent debate. The term 'inputs' is used to designate what Marx terms 'cost-price'. The term 'outputs' is more problematic to render into Marx's terminology but is best thought of as the cost-price of the next period.

Ricardo's theory of the demand for Corn. Stigler (1965, 448) objected to simply selecting the quotations that supported Barkai's case, complaining "Why should we allow the hand-picked quotation to carry an interpretation when we would reject the hand-picked fact as an empirical test of a hypothesis? In fact the two problems are basically the same." He proposed the criterion of *coherence* in his "principle of scientific exegesis" which states that an interpretation should be rejected if it cannot deduce the author's main analytical conclusions from her definitions and premises.

In this case the need for an additional test of meaning is obvious: there are two opposed interpretations of the same quotation. If the second interpretation is correct, we should be able to re-create Marx's reasoning in such a way as to reproduce, faithfully, the conclusions he himself states from the propositions he himself states, supplying the necessary 'correction'. That is, we should be able to generalize further to the case where goods are purchased at prices proportional to values, to the case where they are purchased at prices proportional to prices of production. And this is quite easy to do. Actually, all we need suppose is that, in addition to any propositions governing the equalization of the profit rate itself:[9]

Proposition 3: The value transferred to the product by those commodities that are consumed in order to produce it (constant capital) is equal to price of production of those commodities.

Proposition 4: The value deducted from the living labour engaged in making that product (variable capital), in forming the surplus value created there, is equal to the price of production of that labor's means of consumption.

These are completely compatible with propositions 1 and 2 and we can therefore treat propositions 1-4, together with conclusions 1-3, as a coherent *formalization* of the LTV, to take a term from axiomatic logic. We are moreover justified in attributing it to Marx. Moreover, it has no internal contradictions, allowing for the formation of prices of production in the general case, and thus solving Ricardo's (not Marx's) 'transformation problem'.

---

9   We leave open what these propositions are. This is because the following argument applies independently of how Marx's transformation from values to prices of production is interpreted, provided only the interpretation does not violate propositions 1 or 2.

Now, there may be grounds to *question* propositions 3 and 4; this is both legitimate and essential and should be part of any research agenda dealing with the LTV. It is in this light we should consider the authors' objections to proposition 4, when they argue that variable capital is better defined as the value of wage goods, not their price of production. Consistent with this, they present their own 'dynamic model' and assess in this light the models both of Chinese scholars such as Ding Baojun (Chapter 4), and of earlier Western scholars (chapters 5-7), and modern Western defenses of Marx (Chapter 8).

They further question a view they attribute to TSSI scholars, that the value of inputs is the same as their price of production. We believe this to be a simple misunderstanding: proposition 3 recognizes the distinction between value and price of production, asserting only that the value *transferred* to the product is given by the latter, not the former.[10] However, these misunderstandings are secondary to the issue at hand. The key issue is that the authors assess these propositions from the standpoint 'what is the best way to develop the LTV?' This is unexceptionable. However, it is a *different question* from 'what was Marx's theory?'

The issue in that case is whether propositions 3 and 4 coincide with Marx's *own* formulation of the issue. Coherence is satisfied, because propositions 3 and 4 are consistent with Marx's conclusions. And there is further evidence: Marx describes Price of Production as a 'modified form of value'. Why should he not then suppose that the value transmitted to the product by constant capital is this modified magnitude, not the value with which it emerges from production? Whether or not one believes this is compatible with the LTV, it is entirely reasonable to take it as *Marx's* view.

This proposition is equally open to dispute and study. Indeed, it is perfectly possible to argue both that Marx agreed with propositions 3 and 4, and that he was wrong to do so, or that he *disagreed* with propositions 3 and 4 but was right to do so. TSSI scholars don't concur with either of these, but would be the first to acknowledge that if others want to investigate such possibilities, they should do so.

10   In Chapter 4, they write of Ding Baojun's solution "The gap between the cost-price and value of the capital inputs would be transferred to the value of new commodities as a prerequisite" and add "There is no issue concerning Ding Baojun's treatment of constant capital"

Notwithstanding, it is totally legitimate to look into alternatives to Marx's own theory, just as one may say 'Newton said space offers a fixed frame of reference, and this was wrong, as Einstein later showed when explaining experimental results that contradicted Newton's predictions.' The point is, in order to identify the differences between these alternatives, and Marx's own theory, we have to have a means of judging what Marx's theory actually is.

The concern with interpretation, which has preoccupied modern Western scholars especially the TSSI school, is hence the reverse of a search for doctrinal purity – but, TSSI scholars argue, indispensable to the search for the best possible expression of the LTV.

With this point clarified, it remains to be shown why interpretation matters, even if our primary concern is not with the correct rendering of Marx's TV but with the LTV as such. After all, there are towering individual figures in many branches of knowledge – Newton or Einstein in Physics, Lavoisier or Priestley in Chemistry, Darwin in Biology, Maxwell in the theory of electromagnetic radiation, Mendeleev in atomic theory – but their contribution rapidly becomes collectivized. The process which led them to their ideas then becomes immaterial to the ideas as such.

Their theory then becomes a mental object in its own right, a 'general acquisition of society'. It may get labelled with its founders' name, but 'Newtonian' physics or 'Darwinian' biology are just cyphers for a concept. Nobody would think of 'refuting' the Newtonian concept of space by searching his writings for contradictions or errors or, *pace* creationism, refuting Darwin by interrogating his diary of the voyage of the Beagle. We can with an easy conscience consign such enquiries to the historians of science. Precisely because this theory becomes the common patrimony of a collective body of researchers, its truth or falsity can be judged objectively.

The point is that this is regrettably denied to scholars of Marx, not because of who he is but because of the way his theory is treated. He is systematically judged *subjectively*, not by asking if his theory works, but by offering excuse after excuse for ignoring it.

All the above is simply another way of stating that Marx's legacy is suppressed. Capitalism would have found it difficult to stop masses of people reading Marx and indeed, forbidding it would only make Marx more attractive. Suppression was therefore achieved by a different means: by establishing an academic consensus that Marx's theory is inconsistent and therefore theoretically illegitimate.

But precisely because Marx is remarkably consistent, such charges are only established by misinterpreting him. The misinterpretation of Marx is, in summary, the principal instrument of what should be recognized as a 20th Century *theoretical counter-revolution* against the LTV.

General Equilibrium Marxism

The approach of identifying 'inconsistencies' in Marx was pioneered by Böhm-Bawerk (Sweezy 1949) in his *Karl Marx and the Close of his System*. This work contains no alternative theory at all. It is dedicated to a single purpose: proving a contradiction between Volume I and Volume III. As the authors of this volume note in Chapter 2:

> *His criticism was that Marx had examined commodity exchange in accordance with the labor theory of value in Volume I, but in Volume III he asserted that commodity exchange was based on price of production. Marx had therefore contradicted himself; the reason was the labor theory of value.*

This is no more a work of science than the Catholic Church's indictment of Galileo. Böhm-Bawerk was a partisan. He was three times a Finance Minister in the pre-war Austro-Hungarian government, imposing very unpopular austerity measures and witnessing to his consternation the growing influence of Marx on the working classes of the sprawling territories of Austria-Hungary, a cause of great fear with war looming and the Paris Commune a recent memory. He is commendably explicit about his concerns (Sweezy 1949, 3):

> *As an author Karl Marx was enviably fortunate. No one will affirm that his work can be classed among the books which are easy to read or easy to understand. Most other books would have found their way to popularity hopelessly barred if they had laboured under an even lighter ballast of hard dialectic and wearisome mathematical*

deduction. But Marx, in spite of all this, has become the apostle of wide circles of readers, including many who are not as a rule given to the reading of difficult books.

His aim was not to develop this theory but to stop it in its tracks. This is why we consider his intervention to be what we describe as a theoretical counter-revolution. His method was enviably simple: he enlisted the emerging professional intelligentsia in a project to prove Marx's ideas impossible, to which end he had to purposively distort them. In short, the LTV was suppressed by establishing a plausible lie whose principal function was to discredit its greatest exponent. The lie was that Volume III 'contradicted' Volume I. It is as scientific as if Einstein's detractors had set out to prove that the General Theory of Relativity contradicted the Special Theory.

Nowadays, with the systematic corruption of this same intelligentsia by the narratives of their military-intelligence complexes to 'prove' that military action and economic sanctions are required to combat the fictitious crimes of their enemies, the method of suppression by propagating lies is becoming all too familiar. At the time, it was an innovative masterstroke, whose consequences still echo.

As with today's media manipulators, Bawerk and his circle were happy to extend recognition to critical intellectuals of a Marxist persuasion who assisted this project. The figure of Bortkiewicz enters here; few who cite him have read him carefully enough to establish what he was really trying to say. An exception which makes essential reading is the seminal contribution of Kliman and McGlone (1996). Here, they point out that Bortkiewicz's (1906[1952]:9) objection to Marx is not whether input prices are transformed, but that Marx does not make them *equal* to output prices. Now had Bortkiewicz only been interested in 'correcting' or extending Marx's own transformation procedure, he could easily have incorporated, into his own models, some version of our propositions 3 and 4. But this is not his issue, as he (Bortkiewicz 1907[1906],12) makes clear:

What happens now, when price-calculation (Table II) replaces value-calculation? Production spheres I and V will still be making consumption goods for the workers, sphere II consumption goods for the

17

capitalists, and spheres III and IV means of production. The sum of wages has not altered ... The workers should therefore be able to acquire for this sum the goods produced in I and y, neither more nor less. These goods, however, now have a price of 92+37, i.e. a total of 129. The workers thus must go short, or, put in another way, some of the goods made in I and V find no outlet. In this regard, therefore, the price model breaks down [my emphasis]

The price model 'breaks down' not because inputs are untransformed. It breaks down because if they are transformed as Marx proposes, the system cannot reproduce. There is an insufficient monetary demand – assuming that neither workers nor capitalists have any reserve funds – to pay for the outputs at their modified prices. Bortkiewicz then develops his entire 'correction' to Marx by imposing simple reproduction, which in turn calls for input and output prices to be not just transformed, but *equal*. This is an entirely different, and alien assumption. It amounts to a *fifth and sixth proposition*:

Proposition 5: Prices and values must remain constant throughout production

Proposition 6: Every commodity produced each year must be completely consumed in that year

Finally, he states a 'two-system' definition of value which is the origin of the entire notion of a 'problem' in Marx's transformation procedure:

Proposition 7: The values of commodities in such a system are given, not by the sum of direct labour and consumed constant capital in the price-system, but by their values in a different system, the 'value-system' in which the profit rate is not equalized.

This gives rise to a formalization of the LTV which we provisionally term the 'Bortkiewicz LTV', comprising propositions 1,2 and 5-7 but not 3 and 4. It produces *different numbers* from the 'Marx LTV' which comprises propositions 1-4 but not 5-7. The difference is clear if we consider either the TSSI treatment of Bortkiewicz's examples, or the iterative formalizations of Shaikh discussed in chapter 8, or of Morishima, discussed in chapter 5. In every case, the results are different from the Bortkiewicz TV.

In short, the Bortkiewicz LTV is not the Marx LTV but a different LTV, more accurately a different attempt to formalize the LTV. As the authors correctly note in Chapter 5:

> Above all, [Bortkiewicz] made simple reproduction a restrictive condition. We believe this to be a very mistaken idea. The conditions for simple reproduction concern whether the value or price of production can be realized, which bears little relationship to the transformation of values into prices of production.

They go on to note the perceptive comment of Winternitz (1948, 277):

> Bortkiewicz and Sweezy base their analysis of the transformation problem on Marx's scheme of simple reproduction, i.e., such relations between the main departments of production as will make a continuation of production on the same scale possible. With Marx's method of transformation, the equilibrium of simple reproduction if it obtains with an exchange of equal values would not obtain with an exchange at prices of production. Sweezy finds this result logically unsatisfactory. This objection seems to me not justified. Every change in the price structure normally disturbs an existing equilibrium. A change of prices may necessitate a changed distribution of social labor to restore the equilibrium.

Indeed, the *absence* of equilibrium is integral to Marx's analysis, as is clear in Chapter 10 of Volume III, where he discusses the equalization process. This arises not from the conformity of prices with the ideal equilibrium but from their non-conformity; it is because actual, real-life capitals always seek a surplus-profit, a profit different from the average, that capital migrates from spheres where profit is below average to those where it is above (Marx 1894:169):

> Within each individual sphere of production, there take place changes, i.e., deviations from the general rate of profit...Since the general rate of profit is not only determined by the average rate of profit in each sphere, but also by the distribution of the total social capital

among the different individual spheres, and since this distribution is continually changing, it becomes another constant cause of change in the general rate of profit.

Marxism without Marx: the two-system fallacy

How, and why, does the mere assumption of reproduction create any contradictions for Marx's theory? Bortkiewicz (Sweezy 1949, 199-200) cannot be faulted when he introduces the simplifying assumptions that "the entire advanced capital (including the constant capital) turns over entirely once a year and reappears again in the annual product", which he rightly attributes to the Legal Marxists Dmitriev and Tugan-Baranowski (and, he notes, Kautsky):

Insofar as it is a question of demonstrating Marx's errors it is quite unobjectionable to work with limiting assumptions of this kind, since what does not hold in the special case cannot claim general validity.

If, under these limited assumptions, an inconsistency between Volumes I and III emerged, Bortkiewicz would be justified in claiming Marx's reasoning is itself inconsistent. "[W]hat does not hold in the special case cannot claim general validity" is a correct logical principle. If only it were recognized in respect of TSSI refutations of the Okishio theorem (Okishio 1961, see Kliman and McGlone 1999), Marxist scholarship could be placed on a far saner foundation.

However, Bortkiewicz's demonstration of Marx's error does not depend only on this simplification. It rests on the *further* 'correction' to Marx given in Proposition 7. He supposes that values, and prices, are determined by two distinct economies or 'systems'. In the first, commodities exchange at values, defined as the prices necessary to ensure reproduction if exchange takes place at values. This is the 'value system'. In the second, commodities exchange at prices of production. This is the 'price system'.

He then restates the problem in an entirely different manner from Marx. He identifies two 'equalities' which must both be satisfied, if Marx is to be deemed consistent:

Conclusion B1: Total outputs in the value system must equal total outputs in the price system

Conclusion B2: Total profit in the value system must equal total profit in the price system

These two conclusions cannot in general be deduced from Bortkiewicz's attempted formalization, because they refer to two different economies. They are therefore incompatible with propositions 1 and 2. Either value can be created without labour (if conclusion B1 is dropped) or profit can be produced without labour (if conclusion B2 is dropped). Bortkiewicz's theory is not an LTV but a TV, a *Theory* of Value, a failed attempt to formalize the LTV.

This inconsistency then becomes the 'transformation problem' and Bortkiewicz's failed LTV becomes 'Marx's' Theory of Value. That is to say, Marx's LTV is concealed, and the Bortkiewicz TV is identified as the 'Marx LTV'. *Pace* Samuelson, this is an eraser trick. We write down Marx's theory and deduce a few conclusions from it. Then we wipe out Marx's system and substitute Bortkiewicz's system, including Bortkiewicz's dual-system reformalization of Marx's conclusions. We then find a contradiction and 'hey presto!' Marx is wrong.

The interpretation of Marx's transformation on the basis of Simple Reproduction is particularly outrageous. His Volume III tables do not assume reproduction and don't even cover all the departments in society. Volume III simply does not exhibit a system that reproduces itself. To be sure, he discusses Simple Reproduction – in Volume 2, in an entirely different context. But he also discusses Expanded Reproduction, giving examples in which technology changes, which is incompatible with the Bortkiewicz TV as anyone who takes the trouble can verify.

We can surmise that on the basis of Marx's resolution, in Volume III, of how profit is distributed to all the property-owning classes (which is required to study reproduction at the level of abstraction of Volume III, as noted in the authors' discussion of Shaikh's work), he would have been in a position to present examples of social reproduction on the basis the distribution of profit according to fully capitalist laws. The scientific way to develop the LTV would be to pursue this line of investigation. But the idea that the transformation tables in Volume III can be tacked on to the most primitive reproduction schemas of Volume II to yield a coherent version of Marx's theory is an insult to intelligence. Marx never proposed anything remotely resembling Bortkiewicz's two-system equilibrium presentation of the transformation of values into prices of production.

Nevertheless, his transmogrification was effected by Sweezy's (1942, 71) ringing endorsement:

> *Alone among critics of Marx's theoretical structure, Bortkiewicz grasped the full significance of the law of value and its use...it was Bortkiewicz who laid the basis for a logically unobjectionable proof of the correctness of Marx's method.*

The method itself was, Sweezy (1942, 53) moreover argued, just a variant of General Equilibrium

> *To use a modern expression, the law of value is essentially a theory of general equilibrium developed in the first instance with reference to simple commodity production and later on adapted to capitalism.*

This led him to his conclusion in Steedman (1981:25):

> *This of course is what is known in the Marxist literature as the trans-formation problem. As is by now well known, the way proposed by Marx himself is faulty.*

Sweezy was at one and the same time a recognized academic and a well-known Communist, conferring on him that entitlement which the fearsome combination of rebelliousness, respectability, and prominence alone can offer, and to which two generations of Western Marxists thenceforth aspired. The Bortkiewicz TV became identified as Marx's in both Communist and Western academic circles for half a century or more. Virtually all pre-1980 Western Marxist academic work on transformation proceeds from the assumption that Bortkiewicz's TV was in fact Marx's.[11] This literature is thus built on a single misinterpretation.

---

11 Mandel (1979) is an important exception but, it should be noted, was a professional revolutionary and was explicitly banned from academia for most of his life.

The scientific way to assess these theories is therefore to judge them as alternative attempted formalizations of the LTV. If they cannot reproduce the conclusions from the postulates, they cannot be counted as formalizations of the LTV; having identified what Marx's theory actually is, it then becomes clear the LTV is not to blame. It is for this reason the development of the LTV is, in the present environment, impossible without the militant defense of Marx.

This is indeed the manner in which the authors of this volume present this literature, a salutary corrective to the Western tradition. Therein lies its scientific significance.

The militant emancipation of economics

It is in this respect that the treatment of the authors is an important contribution, new to Western scholarship. For the reader who is new to the subject, it offers a comprehensive introduction. For the reader already familiar with it, it offers a refreshing new perspective.

What does Western scholarship bring to the table? In the West, opposition to the LTV, up to and including its active suppression and calumniation, is a permanent feature of intellectual life, arising from the material circumstances of capitalism. This hostility arises because LTV is a mortal threat to the stability of the capitalist order. As Samuelson's vigorous intervention demonstrates, not to mention the continual favor shown by academia to those respectable Marxists who make the propitiatory sacrifice of 'proving' Marx's errors and omissions, this hostility is not going to dissipate, and constantly re-appears in new forms.

It is not therefore possible simply to proceed as if the LTV were just another body of knowledge in which Kuhnian 'normal science' can be practiced. The process of discovery has to be organized conjointly with militant defense of scientific method, which includes organized resistance to the methods of misrepresentation and delegitimization which constitute the WMD of the anti-Marx counter-revolution.

These are strong words, but justified by the evidence of Marx's treatment at the hands of academics. Its esoteric history is a striving to 'tame' Marx by ridding him of the LTV, which draws all, from left to right, into its orbit. Consider, for example, Joan Robinson's (1960, 21) famous *Essay on*

Marxian Economics, often taken as an example of a friendly and sympathetic Keynesian exegesis. Here is a key passage:

> *I hope that it will become clear, in the following pages, that no point of substance in Marx's argument depends upon the labour theory of value. Voltaire remarked that it is possible to kill a flock of sheep by witchcraft if you give them plenty of arsenic at the same time. The sheep, in this figure, may well stand for the complacent apologists of capitalism; Marx's penetrating insight and bitter hatred of oppression supply the arsenic, while the labour theory of value provides the incantations.*

It is equally possible to kill an idea with neoclassical incantations, provided a Robinson can be induced to administer the arsenic. Her central proposition is that Marx *has* no theory. This is just another way of saying that the theory does not exist. To the extent that the theory exists, or that Marx uses it, she says it either has no explanatory merit ('no point of substance depends upon [it]') or it is just plain wrong, as we find in her dismissal of proposition 3 of the LTV which is the essay's central target.[12] Robinson's protagonist is not Marx: it is the LTV. When even Left Keynesians, themselves the victims of the systematic misrepresentation of their own key thinker, engage with Marx with the sole purpose of discrediting his principal theories, what hope is there of an honest engagement from the economics profession as a whole?

The urge to drive a wedge between Marx and the LTV is also the principal motivating force behind 'Marxism without Marx' (Freeman 2010). This is the idea that the Marx's key conclusions can be derived without recourse to the LTV. The focus is what TSSI scholars term 'physicalism' and is admirably well addressed by the authors in their discussion of Morishima, Steedman and Sraffa. Physicalism is the idea that we can explain how prices are formed, and hence prove exploitation takes place, by studying the exchange of so-called 'physical quantities' of commodities, within input-output models that assume equilibrium.

12   See Freeman (2000) for a discussion of this dismissal. See also Kliman et al (2019) for a discussion of the latest such attempt from Heinrich (2013)

The organizing principle is Morishima's 'Fundamental Marxian Theorem' (FMT) which is held to prove that exploitation must arise in an economy that produces a 'physical surplus', defined as a positive net product. This technical term means the economy in question does not produce less of any commodity than it consumes.

Actually, such models are plagued with even more inconsistencies than equilibrium two-system Marxism.[13] Some of these, such as negative prices and values – arising from Sraffa's treatment of fixed capital mentioned in Chapter 7 of this volume, are recognized by their supporters.

Others, more fundamental yet, arise because the assumptions are untenable. No real economy actually produces a positive net product, because of technical innovation and changes in consumer tastes: actually, thousands of commodities pass into disuse with every day that passes, as they are replaced with new, different commodities fulfilling a similar function or, in cases such as the internet, a radically different function. The net product of all such commodities is negative: a 'physical surplus' simply does not exist.

The FMT, in common with the post-Sraffian physicalist construction in general, is based on a sleight of hand which typifies the equilibrium method. That which is *called* a 'non-negative net product' does not refer to the proportions of the actual economy but to a hypothetical economy which *would* have a non-negative net product *if* it reproduced perfectly. To do so, however, not merely would the prices of this economy depart from reality, but the *quantities* also would depart from reality, and widely so. An economy based on the horse and cart, for example, would never introduce the motor car, nor petrol-driven engines, nor modern roads and would have to go on churning out horses and carts in exactly the same numbers for all eternity, to satisfy the conditions of the FMT.

This is, it should be mentioned for completeness, a far more serious problem than the departure of prices from their predicted equilibrium magnitudes. This latter is sometimes dismissed by claiming that prices behave 'as if' they were in equilibrium and that equilibrium is a 'good approximation' to real prices, and serves as their 'center of gravity' (Freeman 2006). The fig leaf of rationality which conceals the immodesty of this sweeping claim is that if labour

13   See Kliman and Potts (2015) for a full account of these issues.

productivity is rising, prices will tend to fall in both dynamic systems and the corresponding equilibrium systems although, importantly, the rate of profit in a physicalist system will rise even though in the dynamic equivalent, and in the real world, it is falling. But there is no way we can claim that the proportions of production in horse-and-cart economies will function as 'centers of gravity' for those in a motorcar economy. The gap is too large for credulity, and in the physicalist literature, the term 'negative net product' is used without qualification, as a kind of pretense that the issue does not exist.

Once the problem is identified and corrected, the physicalist reasoning behind the FMT collapses. It leads to conclusions that directly counter the claims advanced on its behalf, such as the conclusion that economies exist in which workers can exploit capitalists.

The 'Marxism without Marx' TV is thus riddled with far greater contradictions than those which its protagonists claim for Marx's TV. However, these inconsistencies are not the result of misinterpretation but are a formal result of the physicalist systems themselves. They cannot be wished away. This never seems to act as a deterrent, confirming the deep-seated hostility to the LTV that lies at the heart of the drive to produce such theories.

These inconsistencies highlight the central difficulty of the Bortkiewicz project: it does not lead to the LTV's conclusions. This is what makes it an *inadequate* formalization of the LTV. When it is promoted as the LTV, it can only discredit the LTV. This is why, with Steedman's (1977) renunciation of the LTV, the post-Sraffians erupted in a frenzy of hostility to Marx, who they wrongly identified as the author of their own system.

Material foundations of theoretical counter-revolution

There is a perfectly materialist explanation for this hostility to the LTV, which surfaced while Marx was yet a child, in the opposition to Ricardo arising from the work of the 'Ricardian Socialist' Hodgskin. In 1825 Hodgskin concluded, on the basis of Ricardo's version of the LTV, that profit, just like rent, was a deduction from the produce of labour. This was a perfectly scientific deduction, but James Mill concluded (Dobb 1973:98) "if [Hodgskin's ideas] were to spread they would be subversive of civilised society" and initiated what Marx termed the 'collapse of the Ricardian School', a prolonged

26

retreat from scientific economics against which Marx and Engels were almost alone in holding out.

To economists even in Marx's day, it was *more important* to preserve 'civilized society' than promote the truth. This is no less true today. Economics, in sum, is, as presently organized, a religious, not a scientific, institution.

Mill's reaction summarizes the problem. In economics – a material institution whose members depend on funding, promotion, publication, recognition and a host of other incentives to produce what is wanted, not to mention deterrents to speaking truth to power – a material law frustrates the development of science: the institution sets a higher priority on promoting ideas that do not 'subvert civilised society' than to truth.

Its structure is hierarchical, with its Chief Economists, Senior Economists, Juniors and Trainees. It is a guild, strictly controlling admission and access to funds, status and audiences.[14] It constructs the narratives which politicians and commentators rely on to justify unpopular actions. Through mechanisms such as structural adjustment it has acquired a kind of paralegal status: it is provides 'unwritten' laws of which expenditures are legitimate and which are disallowed which have led to the death of millions – yet there is no court in which its judgements may be contested, nor any scrutiny of its edicts, nor even an internal system of appeal. It is tightly tied into the circuits of finance capital via the banks, capital markets and the International Financial Institutions who offer a kind of revolving door to power, influence and money.

Being determines consciousness. The structure is organized around a doctrine: market perfection. Its theories meet the needs of capitalist classes who can tolerate only sufficient understanding of the market to administer it in their interests. They require that their administrators, technicians and policy makers share, and operate under, theories that provide for this, which enshrine the doctrines that the market is perfect, does not produce crises from within itself, corrects itself automatically when crises arise, and performs sub-optimally if interfered with or regulated; that private property owners are necessary and contribute value to it; and that the capitalist organization of society is naturally-ordained, cannot be improved on, and will not be superseded by any other political system.

14   This is extremely well dissected in Earle et al. (2015)

These requirements explain the primacy of the general equilibrium paradigm which embodies, in mathematically pure form, the above beliefs. Within Marxism, equilibrium 'rewritings' are officially tolerated, all the more so since, if any such re-writing is erroneously taken to be the theory of Marx himself, Marx can be dismissed as a second-rate thinker of no consequence. The effectiveness of this response is evident: it is why economics departments throughout the world are dominated by neoclassical ideas, including in China itself.

The counter-revolutionary function of academic economics must therefore be treated with the utmost seriousness, and any illusion that it is possible, in today's world, to practice 'normal' science within economics, should be discarded. As Marx (1867, 21) noted:

> In the domain of Political Economy, free scientific inquiry meets not merely the same enemies as in all other domains. The peculiar nature of the materials it deals with, summons as foes into the field of battle the most violent, mean and malignant passions of the human breast, the Furies of private interest. The English Established Church, e.g., will more readily pardon an attack on 38 of its 39 articles than on 1/39 of its income. Now-a-days atheism is culpa levis as compared with criticism of existing property relations.

Two things are needed to counter this. The first is the awareness, among growing numbers of ordinary working people, that something is wrong and that they are being lied to. This awareness arises at points in history where the economic difficulties of capitalism become so intractable that they erupt in social and political crisis. It was the 1870 recession that drove the working class to Marx after 1880, because ordinary people learnt from their own experience to distrust what they heard from the Böhm-Bawerks of this world. The Great Recession of 1929-42 similarly accounts for the mass popularity of Keynesianism and its associated welfarism after the Second World war. At such moments, popular consciousness reaches out for an alternative. This is what is happening now.

Discontent among working and poor people is now very widespread, but, due to the lack of a clearly-articulated alternative, is going through a stage in which it gives rise to all manner of morbid reactions such as racism, fascism, Trumpism, and so on.

This highlights the importance of a second condition for a successful scientific political economy: the conscious organization of scientific economics in forms that ensure ordinary people can take possession of it. This is what we mean by 'emancipatory economics'. It does not require a huge effort of dissemination or propaganda, because as in Marx's day, people looking for answers will avail themselves of good ideas – provide these ideas are available. What is required is therefore collective organization to defend the LTV – and hence Marx – against delegitimation, and make the results available to the general public. The encounters between Chinese and Western scholarship, to which this book bears witness, clearly offer an encouraging prospect for this to occur.

Eastern and Western Marx scholarship: a new phase and a research agenda

It is in this light that the book signals the prospect of a new phase of scholarship in the LTV and a Marx's Theory of Value. There are three critical new factors.

1. There is a general agreement between Chinese and Western scholars, summarized below, on a number of key findings of scholarship on the LTV and Marx's Theory of Value.
2. The economic crisis of capitalism and its world order has opened up a wide social and political crisis, leading a new generation to question, in large numbers, the explanations for the misery and danger they undergo.
3. In both China and the West, collective scholarship has emerged with an important degree of independence from the professional institutions of neoclassical economics.

The role of collective scholarship requires special attention. We have spent a good deal of this introduction explaining how the attacks on Marx became the principal vehicle of a more general attach on the LTV. This has prevented what happens in other sciences where, notwithstanding many clashes of ideas, bodies of theory become collectivized; they become mental objects independent of their originators. This is why it makes sense to speak of Newtonian Physics without reference to the writings of Newton. On the other hand, when a theory – such as that of Copernicus (1543) or Galileo in their day or Marx in ours – is a dire threat to entrenched class interests, these classes actively frustrate its general social adoption. In this situation theory becomes the private property of individuals, inaccessible to large masses of people.

This opens the door to all manner of material pressure, the most powerful being the urge for recognition and acceptance. Western Marxist scholarship therefore presents itself as a kind of competitive struggle between individuals who are constantly led to promote their own theories, which become a kind of human capital, an identity, a means to gain acceptance. The scholarly field is then populated with attacks by these individuals on each other, so that to the outside observer it takes the appearance of a battlefield, in which the din makes it impossible to identify the actual nature of the disputes. The same factors create a star culture in which personalities and pundits become a replacement for theories of which they are the mere fetish symbols. The traditional economic methods of proof by rhetoric and proof by misrepresentation attain their highest development in the shape of *proof by authority*: a mere declaration from a recognized cult leader becomes the ultimate criterion of judgement.

The antidote is the development of genuinely collective scholarship, as free as possible from the pernicious inducements of academic economics. It also lightens the burden, which afflicts all Marx scholars, of continually responding to preposterous attacks instead of developing their ideas. By conducting discussions in an orderly and reasoned manner, it creates the foundations of an emancipatory economics by making the scholarship accessible to the critical general public and above all, working people. In short, it brings to the battle a material force opposed to the 'furies of the private interests' which, as Marx notes, dominate and regulate the discussion in the interests of the property-owning classes.

The significance of post-1980s scholarship is, first of all, the common endeavor of defending Marx's ideas. This has however proven insufficient to develop a genuine collective endeavor and this was the cause for the emergence of TSSI and its predecessor, the International Working Group for the Study of Value Theory or IWGVT. The most notable feature of TSSI scholarship, unique in modern Western Marxism, is that it is *not* primarily the work of individuals. Over thirty writers have contributed to the formation of its ideas including its code of conduct.[15] Scholarship in the TSSI framework continues to grow as new writers involve themselves.

In China, collective scholarship in Marx and the LTV is a more normal part of intellectual life. The prominent role of China's schools of Marxism and of CASS itself in developing Marx's economic theories provides an important counter to neoclassical ideas in any case; it also however provides an environment in which scholars can work together with a degree of freedom.

This book thus signals an encounter not just between two bodies of theory but between two traditions of collective scholarship.

This engagement uncovers a set of fundamental points of agreement which offer an agenda for research and development. The two groups of scholars agree that the LTV is valid, insofar as a variety of ways have been suggested which overcome the objections raised by Marx's critics. This is a fundamental step forward. It now remains to devise collective activities and practices to reach common understandings of the best ways to formalize the LTV. This suggests a *research agenda* which we lay down in the form of bullet points for consideration.

- A decisive and welcome agreement is that Marx's LTV is both consistent and the most developed formalization of the LTV so far available.
- A second decisive agreement is that neither Marx, nor any version of the LTV, can be represented by the Bortkiewicz TV or any of its successors, from Sweezy and Morishima onwards. The Bortkiewicz project is at an end, along with the Samuelson critique of Marx, the 'Marxism without Marx' project to reconstruct Marx as a physicalist, and the subsequent post-Sraffian attempt to construct an alternative, physicalist, simultaneous equation TV based on 'linear production' or input-output systems. Not only have the allegations of

---

15   See http://copejournal.com/scholarship-guidelines. The COPE journal site contains an archive of IWGVT writings spanning 25 years and also contains new works of TSSI scholarship.

contradiction against Marx been thoroughly refuted, but the project itself is dogged with its own theoretical contradictions, which it does not deny, and has produced little scholarship of use in understanding the realities of capitalist life today. Solid evidence demonstrates that 'physicalist' Theories of Value have failed reproduce the conclusions of the LTV by other means, which is their principal claim. As the debates reproduced in Kliman and Potts (2015) demonstrate, the 'Fundamental Marxian Theorem' is false; and as many TSSI scholars have shown, these theories predict a rising rate of profit where the LTV correctly predicts a falling rate.[16] There appears to be significant agreement on this judgement also.

- The primary source of error in the Bortkiewicz project is its assumption of simple reproduction, that is, General Equilibrium. A further huge step forward is therefore that Chinese and TSSI scholars clearly agree that the LTV has to be expressed in a fully general, dynamic system that does not depend on the assumption of reproduction. A second source of error in the Bortkiewicz project requires further discussion: the two-system formulation which substitutes conclusions B1 and B2 for conclusions 1 and 2, imposing a requirement that necessarily violates the LTV. It has been shown that non-dynamic formalizations, such as the 'Simultaneous Single System' approach of Wolff, Callari and Roberts, or Moseley, do satisfy propositions 1 and 2 and do yield conclusions 1 and 2, as does the New Solution in some presentations. But they do so only under the limited condition of simple reproduction and for this reason suffer a serious weakness; namely they contradict the LTV for any system in which simple reproduction does not hold, for example in which there is technical change, or when for any reason supply and demand do not match. For this reason also, they do not yield conclusion 3 and therefore cannot explain the tendential fall in the profit rate. This is a further serious weakness in that this conclusion is the basis both of Marx's

---

16   By 'correctly' in this context we mean the inductive or empirical criterion applies: the LTV predicts what is actually observed to happen better than any alternative. See Freeman (2009)

theory of crisis and his analysis of the laws of motion of capitalism. There is agreement that the restriction to Simple Reproduction is a weakness, but it is not clear that there is agreement that the two-system formalization necessarily contradicts the LTV, nor has much progress been made on either side in the investigation of expanded reproduction with technical change, arguably the most important generalization of Marx's LTV now required. I would hope this can be recognized as an urgent task by all concerned.

- The issue that requires the most discussion is undoubtedly that of money, and Marx as a monetary theorist, which is one of the most promising modern trends, and also owes a debt to Japanese scholars such as Itoh. Chinese scholars are not convinced of the case for the 'Monetary Expression of Labour Time' or MELT, proposed by Ramos (1995) and based on the exegesis of Marx's 'dual concept of value' in Ramos and Rodriguez (1996). Since the concept of the MELT has now been adopted by New Interpretation scholars (though without reference to Ramos) this is an important issue also for Western scholars to discuss further. This clearly needs to be accompanied by the study of Marx's theory of money in general, a neglected subject of great controversy, and also of money-dealing, banking, and financial capital.

- A further important focus is: what exactly distinguishes the LTV from neoclassical and other theories? Answers are required not simply because the question is often asked, but for the reasons given in this article: the LTV explains the 'real world' better, so it is important to identify exactly why. To the authors persuasive case we can add a neglected argument of Marx's, in Chapter 5 of Volume 1 which we might term a 'conservation of value' argument. Though attacked by Mirowski (1991) on the spurious grounds that the marginalists discarded it, the idea is sound: value by definition cannot be created in circulation, the pure exchange of property titles. So, if we want to distinguish production from circulation, we need a theory of 'what is produced' – value – which recognizes that value cannot be created in circulation. Only the LTV satisfies this criterion. It is important to research why this is the case. This study includes such issues as productive and unproductive labour, broached at length in Volume 1 of this work.

- There is a need to make explicit as a research topic the issue of whether Marx provides a valid formalization of the LTV which, we have argued is a distinct question from whether the LTV is valid. Chinese scholars are less focused on this issue, because attacks on Marx in China are less intense and the methods employed less mischievous. Among Westerners, only TSSI scholars and Moseley (2017)[17] give it any attention, though there are strong disagreements between these two. Yet for all the reasons given, we believe this an important issue for scholarship.

- An area that requires further exploration is the 'historical method' on which Chinese scholars set great store. Chris Arthur (2008) of the Value Form school,[18] argues that the notion of a 'Simple Commodity Production' stage of history was wrongly attributed to Marx by Engels, and that Marx did not fully subscribe to this idea. That said, it is clear from Marx's own writings in the *Critique of Political Economy*, that he set great store by the historical method. This clearly requires further discussion.

- Volume 1 of this work places the issue of the *intensity* of labour squarely on the agenda. The issue has been insufficiently covered by Western Marxists and requires their attention.

- The agreements listed above, together with the areas for discussion, move the study of the LTV, and of Marx, in the healthy and welcome direction of making the theory more *general* and more *concrete*. If the LTV can be developed to cover fully dynamic systems in which there is technical change, in which equilibrium is not assumed to hold and in which the value of money is not assumed to be constant, it will be in a position not only to provide a very practical understanding of

17 Moseley's book, which appeared after the original (Chinese) edition of this work was published, is not covered in this volume.
18 The work of the Value Form School is not assessed in this volume, probably because Value Form scholars rarely if ever comment on the Transformation Problem as such.

34

capitalist reality but, as is already clear from the results of this theory in its present form, present a formidable challenge to neoclassical orthodoxy. To achieve this aim, it is necessary also to consider in a more developed way the *social reproduction of capital,* which means not just 'technical' reproduction but the reproduction of capitalism's classes. This appears in any case to have been the prime objective of Volume III, whose most neglected chapters are those dealing with commercial capital, landed capital and moneyed capital. This objective also requires a fuller discussion on productive and unproductive labour, on which (from the analysis in the first volume of the present work) substantial agreement is likely.

- Such an analysis inevitably becomes a work of political economy, because in considering the revenues and expenditures of the various capitalist classes, one enters a domain in the *actions* of classes are taken into account. Thus, ultimately, an assessment of the role of the state and the nation, which as is known Marx fully intended to deal with, is required. The role of collective forms ownership here also becomes important.

- This analysis, finally, requires an assessment of Marx's 'general law' of capitalist development, the process of accumulation, the process of technical change, and the causes and course of crisis.

- The role of the nation in both the LTV and Marx's scholarship (see Desai 2013), and of Foreign Trade. This also calls for a long-overdue re-assessment of the contribution of the early Communist theorists of Imperialism, of the Dependency School and hence of Unequal Exchange. The empirical phenomena to be explained include the division of the world's nations into two great blocs of rich and poor (Freeman 2019b, King 2018). There are many Chinese contributions to this analysis, but it is underrepresented in Western Scholarship.[19]

---

19   An important exception is King (2018) who also provides useful references to works by other relevant scholars.

2

Implications and methods of studying value transformation

In the three centuries after Petty (1662) articulated the labor theory of value, Adam Smith and David Ricardo extended it and Marx took it to new heights, building the Marxist economic system.

However, from the early years of the 19th century the theory came under attack from all sides. The so-called transformation problem – of transforming values into price of production – was seen by many economists as a weapon to overturn it. Before Ricardo, neither the classical economists such as Petty, Smith, or Boisguillebert, nor the Physiocratic school such as Quesnay or Turgot, had considered this issue.

Ricardo, Say and Malthus, who championed the labor theory of value, originated many debates with its opponents. They found that on the basis of this theory in its current form, equal magnitudes of capital could not yield equal magnitudes of profit. However, a general rate of profit in fact existed. As a result, Ricardo was in a dilemma, of which his opponents took advantage to increase their criticism of the labor theory of value.

Ricardo, like his successors James Mill and McCulloch, failed to distinguish labor from labor-power, and value from price of production. This led to the collapse of the Ricardian school. It was not until 1867 when the first volume of *Capital* was published that new life was breathed into the labor theory of value. However, it was not until 1894, when Volume III was published, that a new solution to the transformation problem was found.

Arguments concerning transformation

Marx's statements

In Volume I and Volume II of *Capital*, Marx began his analysis of value and transformation by making the law of value a determining factor of commodity price. However, in a letter to Engels, He noted: "the changed form of manifestation that the previously developed and still valid laws of value and surplus value assume now, after the transformation of values into prices of production." (Marx to Engels 30 April 1868) He also claimed that he would relate the analysis of transformation in Volume III to that of capital circulation in Volume II.

In Volume III, Marx argued that since the organic composition and turnover time of capital was different across different departments, profit would vary when the capitalist economy had developed to a certain stage. But due to capitalist competition, the rate of profit across departments tends to gravitate to a certain point, forming the general rate of profit. As a result, the law of price of production began to replace the law of value as the basic economic law of capitalist societies.

In Volume III of *Capital*, Marx elaborated on these issues: surplus value is divided among different departments in proportion to the magnitudes of capital advanced, surplus value is transformed into average profit, and value is transformed into price of production. A general rate of profit

$$r = \frac{\Sigma \, s_i}{\Sigma \, c_i + v_i}$$

is formed across all departments (where s_i is the surplus value in department i (i=1...n), c_i is the value of constant capital advanced and v_i that of variable capital advanced), along with a price of production p_i in each department where

$$p_i = (c_i + v_i) \, (1 + r).$$

The starting point of the transformation process is that, in the absence of any transformation, the rate of profit in each department will be different, because the organic composition and turnover time of the capital of each department is different.

The outcome of the transformation process is that equal magnitudes of capital in each department yield equal amounts of profit. Marx (1894, 158) argued that:

> [A]lthough in selling their commodities the capitalists of the various spheres of production recover the value of the capital consumed in their production, they do not secure the surplus-value, and consequently the profit, created in their own sphere by the production of these commodities. What they secure is only as much surplus-value, and hence profit, as falls, when uniformly distributed, to the share of every aliquot part of the total social capital from the total surplus-value, or profit, produced in a given time by the social capital in all spheres of production.

Therefore, total profit equals total surplus value, and total price of production equals total value. These two equalities both hold.

To briefly illustrate Marx's transformation process, let us assume an economy with three departments such that:

a. The magnitude of capital in each department is 100, but the organic composition of capital in each department is different;
b. The rate of surplus value throughout society is 100%;
c. The constant capital of each department is consumed once in each period;
d. The value transferred to the output of each department by its constant capital is equal to the value of that constant capital consumed;
e. The turnover time of constant capital in of each department is the same.

We can then calculate the value and the surplus value produced in each department, the total profit and hence the average rate of profit, and thereby the price of production of the output of each department. These are listed in table 2.1.

Table 2.1

Department	Capital composition	Rate of surplus value	Surplus value	Value produced	Rate of profit	General rate of profit	Production price	Average profit
I	80c+20v	100%	20	120	20%	30%	130	30
II	70c+30v	100%	30	130	30%	30%	130	30
III	60c+40v	100%	40	140	40%	30%	130	30

Table 2.1 illustrates Marx's treatment. The two equalities are both valid. Marx's method was to add a certain amount of surplus value to the value of consumed capital to obtain the price of production, without transforming the cost of this capital. In other words, he simply readjusted the magnitude of surplus value in each department rather than the magnitude of total surplus value. The proof of the validity of the equalities was therefore obvious.

Some scholars argued that for Marx's treatment to be valid, it should meet at least one of the following two conditions:

1. It should be assumed that all departments have an average organic composition of capital;
2. It should be assumed that all inputs were produced outside the system and hence purchased at their value.

However, these two conditions were unrealistic.

Supplementary issues and questions arising

As this example shows, Marx's transformation procedure dealt only with commodities generated by the production process and the transformation of their values into prices of production. However, he did not go on to treat these prices of production as inputs to the next circuit of the production process. Marx actually mentions this issue many times. Thus in Volume III of *Capital*, (Marx 1894, 160) he pointed out that:

> *This statement seems to conflict with the fact that under capitalist production the elements of productive capital are, as a rule, bought on*

40

the market, and that for this reason their prices include profit which has already been realised, hence, include the price of production of the respective branch of industry together with the profit contained in it, so that the profit of one branch of industry goes into the cost price of another.

He added (Marx and Engels 1998, 160) that:

However, this always resolves itself to one commodity receiving too little of the surplus value while another receives too much, so that the deviations from the value which are embodied in the prices of production compensate one another. Under capitalist production, the general law acts as the prevailing tendency only in a very complicated and approximate manner, as a never ascertainable average of ceaseless fluctuations.

Moreover, he pointed out (Marx 1894, 165) that:

It is necessary to remember this modified significance of the cost price, and to bear in mind that there is always the possibility of an error if the cost price of a commodity in any particular sphere is identified with the value of the means of production consumed by it. Our present analysis does not necessitate a closer examination of this point.

For that reason, Marx started to solve the transformation problem from a historical perspective. The reason he believed that there was no need to examine the issue further was that

1. He emphasized the influence of the gross average on the whole capitalist production process. As a result, the deviation from value contained in commodities' price of production would be offset;
2. Since gross magnitudes were emphasized, Marx did not bother to examine the distribution of these magnitudes across different departments;
3. His real purpose in studying transformation was prove that the total surplus value was redistributed among capitalists and thus reveal class antagonisms. As a result, the surplus value arising from the law

of value and the total surplus value realized was equal to total profit. What really concerned the capitalists was the distribution of surplus value or profit in proportion to the capital advanced.

He therefore pointed out (Marx 1894, 165) that:

> For no matter how much the cost price of a commodity may differ from the value of the means of production consumed by it, this past mistake is immaterial to the capitalist. The cost price of a particular commodity is a definite condition which is given, and independent of the production of our capitalist, while the result of his production is a commodity containing surplus value, therefore an excess of value over and above its cost price.

To sum up, Marx recognized that if precisely calculated, the cost-price[1] should be calculated in accordance with the price of production of inputs from previous production, but not from immediate production; therefore, if the cost-price of these inputs differed from their values, then the cost prices of outputs would deviate from what they would have been, if the inputs had been purchased at their values; but finally, such deviations basically did not impact the conclusion, so there was no need for further research. (Bai 1999, 85)

In other words, Marx anticipated deviations from his calculation after inputs were transformed into production prices. However, he did not take any measures to deal with it. This is what gave rise to what is now termed 'the transformation problem'.

A majority of Western scholars believe that Marx made serious mistakes in his treatment of this problem, because they claim that when inputs are transformed into prices of production, the equalities could not still both be true, except under restricted conditions. Other scholars believe that it is unnecessary to transform the values of inputs into prices of production. Clearly the transformation problem has given rise to wide controversies.

---

1   In *Theories of Surplus Value* Marx uses the term 'cost price' but in Volume III of *Capital* he refers to this as 'price of production'. In Volume III of *Capital* the term 'cost price' is used in a different sense, referring to the sum of constant and variable capital consumed in production, without the additional surplus-value created by the worker (and hence without the profit appropriated by the capitalist)

Controversies over the transformation problem

Immediately after Volume III of *Capital* was published in 1894, it began facing challenges.

Loria (1895) argued that Marx had switched from the labor theory of value in Volume I to the theory of price of production in Volume III, which he characterized as absurd, a theoretical bankruptcy and scientifically suicidal. Masaryk (1895, see Kuhne 1979, 73) also believed that Marx had failed to give full consideration to empirical reality. Now he had to face it and admit that his theory of value deviated from the real facts. However, both Loria and Masaryk failed to elaborate or comment substantively on Marx's transformation procedure.

Böhm-Bawerk (1884) had also previously criticized the logic of Marx's labor theory of value , arguing that it contradicted the determination of commodity prices. In 1894, with the publication of Volume III, Marx's theory of price of production was thoroughly elaborated. In 1896 he then published *Karl Marx and the Close of His System* (see Sweezy 1949). His criticism was that Marx had examined the commodity exchange in accordance with the labor theory of value in Volume I but in Volume III he asserted that commodity exchange was based on price of production. Marx had therefore contradicted himself; the reason was the labor theory of value.

Böhm-Bawerk argued that on the basis of Marx's value theory, price of production was the aggregate of cost-price and average profit. Cost-price, however, was not equal to value but to price of production. According to this reasoning, the price of production could be divided into two parts or determinants: total wages in different stages of production and total profit calculated in accordance with the general rate of profit, which was actually very close to the second definition of value given by Adam Smith. Böhm-Bawerk concluded that this fact just reflected the contradictory nature of Marx's theoretical system.

We believe Böhm-Bawerk failed to develop a deeper understanding of the implications of value and price of production as well as the role they once played at different periods of history. In essence, he confused price of production with price. Although Böhm-Bawerk approached the issue from an academic perspective, his passion overcame rationality.

In 1904 Hilferding (Sweezy 1949) refuted Böhm-Bawerk's attack, arguing that Marx's theory of value and price of production corresponded to historical categories. Value could only be transformed into price of production in the capitalist system. Seen from this historical perspective, value did not contradict price of production. Hilferding also argued that Böhm-Bawerk could not develop a better understanding of Marx's theories on the basis of psychology-based marginalism.

Both Böhm-Bawerk and Hilferding concerned themselves only with the relationship between Volume I and Volume III of *Capital*. Böhm-Bawerk held that the theory of value contradicted the theory of price of production while Hilferding sustained that price of production was just a variant of value; the two theories were logically related to each other and were not mutually contradictory. However, according to Sweezy (1949, 24) Hilferding also argued that both theories had not so far evolved into actual procedures which could be employed to critically examine transformation.

Bortkiewicz (1952[1906], 1984[1907]) approached the problem from a logic-mathematical perspective. He was not a Marxist, but he sympathized with Marx's ideas. In terms of his academic position, he tended to defend the Ricardian tradition. He was also an ardent follower of Walras with whom he corresponded from the age of 19 (Freeman 2010,11), and held that Marx's theory of value should be developed along Walrasian principles, in the same way that Marshall had developed Ricardo:

> *Alfred Marshall said once of Ricardo: 'He does not state clearly, and in some cases he perhaps did not fully and clearly perceive how, in the problem of normal value, the various elements govern one another mutually , not successively , in a long chain of causation'. ... Modern economics is beginning to free itself gradually from the successivist prejudice, the chief merit being due to the mathematical school led by Léon Walras. (Bortkiewicz 1952[1906]:23-24).*

He considered the labor theory of value and the theory of surplus value to be Marx's most important contributions. However, he also believed that there were serious flaws in Marx's statements about cost-price. This was because price of production was formed through business transactions which guaranteed the equilibrium of social reproduction. As a result, the cost-price of the commodities purchased by each capitalist would be the selling price of other capitalists, which was the price of production.

Bortkiewicz saw this as the principal theoretical dilemma and proposed a transformation procedure based on a linear model containing simultaneous equations which expressed the condition that input prices and values, at the start of a circuit of capital, should be the same as input prices and values at the end of the same circuit. From this he drew the conclusion that total price of production was not equal to total value.

Bortkiewicz elaborated the logic of the transformation problem quite thoroughly, though from his own perspective in which he sought to 'correct' Marx for failing to include the condition of social equilibrium in his procedure. It could be argued that Bortkiewicz was the first scholar who treated the transformation problem seriously. His solution had important influence on subsequent scholars and consequently formed what was called "the classical solutions." Dimitriev (1898) had proposed a similar solution, but it did not attract people's attention. Neither did Bortkiewicz's solution capture worldwide attention until Sweezy (1993[1942]) wrote his own introduction to Bortkiewicz's solution.

Winternitz (1948) criticized Bortkiewicz's solution. He held that Bortkiewicz's solution contradicted the theoretical foundations of Marx's theory of price of production. He criticized the assumption, proposed by Bortkiewicz and Sweezy, that the value of the commodity serving as money should be 1 ($z = 1$ in Bortkiewicz's notation) which he said was irrational, because it meant total price of production would not be equal to total value, which, he argued, conformed more closely to the Marxist thought system.

Winternitz further argued that it was unnecessary for the Bortkiewicz-Sweezy solution to make simple reproduction the prerequisite. The general case required expanding social reproduction. Winternitz therefore introduced a fourth equation asserting that total price of production was equal to total value, which he used in place of the assumption $z = 1$. This perspective reduced transformation to the distribution of social labor. In essence, it departed from the fact that price of production was a particular expression of value and, as a result, the relationship between the two became without foundation .

May (1948) held that Winternitz had made a profound contribution to the relationship between value and the price of production by using mathematical methods. However, he criticized Winternitz's solution because it made total profit deviate from total surplus value, contradicting the original thesis of Marx's theory of value. May also emphasized that the price of production was not a price, but a form of value; this was why it was important to solve the transformation problem.

Dobb (1955, 1973) criticized both the Bortkiewicz-Sweezy solution and the Winternitz solution. He regarded the relationship between value and price of production as a mechanism which included the distribution of labor power, arguing that when value is transformed into price of production, the real wage and the quantity of labor power should be viewed as constant. This had a significant influence on Meek.

Meek (1956a,1956b) abandoned Marx's thesis that total price of production was equal to total value and argued that

$$\frac{\sum a}{\sum v} = \frac{\sum a_p}{\sum v_p}$$

(1)

where a represents the sum of the values of outputs, v is variable capital, and the subscript p indicates the price of production transformed from the values a and v. He believed that this was more consistent with Marx's original thesis. He also made the requirement that total profit be equal to total surplus value a prerequisite for solving the transformation problem.

Using the three departments suggested by Bortkiewicz as an example, and assuming the organic composition of capital of Department II to be equal to the average social organic composition of capital, Meek obtained the results he expected. This solution suggested that the equalities could not both be valid, showing that Meek clearly understood his solution would not solve the transformation problem. He therefore turned to trying to solve the problem from a historical perspective. In other words, he shunned the theoretical analysis.

He then (Meek 1977) proposed a second solution, basically in Bortkiewicz's framework but with a different understanding of the fourth equation. Earlier (Meek 1975) he had attempted a further, different method, trying to deduce price of production from input-output relations. This was deeply influenced by Sraffa and ultimately turned out to be studying price of production on the basis of the quantities of commodities, rather than the value of commodities.

Dickinson (1956) criticized Meek's first solution. He argued that Marx's value theory and his price theory were two concepts at different levels. It was therefore meaningless to compare the two concepts. Dickinson believed that it was adequate to determine the relative ratio and the rate of profit of each commodity type in accordance with the value relationship; there was hence no need for the controversial fourth equation and the transformation problem should be solved without making special assumptions. Okishio (1974) expressed a similar point of view.

Seton (1957) divided the economy into n departments and used mathematical methods to analyze the transformation problem. Seton shared the basic view of Bortkiewicz, Sweezy, Winternitz and Meek on the transformation problem. However he also agreed with Dickinson that price ratios and the rate of profit should be determined without a fourth equation. Seton however argued that with simple reproduction across the three departments, if the organic composition of capital in the department producing luxury goods was equal to the social average composition of capital, Bortkiewicz's $z = 1$ condition could be satisfied along with both equalities. Seton's solution had many limitations, and he eventually concluded that Marx's labor theory of value made no contribution to solving the transformation problem, and was actually an obstacle to a solution.

Brock (1962) thought Seton's approach solved the transformation problem; Samuelson also thought highly of Seton's solution. However, we feel this praise is not appropriate. Seton's logic was widely accepted by Western academia who questioned it no further. Debates now turned to whether or not the labor theory of value was valid.

Samuelson (1971) argued that value and price were replaceable but not reconcilable. He believed that values and prices, as defined by the transformation problem, were mutually exclusive. Initially he accepted the basic ideas of Marx's theory of price of production, that when profit was zero, or in the departments where the organic composition of capital were the same, equivalent exchange based on equal labor could be valid. However, he argued that under these conditions it was unnecessary to prove the labor theory of value or its extension to prices of production. By employing input-output equations, scholars could analyze similar equilibrium price systems without recourse to values determined by the amount of labor. This led him to criticize the Bortkiewicz tradition, formulating his famous 'eraser' critique of the Bortkiewicz solution which he wrongly attributed to Marx himself: Marx first writes down a set of equations determining value, he said, and then erases it and writes down another set determining price. Scorning the resultant scholarship, he tried to show that the "reverse transformation" from price to value could take place. As he said, "just as Marx could turn Hegel upside down, we can turn Marx upside down." (Samuelson 1971)

Steedman's (1977) *Marx after Sraffa* then argued Marx's theory of value could – and should – be replaced by a type of political economy, using Sraffa's (1960) theory based on relationships between physical quantities. He argued that price of production could be deduced without relying on the concept of value, using mathematical relationships determined by technology and the wage level. From this perspective, Marx's concept of value was unnecessary and also contradictory. Steedman argued that Marx expressed the rate of profit in terms of value and so derived price of production from value, but that price of production could actually be derived directly from physical magnitudes. Moreover when this was done, it turns out that the value profit rate is incorrect. The whole transformation process was therefore incorrect. Steedman (1977, 30) thus believed that input prices had been transformed, but the results were fraught with conflicts (Steedman 1977, 30).

Morishima (1973) rebutted Samuelson's view by clarifying Marx's dual value concept and showing that the value system and the price system were not inconsistent. Morishima and Catephores (1978), by employing a Markov process with multiple iterations, transformed both input and output values into prices of production In such a way that the two equalities were both valid.

Morishima also correctly pointed out that when Marx solved the two equalities equations in his transformation procedure, he abstracted from the concept of time in the transformation process. This was why it was hard for him to make the two equalities both valid, which could help shed light on the quantitative relationships in the transformation problem. However, Morishima insisted on his own particular model and believed that the labor theory of value was meaningless. He also rejected the idea of 'historical transformation.'

From the 1980s onwards, two broad camps on the transformation problem gradually formed. One camp was strongly against Marx's labor theory of value and denied his approach to transformation. It argued that

1. The labor theory of value was useless. The relative price of commodities could be deduced from the technological relation between physical inputs and outputs, as Samuelson and Steedman had argued;
2. There was also no connection between luxuries, or departments producing non-basic commodities and the social general rate of profit.

The others argued that

1. The labor theory of value was scientific and should be made the theoretical basis for solving the transformation problem;
2. Prices of production could be deduced from the value system. Essentially, Marx's statement that value could be transformed to price of production was correct;
3. Marx's transformation did not testify to a ratio relationship between price of production and value but to a deviation of the former from the latter;
4. There should be some prerequisite for the validity of the equalities;
5. Marx failed to transform inputs into price of production and consequently slipped into an technical error when dealing with transformation.

From the 1980s onward, few scholars criticized Marx's transformation theory as such. Instead, scholars from the pro-camp or half-pro-camp proposed new solutions for the transformation problem.

Shaikh (1977, 1984) argued that the key issue of the transformation problem was how to develop a deeper understanding of Marx's value theory. He abandoned the Bortkiewicz tradition and rejected Böhm-Bawerk and Samuelson's criticism of Marx's transformation procedure. He insisted that by using the 'feedback' method to extend Marx's solution, scholars could expect to see the transformation of value to price of production. And, under the conditions of equilibrium growth, the equalities could be valid simultaneously.

Shaikh however began by making total price of production equal to total value the assumption and, to make this assumption valid, adjusted monetary wages in each step of the transformation process. Clearly, this was not logical.

Duménil (1980, 1983) provided a new interpretation of the transformation problem. He argued that Marx's labor theory of value was a basic theory which should be adhered to, but that the equalities should be reconsidered. He contended that the statement that total profit was equal to total surplus value was meaningless, while the statement that total price of production was equal to total value was also not valid. He argued that the phrase 'total profit is equal" should be replaced with a statement like "total income arising from net sales in a given period is related to the total labor expended in that same period." He held that inputs into the next period of production would be revalued; to deal with this, instead of stating that total price equals the total value of a given period, we should state that the total income equals the total labor power of that period. Duménil also criticized Marx's assumption of a uniform rate of surplus value.

Foley (1982) and Lipietz (1982) independently articulated similar viewpoints, differing only in the way they presented and thought about the issues. The solution provided by Foley and Lipietz is sometimes called the New Solution or the New Interpretation.

Richard D. Wolff, Antonino Callari and Bruce Roberts (1984) further elaborated on the transformation problem but within a static general equilibrium analytical framework. Their solution is usually called the Wolff-Callari-Roberts (WCR) solution or following Kliman's (2007) terminology, the 'Simultaneous Single System Interpretation' (SSSI). WCR argued that it was important to adhere to Marx's labor theory of value and of price of production. However, they held that the magnitude of value transferred to the product by constant capital was equal to the price of production of the means of production consumed. They argued that only in this way could social reproduction proceed normally. They further argued that the cost of variable capital to the capitalists would be the price of labor-power rather than its value. As a result, WCR's argument that the fixed capital could transfer value while the variable capital could generate value is disputable. The argument that the two invariant equalities could both be valid is also contestable.

In the 1990s and at the turn of 21st century, A. Freeman and A. Kliman, and other writers from the 'Temporal Single System Interpretation' (TSSI) school offered solutions to the transformation problem which captured wide attention (Freeman and Carchedi 1996). Their objective was not however to offer yet another solution but to demonstrate the validity of Marx's own solution. To this end they also sought to develop a better understanding of the theory of value, the basic theory of Marxist economic system, and of Marx's transformation theory, arguing that if Marx was properly understood the transformation problem did not really exist. This distinctive idea endowed the transformation problem with new implications.

The TSSI school approached the transformation problem by articulating two ideas: that of the single system and that of the temporal system.

Put simply, the idea behind the single system is that the value of the capital advanced, and hence that of the constant capital consumed, depends on the price of commodities when purchased by the capitalists that consume them as inputs, rather than the value of these same commodities when produced as outputs of the previous circuit. Price is from this perspective simply a quantitatively modified form of the original value.

The idea behind the temporal system is that value and the price were determined in time rather than simultaneously. Crucially, this rules out the simultaneous equation determination of Bortkiewicz tradition, including in particular the calculations proposed by Sweezy, Winternitz, Seton, Meek and Steedman, in which – consistent with the notion that Marx's value theory should be understood as a variant of Walrasian general equilibrium – it is supposed that values at the end of a period of production must necessarily equal those at the beginning of the same period, and that prices of production at the end of the period must necessarily equal those at the beginning of the same period. Instead, TSSI supposes that values and prices at the end of a period are equal to values and prices at the start of the *next* period, mathematically a completely different assumption.

The TSSI shared some connection with other solutions that came about at the same time. Like WCR and New Solution theorists, it recognizes, following Ramos (1996) that value, for Marx, has two expressions – its intrinsic expression as a quantity of labor time and its extrinsic expression as a sum of money. The ratio between the two is what Foley terms the 'value of money' and its inverse is termed by Ramos (1995, see also Ramos and Rodriguez 1996) the 'Monetary Expression of Labour Time' or the MELT. However, in common with WCR it differed from the New Solution by proposing that constant capital, as well as variable capital, was modified by transformation. And in distinction from TSSI, WCR based themselves on the simultaneous determination of values and price, although it could be argued that their treatment of transformation was independent of their simultaneism.

TSSI scholars were also informed by Markov chain or iterative approaches such as that of Morishima and Catephores mentioned above. However, unlike Morishima and Catephores who proposed that the sequence in which successive values and prices were formed should be regarded as purely logical, TSSI scholars argued that the process took place in real, that is historical time, and hence corresponded to the actual sequence of values and prices found in a real capitalist economy.

Finally, TSSI scholars did not claim to have produced a new solution to the transformation problem, but argued that they were clarifying Marx's own value theory. Although the TSSI school maintained that Marx's labor theory of value and the theory of price of production should be made the theoretical foundations of the transformation problem study, their reinterpretation of the concept of value simplified this concept. However, the single and temporal systems also contained conflicts. They led to the conclusion that the two equalities could both be valid, and that conclusion followed naturally without being proved.

Seen from the standpoint of the history of the study of transformation problem, we argue that differences between transformation scholars, whether pro-transformation theory scholars or anti-transformation theory scholars, dependent on differences in theoretical background. The reason for these differences lay in how scholars saw value theory and the theory of price of production, as well as in how they understood the theoretical foundations and essence of the transformation problem.

Implications of studying value transformation

The theory of value and its transformation are the basic theories of Marx's economic system, which Marx first elaborated as the theory of value and then as the transformation of value into price of production. However, Marx maintained that value formed the basis of price of production and that its transformation did not contradict the labor theory of value, As regards the labor theory of value, the theory of price of production elaborated the transition of value from its abstract to its concrete form. As regards the theory of surplus value, it elaborated on the transition of surplus value from its general form to its particular form.

Marx's theory of price of production, however, defused the tension between the law of value and the existence of prices of production. The fact that equal quantities of capital yielded the same amount of profit did not mean contradict the labor theory of value but constituted its application when capitalist economic relationships had reached a certain stage. Similarly, the emergence of an average profit and of prices of production did not signify the end of the labor theory of value but, on the contrary, was a true reflection of that theory's validity.

The theory of value transformation was one of the most controversial issues in Marxist economics and one of the most frequent targets of anti-Marxist economics. Nevertheless, a uniform perspective on the transformation theory so far has not formed, either in the Marxist or the anti-Marxist camps. This is why the transformation problem has important implications.

Firstly, the labor theory of value is the bedrock of Marxist economics. If it is disproved by the transformation problem the whole Marxist economic system is undermined. To take an example consider the equality of total price of production and total value. If this thesis lacks validity, price of production cannot be a necessary reflection of value; however it underpins many issues elaborated in Volume III of *Capital*; If the transformation is wrong, we must hence conclude that the law of value *per se* has serious weaknesses.

Many Western economists made this their point of attack on Marx's labor theory of value. Therefore, the equality is not a mere technical issue, but concerns the foundations of Marx's economic system.

Seen from the perspective of the second equality, if total profit does not equal total surplus value, it would mean that average profit is not redistributed on the basis of a division of surplus value in proportion to capital advanced; also the thesis that surplus value is the source of profit would not hold.

The transformation problem therefore had, and continues to have, profound implications for defending the Marxist economic system.

Furthermore, transformation theory is the premise of social distribution theory. Value transformation is actually a process of distribution at the macro level. In this process, surplus values are divided between the capitalists of different departments while the use value of commodities are realized throughout society in the form of prices of production. As a result, relationships of distribution in all walks of life are formed. Clearly, these relationship cannot be explained without a rational transformation theory.

Finally, the construction of a theory of price on the foundation of labor theory of value was a remarkable sign of distinction between Marxist and non-Marxist economics. Non-Marxist economists tend to try and disprove it by choosing to criticize Marx's transformation theory, or even by replacing price of production with value. We believed that by studying the transformation problem, Marxist economics can rebut the irrational arguments of anti-Marxist economists, and in so doing, defend the scientific nature of Marxist economics.

Research methods for studying value transformation

As Marx pointed out, human beings constantly create principles, concepts and categories in accordance with their social relationships. The category of the 'economy' was not a product of pure reason but a theoretical reflection of actual relations of production. Since this category is the theoretical expression of the relations of production, and since the development of these relations is a historical process, then the development of the category should also be a historical process, just like the relations of production.

Generally speaking, the development of productivity results in changes in the relations of production. Since the category of the 'economy' is a theoretical expression of the relations of production, we should expect it to evolve and develop with these relations. The concepts and implications of Marxist economics are not changeless, but evolve constantly, nourishing itself from many sources. Only by adhering to historical materialist philosophy and dialectical method can we develop a better understanding of any concept in Marxist economics: the transformation problem is no exception.

In this way we should seek a deeper understanding of the fact that average profit and price of production are just the form in which surplus value and value are distributed. This helps capture the essence of the transformation problem, making it easier to understand the relationship between the many variables of distribution.

In addition, in this volume we will adopt the following research methods:

1. We integrate the study of the abstract with that of the concrete. This allows us to distinguish content from form within the complex. For instance, by studying the intermediate stage in which surplus value is transformed into average profit, Marx rightly concluded that average profit and price of production were expressions of surplus value and value. Ricardo ran into trouble on this point and Samuelson and neo-Ricardians also fell short, drawing the wrong conclusion that Volume 1 of *Capital* contradicted that of Volume 3.

2. We integrate the logical analytical method with the historical and dynamic analytical method. Logical method should be based on historical research, but logical method independent of historical process is frequently used by Western economists. This is why the vast majority of Western scholars reject the transformation of value to price of production in history. This prevented them developing a deeper understanding of the transformation problem. The concept of price of production reflects not only a stage of historical development but the fact that social reproduction is a dynamic, continuous process. At the same time, the concepts of input and output are not absolute. So, the equality between total price of production and that of values is not a mere question of 'magnitude'. From the point of view of Bortkiewiczian mathematics, we should not expect this equality to hold. But dynamic analysis shows that it does indeed hold and indeed, if it did not, Marxist economics would lose the scientific nature it was supposed to have. Most transformation scholars failed to integrate dynamic analysis with static analysis, choosing to approach the problem from the allegedly logical standpoint of equilibrium

analysis. They then seized on the wrong conclusion that total price of production was not equal to total value and concluded that Marx's labor theory of value contradicted the theory of price of production.

3. We integrate qualitative and quantitative methods. The most important issue in researching the transformation problem is that of the essence of the capitalist relationship of production. "We need present only the inner organization of the capitalist mode of production, in its ideal average, as it were." (Marx 1998, 818) Therefore, qualitative analysis is a must. However, everything in this world had both a qualitative and a quantitative aspect. In other words, everything must have a quantitative limit. We believe that quantitative relationships are an integral expression of phenomena. Therefore only if we conduct quantitative analysis can we capture the essence of the phenomenon, and the transformation problem therefore needs a mathematically precise proof. (Marx 1998, 197) This section elaborates on the transformation problem by combining qualitative and quantitative methods.

Structure of Book II

Book II can be thought of as composed of three sections, the first outlining the issue, the second presenting our own approach, and the third analyzing the approaches of Western scholars.

In Chapter 3 we outline the origins of the transformation problem and present a roadmap of research. We also present the implications of studying the transformation problem and provide a research methodology and framework.

Chapter 4 constitutes the core of Book II. It provides a brief introduction to the theoretical foundations of our construction, then defines the implications of the price of production and average profit from different angles as the two key concepts involved. By conceptualizing them, we believe the essence of the transformation problem can be captured and the main research questions identified. This chapter also provides a brief explanation of the mathematical issues in the transformation problem. It presents the authors' construction of this problem, presenting a static transformation model and a dynamic transformation model based on our historical, logical and dynamic analysis. We also elaborate on the two equalities.

The models are then tested to see whether the transformation of value into prices of production in Marxist transformation theory is rigorous and exact, which we think of as the transformation problem in a narrow sense.

The following chapters then elaborate on the arguments of Western scholars on transformation, finding that they have a negative attitude towards Marx's labor theory of value and question the need to transform values into price of production, which we think of as the transformation problem in a broad sense.

Chapter 5 gives a brief introduction to the classical solutions of the transformation problem. These include the models of Bortkiewicz and Winternitz, and Meek's solution A. We argue that these models share Bortkiewicz's tradition and are sympathetic to Marx's transformation theory.

In chapter 6 we elaborate on the Seton and Morishima models. These two test whether the two equalities can both be valid. However, they impose stringent conditions. Outwardly, they are presented as perfecting the logic of Marx's transformation theory, but actually, they were trying to find a proof that the labor theory of value should be abandoned.

The next chapter provides an introduction to Samuelson, Steedman and Meek's Solution B approaches to the transformation problem. One of their points in common is that they abandon the labor theory of value as the theoretical foundation of transformation study. Instead, they approach it by deducing the input-output price of production from within Sraffa's analytical framework. In so doing they actually deny the existence of the transformation problem.

The final chapter offers a detailed introduction to the new solutions to the transformation problem. These include that of Shaikh, the New Solution/Interpretation, the Wolf-Callari-Roberts model and the TSSI school, all proposed in the 1980s. A common point of these new solutions is to restore the labor theory of value as the theoretical foundation of the transformation problem. However, they do not confine themselves to the traditional goals of transformation scholarship. Some of these models, therefore, also modify the concept of value of the Marxist economic system.

3
Theoretical foundations and research methods

Many solutions to the transformation problem have been proposed, based on many theories. Some Marxist scholars sought to revise Marx's labor theory of value, some to revise that of production price, and still others to revise the concept of value as such. All these revisions were intended to solve the problem, but backfired because their theoretical foundations led to wrong conclusion. The solutions suggested by opponents of Marx's theory was of course non-Marxist. Our conclusion in summary is that the theoretical foundations adopted, in addressing the transformation problem, dictate way its study is scientifically conducted. Before constructing our model of transformation, we therefore elaborate these foundations.

Theoretical foundations of the study of value transformation

The labor theory of value

Labor and value

Marx's concept of transformation was built on the labor theory of value. Without understanding it scientifically, no true understanding of the problem is possible, and hence neither is any correct theory. Western Marxist scholars generally propose conflicting solutions; this arises from their inadequate understanding of the labor theory of value. Samuelson, Steedman and others then sought to drop the labor theory of value as the theoretical foundation of the transformation problem and instead make price the starting point. But they too reached the wrong conclusion, getting bogged down in theorizing value. Both show why we need to elaborate the scientific character of the labor theory of value.

Labor, its instruments, and its subject are sources of material wealth from a use-value perspective. But to human beings, a commodity is not just an economic category but also has important social implications. When commodities are exchanged, their commonality is labor above all else. As for use value, its general form depends on the specific form of each distinct use-value, and so can never be the basis on which different commodities are exchanged. When Marx set out to prove that living labor was the only source of value, he neither used the elimination method like Böhm-Bawerk, nor did he confine himself to the non-empirical method. His elaboration combined normative and empirical analysis.

The labor theory of value came into being before Marx. However Petty, Smith, and Ricardo chose to use the metaphysical method and the non-historical perspective to study labor and value. Although they had made significant contributions to the study of value, exchange value and magnitude of value, they failed to grasp the essence of labor and value. It was not until Marx proposed the duality of labor that the problems related to the theory of value in classical economics were resolved.

Marx, having thoroughly analyzed the essence, magnitude and forms of value, found that value was no more than the social expression of labor. Under specific relationships of production, the product of labor was commodities and the exchange of labor was conducted in the form of commodities. Marx therefore argued that value was actually a kind of social relationship and contended that living labor was the only source of value. On this basis, he examined the capitalist mode of production and created the theory of surplus value. This theory evolved into the theoretical basis for theories of capital, profit, rent, social reproduction, and economic crisis. In sum, the labor theory of value became the theoretical foundation of Marxist economic theory.

The scientific basis of the labor theory of value

Joan Robinson once argued that none of the essential points of the Marxist system depended on the labor theory of value (Zhu 1991, 19; Robinson 1960,

21). The truth, we argue, is the opposite: every essential point in Marx's economic system is built on the labor theory of value. Since living labor is the only source of the value of commodities, only variable capital can create new value and surplus value.

From this, the following can be deduced:

1. the magnitude of surplus value is positively related to variable capital but unrelated to constant capital;

2. the greater the proportion of constant capital in value magnitudes, the lower the rate of profit. The fact that the capitalists rack their brains to save means of production and increase the rate of profit bears testimony to this principle;

3. the same magnitude of capital with different organic composition of capital across different departments creates varying rates of profit, given equal rates of surplus value.

Therefore, only by relying on the labor theory of value can we develop a clear understanding of the capitalist mode of production (Mandel 1979, 353-4 see also Mandel 1974).

However, the labor theory of value's explanatory power, in interpreting economic phenomena, was not expressed very directly. For example, Marx's study of market price and the tension between supply and demand was not limited to simple commodity production, and he cast doubt on the use of studying the supply-demand relationship and market price within the boundary of simple production, arguing that the factor of capital should instead be made as an assumption. The supply-demand relationship and the fluctuations of market prices were then subsumed under the category of capital flows and capital competition, figuring prominently in the latter. In addition, Marx also proposed a systematic theory of superprofit, providing theoretical evidence for the study of land tax and monopoly profit.

This theory further laid the foundations for using income capitalization theory to explain land price, stock prices and bond prices. All of these were explained by the labor theory of value. In like vein, when the development of the capitalist economy had risen to a certain level, equal magnitudes of capital could secure equal magnitudes of profit. However, to prove this Marx also developed the theory of price of production.

Price of production

In a simple commodity-based economy, the whole production process is rather simple and basically depends on living labor. Commodities are exchanged according to the principle of equal value. Therefore, the issue of equal profits for equal capital magnitudes does not exist. However, once simple commodity production reaches the stage of a capitalist commodity-based economy, the means of production assume an increasingly important position, and the proportion of constant capital in capital advanced also rises. But since productivity across different departments varies, so does the organic composition of capital and the rate of capital turnover.

in contrast, competition between workers levels out the rate of exploitation between departments. Rates of profit then inexorably tend to equalize across departments and surplus value thus completes "the first kind of transformation" to profit. Seen from another perspective, the flow of capital is always towards those places where the rate of profit is highest. At the same time, capital withdraws from spheres with a low rate of profit and invades others which yield a higher profit (Marx 1894, 195).

> Through this incessant outflow and influx, or, briefly, through its distribution among the various spheres, which depends on how the rate of profit falls here and rises there, it creates such a ratio of supply to demand that the average profit in the various spheres of production becomes the same, and values are, therefore, converted into prices of production.

Therefore, it can be seen that the formation of prices of production and the general rate of profit are not assumptions but a theorem, about a phenomenon which comes to the surface only when the economy reaches a certain stage. This theorem rested on the assumptions that competition and resources can flow between departments and that rates of profit are not equal across different departments. That was to say, the existence of production prices precedes the formation of the general rate of profit.

It should be noted that the general rate of profit is formed on the basis of the actual inputs of the capitalists. This point, however, is likely to be overlooked as Marx's transformation in Volume III does not convert inputs into

62

production price. Consequently, if inputs are measured in accordance with value, the general rate of profit can be expressed as follows:

$$r_1 = \frac{\sum m_i}{\sum(c_i + v_i)} \tag{1}$$

Here c_i, v_i and m_i stand for constant capital, variable capital and surplus value in Department i. If inputs are calculated on the basis of production price, the average profit is:

$$r_2 = \frac{\sum m_i}{\sum(a_i c_i + \beta_i v_i)} \tag{2}$$

where α_i and β_i stand for the production price-value coefficients of constant and variable capital. At this point, r_1 and r_2 stand for the stable general rate of profit. Clearly, total profit is equal to total surplus value. If the average rates of profit were not equal to r_1 and r_2 – say, for example, that total profit was 10% higher than total surplus value, then the capitalists would have no choice but to raise their selling price by 10% whilst still purchasing at the same purchase price. This was the way it should be. In terms of the relationship between the sum of capital and the sum of labor-power, this situation could only be temporary. In order to live, the workers must obtain the basic wages necessary for their daily life. But the rise in wages would pull things back to the original situation. Therefore, total profits would have to equal total surplus value and total production price would have to equal total value. In the final analysis, production price is determined by, and deduced, value instead of from the general rate of profit, even though total production price is related to the general rate of profit.

Thus it can be seen that production price is an exact expression of value. Production price, and price as such, are actually two concepts belonging to different levels. As Rosdolsky (1982) notes, Marx's production price is by no means the market price. Instead, it is the modified value after calculating the average profit rate. May (1948) also defends the concept of production price proposed by Winternitz:

but in relating these two concepts to actual prices, to the actual ex-
changes, which, it must be remembered, are not involved in the defini-
tions of value and production price in terms of labor time involved in
the productive process.

Okishio (1955) and Dickinson (1956) sympathize with May on this point. The afore-mentioned analysis is clearly conducted without reference to the monetary factor. Laibman (1983) points out that if production price was expressed by commodity money whilst value was expressed in the form of labor time, then the two would have no relations. But production price and value belong to the same level, whose unit is labor time.

Even if money is taken into consideration, price of production should not be confused with price. Not only Bortkiewicz and Sweezy but also many other scholars view price of production, wittingly or unwittingly, as price. According to their view, since production price is determined by the organic composition of capital of the department producing the money commodity, then it is important whether or not total production price equals total value. On the other hand, Marx's production price can be studied from its monetary expression. But the production price expressed in the form of monetary units refers to the redistribution of total surplus value among all capitalists. So it is essentially unimportant to express production price in monetary units.

Thus, for value, its composition can be measured and expressed in the form of labor time: cost-price plus profit. However, it can also be expressed or measured in terms of other types of commodities. In like manner, the same method can be applied to measure or express production price as the sum of cost-price and average profit.

We conclude that production price is no more than a variant of value which still belongs to the category of value. The law of value, as the basis of the law of production price, is then expressed as follows: in some depart-ments, value is not equal to production price. But the sum of production prices in all departments taken together is subsumed under the category of the sum of values. The way in which the law of value determines a commod-ity economy is reflected in the law of production price: the law of value does not contradict the law of production price, and Volume III of Capital does not contradict Volume I of Capital.

Comparison of Marx's theory of production price to Sraffa's theory of price

In 1960, Sraffa published *The Production of Commodities by Means of Commodities*. In it, he set out to build a production system which did not begin from the concept of 'margin'. Instead he sought to make the inputs of labor and means of production endogenous variables, so as to study the effects of changes in the wage, rate of profit and relative prices of commodities.

The neo-Ricardian school then tried to turn Sraffa's theory into a type of value theory, and use it to reexamine classical and Marxist economics. Sraffa's theory was widely held to have important implications for solving the transformation problem. Many transformation studies by Western scholars were actually conducted in Sraffa's framework. For this reason, we need to examine Sraffa's price theory and compare it to Marx's theory of production price theory.

We first examine the price theory based on Sraffa's logic, which theorizes a production model producing a surplus, of which the workers can take possession of part. This yields a price system:

$$
\begin{cases}
(A_a P_a + B_a P_b + \cdots + K_a P_k)(1 + r) + L_a \dot\omega = A P_a \\
(A_b P_a + B_b P_b + \cdots + K_b P_k)(1 + r) + L_b \dot\omega = B P_b \\
\cdots\cdots\cdots\cdots\cdots\cdots\cdots\cdots\cdots \\
\cdots\cdots\cdots\cdots\cdots\cdots\cdots\cdots\cdots \\
(A_k P_a + B_k P_b + \cdots + K_k P_k)(1 + r) + L_k \dot\omega = K P_k
\end{cases}
\tag{3}
$$

where

a, b, ..., k stand for commodities produced by departments,
A, B, ..., K stand for the annual output of a, b, ... , k;
A_a, B_a, ..., K_a stand for the amount of a, b, ... , k used in producing A etc.;
L_a, L_a, ..., L_a stand for the labor-power needed to produce A, B, ..., K
$\dot\omega$ stands for the wage derived from each unit of labor;
and P_a, P_β, ..., P_k stand for the prices of each type of commodity.

P_k, the rate of profit r, and the wage rate $\dot\omega$ are all unknown variables.

Assuming this system can have a surplus, we also have:

$$\begin{cases} A_a + A_b + \cdots + A_k \leq A \\ B_a + B_b + \cdots + B_k \leq B \\ \cdots\cdots\cdots\cdots\cdots\cdots\cdots\cdots \\ \cdots\cdots\cdots\cdots\cdots\cdots\cdots\cdots \\ K_a + K_b + \ldots + K_k \leq K \end{cases} \tag{4}$$

This system contains k independent equations and unknown $k + 2$ variables. If one commodity is selected and its value made the standard, then assuming its price is 1, and either r or $\dot\omega$ is determined exogenously, then all unknowns can be calculated.

On the basis of this model Sraffa studied

1. differences between the percentage of labor power and means of production consumed by different departments;
2. the measurement of value;
3. the conversion to the labor power of a particular period.

Meek (1973) and Steedman (1977) maintained that the Sraffa system was the result of the Marxist system. Only by sticking to Sraffa's production conditions and quantitative analysis based on real commodities, could we determine the rate of profit and production price and develop a clear understanding of the conflicting relationship between wage and profit, and that between surplus value and profit, all of which were beyond the reach of Marx's value analysis. By relying on the Sraffa system, scholars could bypass the difficulties caused by the transformation problem. Moreover, they could demonstrate the exploitation in the capitalist system which Marx had always been bent on obtaining. From this perspective, we argue that the Sraffa system does have many strengths. Let's take a look at them.

Firstly, the Sraffa system is quite consistent with Marx's method of logical-historical analytical method. As Meek argued: "as long as the clarification of the proof of the system was provided, with very few modifications and improvement" (Meek 1977, 133), Sraffa can be related to Marx and "the sequence of Sraffian models can be made to do essentially the same job which Marx's labor theory of value was employed to do." (Meek 1977, 133) Meek exhibits five production models which are also consistent with the logical-historical analytical method.

Sraffa held that since the ratio of labor to means of production consumed by different departments was different, and since this ratio determined production prices, changes in the distribution of wages and profits would impact the rate of profit and the relative price of commodities (Ding Baojun 2001). Moreover, Ding notes, "Sraffa holds that the key research question is his study of the impact of wage fluctuations on profit and prices of various commodities."

On this point, Marx's method of analyzing the impact of organic composition across departments on the general rate of profit and prices of production shares similarities with Sraffa. Sraffa's criticism of marginal utility and marginal productivity distribution theory was also commendable.

However, as we have noted, there were dramatic differences between Sraffa's price theory and Marx's production price theory.

Above all, Sraffa's price theory was built on static equilibrium analysis. He was hence unable to refute neo-classical theory thoroughly and build a dynamic economic system, nor could his system be used to analyze the transformation from values to production prices. As we have shown, the transformation problem can only be solved by means of dynamic disequilibrium analysis on the basis of the labor theory of value, combined with scientific evidence for the formation of production prices. It is hence absurd to argue that Sraffa's price theory can replace Marx's theory of production price.

Next, the Sraffa system made labor and the means of production endogenous variables. In doing so, relative price ceased to be the index of the input of labor and means of production. This made the connection between relative price, cost, and output uncertain. The real relationships between variable capital, surplus value, average profit and production price were concealed. Rowthorn (1971) also wrongly argued that profit derived from the circulation and exploitation arose in the sphere of distribution. Furthermore, Sraffa's theory concealed the process of capital accumulation and creation of surplus value. Not surprisingly, it failed to show how profit was created. Sraffa's price theory was thus inadequate in helping understand how transformation took place, and could not solve the transformation problem.

Thirdly, profit and price are completely determined by the material conditions of production and the wage rate. Value as such plays little role in determining the general rate of profit or production price. It has become a redundant concept in analyzing the exchange relationship. But in fact, it is the labor process that determines the numerical values or indexes of material goods production. Human labor determines the different types of inputs and outputs and the labor process materializes value in different types of use value. Therefore, it is value that determines the various indices of material goods production.

As Shaikh (1990) points out in *The Poverty of Algebra*, Sraffa makes two mistakes. He first views production as a technological rather than a labor process, so the social process emphasized is not production but distribution. He then overlooks the actual process by which labor time brings about adjustments in exchange, and calculates value from data about material goods. But the latter cannot determine the former, just as calculating the earth's weight cannot tell us what produces that weight.

Seen from another perspective, to derive production price from production price is not an impossible method. But if the principle is to integrate historical with logical analysis, it is more consistent to deduce both price of production and market price from the standpoint of value. "In Marx's time, Sraffa's method did not come to the surface. So what he could use was the deductive method, deducing value from price." (Meek 1977, 385-6) But without the value standard as basis, average profit and cost-price are imaginary and unfounded terminologies. As a result, scholars risk using circular arguments.

The fourth problem (Ding Baojun 2001) concerns Sraffa's so-called 'reduction to dated labor', illustrated by the production equation of commodity a:

$$(A_a P_a + B_a B_p + \ldots + K_a P_k)\,(1 + r) + L_a \dot{\omega} = AP_a \qquad (5)$$

Its conversion equation is:

$$L_a \dot{\omega} + L_{a1} \dot{\omega}\,(1 + r) + L_{a2} \dot{\omega}\,(1 + r)^2 + \ldots + L_{an} \dot{\omega}\,(1 + r)^n + \ldots = AP_a \qquad (6)$$

where $L_a \dot{\omega}$ stands for the value of direct labor power used, and

$$L_{a1} \dot{\omega}\,(1 + r) + L_{a2} \dot{\omega}\,(1 + r)^2 + \ldots + L_{an} \dot{\omega}\,(1 + r)^n + \ldots$$

stands for the value of indirect labor power consumed as means of production in each stage of production.

Sraffa hence deduces the value of commodity *a*, or the labor power condensed into the commodity, by relying on the production price of a particular department. Now after value has been transformed into price of production, total production price equals total value. But for a particular department, production price does not equal value, because the inequality between the two arises from the ratio of the organic composition of capital of a given department to the average composition of social capital. Therefore, it is impossible to deduce value from production price via Sraffa's conversion equation. Sraffa is in effect trying to convert value into labor power purchased rather than labor power consumed. Seen from a different perspective, no matter how far the conversion could be pushed back, there was always a "commodity remainder" outside the labor items. As Hu Daiguang (1988, 119-120) criticized:

> it was totally impossible. The reason why Sraffa arrived at such a conclusion was that it rested on the assumption that all production activities employed the same technologies and there were constant returns. However, in real economic life, production techniques were under constant change and development......it was hard eliminate the 'commodity remainder' from commodity value.

Finally, let us take a look at the invariable standard of value in Sraffa's price theory. Sraffa noticed that the rise and fall in wages could cause fluctuations in prices. However, was there a department producing a 'standard commodity' for which the rise and fall in wages would not cause a deficit or surplus, which could show an equilibrium between wage and profit? Sraffa believed that as long as the ratio of labor to means of production of this department was just sitting on the dividing line between deficit and surplus, then the standard commodity did exist. Sraffa then obtained a 'composite commodity' for which, when adopted as the standard commodity, the price remained constant despite changes in distribution. If adopted as an invariant value standard, it could be used as a standard of price.

This was not a value standard in a true sense, and in its implications, was dramatically different from Ricardo's invariable standard of value. Marx had already made a clear distinction between the intrinsic, or inner standard of commodity value and its extrinsic, or outer standard. He pointed out that the value of any commodity was constantly changing. Sraffa's "standard commodity' had positive merits, but it was totally different from the commodities produced by departments with the same average organic composition of social capital in Marx's theory of price of production.

Therefore, Sraffa's price theory and Marx's theory of production price were speaking different languages, and could hardly be related to each other. Sraffa's price theory actually contributed little to the solution of the transformation problem.

Sraffa's price theory emphasized the relationship between material goods in production, and that between wage and profit. It represented on the one hand a regression to the classical school and on the other a challenge to the neo-classical school which prided itself on being able to employ equilibrium analysis of production and demand at the same time as marginal analysis. We believe that Sraffa's price theory did not really touch on the transformation problem at all. So it is inappropriate to say that this theory has solved the long-disputed and riddle-ridden transformation problem, and to argue that Sraffa's price theory had provided a new tool to study the transformation problem (Meek 1977, 124), because Sraffa's analysis was devoid of the concept of value from the outset. According to Sraffa, even though he tried to convert the price of means of production to labor, value was essentially the equivalent of price.

The nature of value transformation

Marx elaborated on the transformation problem as early as the 1861-1863 *Economic Manuscripts* and in *Theories of Surplus Value*. He criticized Ricardo for failing to understand the logic of how the general rate of profit was formed, thus confusing value with production price.

In Volumes I and II of *Capital*, Marx studied the production process of surplus value, and the circulation and reproduction of surplus value respectively. In the first section of Volume III, he examined the transformation of surplus value into profit, commenting on cost-price, profit and the rate of profit. He then moved to the second section of Volume III, where he studied how profit was transformed into the average profit and how commodity value was transformed into price of production. In conclusion, Marx pointed out that average profit was simply surplus value equally distributed in proportion to capital advanced.

Marx's exploration of the transformation problem was going progressively deeper by relying on the concept of value and the law of value as defined in Volume I of *Capital*. The topics in Volume III cover many forms of capital flows, bringing the illustrations closer to the real world by studying the interactions between different types of capital. By analyzing these interactions, Marx also studied the necessity of these forms. His dynamic analysis adopted the dialectical approach of moving from simplicity to complexity.

However, some scholars argue that the views in Volume III conflict with those in Volume I. We will argue this is a misunderstanding, arising from their failure to develop a deeper understanding of the methodology of Marxist economics. Marx, while discussing, adopted very different methods from Ricardo. He analyzed the extended forms of value by insisting on the concept of value as theoretical basis. He developed intermediary categories like surplus value, the distinction between constant and variable capital, the organic composition of capital, the rate of profit and the general rate of profit. The law of production price did not therefore contradict the law of value but was the concrete form of that law when economic development reached a certain stage. If conflicts emerged in fact, these belonged to the conflict between nature and phenomenon, rather than within his system. In a letter to Kugelmann Marx (May 31st 1873) said:

> *Science consists precisely in demonstrating how the law of value asserts itself. So that if one wanted at the very beginning to "explain" all the phenomenon which seemingly contradict that law, one would have to present science before science. It is precisely Ricardo's mistake that in his first chapter on value [On the Principles of Political Economy, and Taxation , Page 479] he takes as given all possible and still to be developed categories in order to prove their conformity with the law of value.*

Marx concluded that average profit was the distributional form of total social surplus value and the production price was the distributional form of total social value. In other words, surplus value was the core of average profit and value was the core of production price. The question 'is the magnitude formed after distribution (average profit and production price) equal to the magnitude prior to distribution (surplus value or value)' was not the real problem. The real problem was to clarify how distribution affected the interrelationships between these magnitudes at the level of sub-components of the economy as a whole.

Admittedly, Marx's quantitative analysis into his testing of the logic can be improved. We believe that only by so doing could Marx have best elaborated on the essential relationship between average profit, production price, surplus value and value.

Mathematical calculation in value transformation

Mathematical calculation has always played a major part in the narrow and broad transformation problems, and featured strongly in all the important models built to deal with the transformation problem in the last Century. These effectively presented the problem as mathematical. We therefore need to go into more detail on the mathematics of these models.

Applying quantitative methods to economic study as many advantages, as it can minimize ambiguity. Some assumptions can only be tested on the basis of precise mathematical calculation. But the instruments employed cannot focus only on accuracy whilst overlooking the premises, implications and relevance of these assumptions as well as the actual implications and real relevance. The British geologist Hykes argued that mathematics was like a millstone. It could grind what was under it and throw away the husks, but could not create flour without corn. Similarly, formulas may fill one paper after another, but we cannot produce truth if our assumptions are wrong (Cheng and Hu 2002, 298).

Marx attached great importance to mathematical methods in his economic studies. In Volume III of *Capital*, He made significant use of mathematical calculation. However, he stuck strictly to the principle that purely mathematical findings or claims must be examined on the basis of economic situations, before making them independent of inherent economic laws. In a letter to Engels in 1873, Marx not only championed the use of mathematical methods in economic studies, but outlined the principles to which these economic studies should adhere.

As regards the use of mathematical instruments to address the transformation problem, Meek correctly pointed out that in statistical tables, fluctuations in prices, discount rates and other variables take curvilinear forms. In analyzing crises, Meek frequently tried to identify the rules governing the rise and fall of these variables and obtain the law of crises using mathematical methods. He believed that given sufficient empirical data, this was possible (Cheng and Hu 2002, 77).

> The simple mathematical illustration in Marx's Capital was very similar to the role in Ricardo's Principle but entirely different from their function in much or the work or modern mathematical economists. They are designed to illustrate arguments (or steps in arguments), and not to prove them; and they are usually designed to do this only on a very elementary level. To suggest that any argument in Capital stands or falls by Marx's arithmetical illustrations (or by the lack of them) is to betray a serious argument. (Meek 1963, 221)

May (1948, 211) similarly argued that

> Marx, who used calculations primarily as illustrations to accompany verbal arguments which combined process and cross-section analysis in a way which could hardly be fitted to the mathematical techniques available even today. So, the implications of mathematical calculation in Marxist transformation theory was to illustrate the economic theory instead of proving economic theory. Just as Lenin had once argued: 'The important thing here was not the absolute numbers, but the relationship these numbers had revealed.'

In economics, the mathematical method can be used to describe the motion, state, size and tendency of the development of things. However, interpersonal relationships figure prominently in economic study, defying mathematical analysis. In studying transformation, Marx integrated the historical and logical method and, in so doing, elaborated on the characteristics of relationship of production in the stage of laissez-faire capitalism, whilst also clarifying the two equalities. in contrast Bortkiewicz and others, relying on mathematical calculations alone, having bogged themselves down in the validity of the two equalities, immediately declared Marx's transformation theory and even his labor theory of value problematic. Yet they failed to examine how transformation figures in production, and did not develop a clear understanding of labor and value.

Value measurement should be made the basis the mathematical calculations that inform transformation or the problem cannot even be properly understood, let alone resolved scientifically.

This is especially clear in the work of Samuelson, who hated value measurement the most. In Samuelson (1971) he argued that to clear away the logical confusion it was unnecessary to make any detour via the value analysis of Volume I: that is, it was totally unnecessary to make value measurement the basis. Instead, it was sufficient to rely on such concepts as price and profit. He argued that since the equilibrium price system could be solved using Leontief-Sraffa input-output equations, the value system based on labor power could be dispensed with and the problem solved without the help of value and surplus value. But as Alan Freeman points out, the transformation of value into price is not a type of calculation but a study of a social process in which production and distribution are kept clearly separate, and it is recognized that value originates in production. If value is known, price can be deduced. Mathematical calculation that is not founded on a value calculation will make it appear that profit can be created in circulation. Purely mathematical study thus misanalyses the underlying socioeconomic relations.

Samuelson also held that value could not be observed directly, while the monetary form of price and profit could be deduced through mathematical calculations. But as Shaikh (cited by Hu 1990, 174) notes:

> [T]he capitalists clearly know that capitalist society is unplanned. They produce commodities without scruples, for the purpose of earning profits: however, they also know that their profit is not always guaranteed, and therefore know that price and profit fluctuate constantly, and that a uniform rate of profit never exists. So, there is no reason to suppose that production price exists. Based on this, we could

draw the conclusion that the basis on which the capitalists made deci-
sions is price, a single rate of profit or even the average rate of profit
which are never equal to production price or the uniform rate of profit.

P. N. Junankar (1982, 64) also points out that:

[P]rices of production are also non-observable. Capitalists react to
variables at market price, or to non-observable expected prices. Unless
they have rational expectations and their expected prices are the long-
run equilibrium prices, prices of production and rates of profit at pric-
es of production are also not observed by capitalists. Thus we have to
choose between two sets of abstractions: one that uses value analysis
and one that does not.

However, we can argue that though production price and a general rate of
profit never manifest themselves directly in actually realized prices or profits, they nevertheless exist as an average which does indeed constantly enter
the determination of fluctuating market prices and rates of profit. In this
sense, value, and profit based on it, appears even more important because it
enters the determination of production price and the general rate of profit.
This was what Marx had been endeavoring to prove. As a result, it is unrea-
sonable for Samuelson to dismiss value measurement under the pretext that
it cannot be observed.

The reason that mathematical calculation should be based on value calculation is that otherwise, the numbers become the instruments of measurement and cannot prove anything. Calculation based on price is the typical
method employed in preference to value calculation. Sweezy (1993, 147) offers an insightful analysis of the relationship between the two.

The entire social output is the product of human labor. Under capi-
talist conditions, a part of this social output is appropriated by
that group in the community which owns the means of production.
This is not an ethical judgment, but a method of describing the re-
ally basic economic relation between social groups. It finds its most
clear-cut theoretical formulation in the theory of surplus value. As
long as we retain value calculation, there can be no obscuring of

the origin and nature of profits as a deduction from the product of total social labor. The translation of pecuniary categories in social categories is greatly facilitated. In short, value calculation makes it possible to look beneath the surface phenomena of money and commodities to the underlying relations between people and classes. Price calculation, on the other hand, mystifies the underlying social relations of capitalist production. Since profit is calculated as a return on total capital, the idea inevitably arises that capital as such is in some way 'productive'. Tings appear to be endowed with an independent power of their own. From the point of view of value calculation it is easy to recognize this as a flagrant form of commodity fetishism. From the point of view of price calculation it appears to be natural and inevitable. It is not only a question of obscuring the basic social relations of capitalist production, however. Every one of the theories of profit which have been developed starting from price calculation is open to serious objection.......It is perhaps significant that modern theorists have largely given up the attempt to explain the origin of profit and now confine themselves to analyzing changes in the level of profit and the division of profit among entrepreneurs and interest-holders. But despite this attitude of indifference on the part of modern theorists towards the problem of origin and nature, the issues involved are of profound significance. They affect not only our attitude towards the economic system in which we live but also our choice of the theoretical tools with which we seek to understand it. It is from this circumstance that the dispute over price calculation versus value calculation derives its real importance.

4

A model for studying transformation

In this chapter, we construct a model to study transformation based on the theoretical foundations established in our last chapter, namely Marx's labor theory of value and prices of production. To avoid the error of deducing prices of production from prices of production, we divide transformation into two parts. We exhibit two models, a static transformation model characterized by measuring inputs at their values and a dynamic transformation model in which they are measured at their production price. We argue that this is consistent with the distinction between historical and logical transformation.

Some assumptions

For ease of presentation, we briefly explain some important assumptions which apply to both models.

Equalization of the rate of surplus value across different departments

If the rate of surplus value across different departments is not equalized, it may complicate the process. See Table 4.1

Table 4.1

Dept	Constant capital	Variable capital	Surplus value	Value	Rate of Surplus Value (%)	Organic composition of capital (%)	Rate of profit (%)
	c	v	s	c+v+s	m/v	c/(c+v)	s/(c+v)
I	75	25	50	150	200	75	50
II	50	50	50	150	100	50	50
III	25	75	50	150	66.6	25	50
Σ	150	150	150	450	—	—	—

Here, the output of each of three departments is 150 units and its input is 100 units. The profit rate is 50%. In this case, the same amount of labor creates the same amount of value and the same amount of capital creates the same amount of profit. There is actually no transformation to prices of production, because rates of surplus value are unequal.

However, although an equalized rate of surplus value across different departments is only an assumption, it is nevertheless consistent with real-world situations. This is because competition levels it out. As Marx (1894, 174) pointed out:

> Such a general rate of surplus value — viewed as a tendency, like all other economic laws — has been assumed by us for the sake of theoretical simplification. But in reality it is an actual premiss of the capitalist mode of production, although it is more or less obstructed by practical frictions causing more or less considerable local differences, such as the settlement laws for farm labourers in Britain. But in theory it is assumed that the laws of capitalist mode of production operate in their pure form. In reality there exists only approximation; but, this approximation is the greater, the more developed the capitalist mode of production and the less it is adulterated and amalgamated with survivals of former economic conditions.

(Sweezy 1993, 84) argued that

> [T]he equalized rate of surplus value must rest on two implied assumptions: First, there must be a homogeneous, transferable, and mobile labor force. Second, the labor used by all branches of industry and in all firms within each industry should be exactly the same labor required by socially necessary labor under existing conditions. In other words, no producer ran his firm with excessively high or excessively low technologies.

Although these conditions are only partially met, an equal rate of surplus value in all branches of industry and in all firms within each industry is a reasonable assumption compatible with the real-world situations as long as competition, such as the movement of workers from low-wage areas to high-wage areas and the disposition of producers to use the most sophisti-cated technologies, was in effect.

Unequal organic composition of capital across different departments

Following Marx, we define the organic composition of capital of Department to be

$$k_i = c_i/v_i \tag{1}$$

And further define

$$k_i' = c_i/(c_i + v_i) \tag{2}$$

The values of and evolve in the same direction. Since lies between 0 to 1, it is a more convenient indicator for studying the problem. The or-ganic composition of social capital can be expressed as follows:

$$k = \Sigma c_i / \Sigma(c_i + v_i) \tag{3}$$

In the real world, very few departments will have an organic composition equal to the social average. However should this be the case, the result will look like Table 4.2.

Table 4.2

Dept	Constant capital	Variable capital	Surplus value	Value	Rate of Surplus Value (%)	Organic composition of capital (%)	Rate of profit (%)
	c	v	s	c+v+s	m/v	c/(c+v)	s/(c+v)
I	100	50	50	200	100	66.6	33.3
II	50	25	25	100	100	66.6	33.3
III	50	25	25	100	100	66.6	33.3
Σ	200	100	100	400	—	—	—

Under these conditions, the assertions that equal amounts of labor create equal amounts of value and that equal capitals generate the same amount of profit are consistent with each other. As a result, in this particular case, cre-ated to illustrate the issue, the problem of transforming values into prices of production does not exist.

The same capital turnover in each department

A change in the data for Department III in Table 4.2 gives us Table 4.3:

Table 4.3

Dept	Constant capital	Variable capital	Surplus value	Value	Rate of Surplus Value (%)	Organic composition of capital (%)	Rate of profit (%)
	c	v	s	c+v+s	m/v	c/(c+v)	s/(c+v)
I	100	50	50	200	100	2/3	1/3
II	50	25	25	100	100	2/3	1/3
III	100	20	20	140	100	5/6	1/6
Σ	250	95	95	440	—	—	—

Here the rate of profit of the three departments is not equal and the rate of profit in Department III is only half of that of the other two Departments. However, if the turnover time of capital in Department III were to double, then the rate of profit across the three departments within the same period of time would be the same. The transformation from value to prices of production would not take place.

It should be noted that the above conclusions were reached on the basis of special assumptions for ease of illustration, so they should not impact the final conclusions. But even without these assumptions, the same conclusions can still be drawn. This point is evident in the following analysis.

The static transformation model

A mathematical example

Logically and historically, the theory of prices of production is consistent with the labor theory of value. Logically, production price is the transformed form of value and value the basis for prices of production. This is because firstly, a change of labor productivity often involves a change in the value of commodities, bringing about a change in prices of production; secondly, from the standpoint of the sum of social capital, since the sum of commodity values is equal to the sum of prices of production, the variation in market prices based on prices of production is essentially the same as the variations based on values. Looking at the development of a commodity economy, we argue that the transformation of value into prices of production is an inevitable tendency. In a simple commodity-based economy, the producer of a given type of commodities takes control of the means of production and engages in their production and exchange. As a result, the amount of the means of production and the values consumed varies with different types of products within the same department. Consequently, cost prices of products based on the means of production also vary. Values in of each department also vary with labor intensity and with the labor time devoted to each unit of the commodity. Even if this labor intensity and labor time were the same, the value of each commodity would be different. Even so, once the commodity is sold, each department can compensate for the values of its means of production and obtain new values created by labor.

If each individual laborer takes control of means of production, their ownership belongs in each department and it is quite difficult to switch them from one department or place to another. As a result, the requirements for the equalization of profits are not satisfied. "The exchange of commodities at their values, or approximately at their values, thus requires a much lower stage than their exchange at their prices of production." (Marx 1894, 176)

As Marx (1894, 179) claims

> What competition, first in a single sphere, achieves is a single market value and market price derived from the various individual values of commodities. And it is competition of capitals in different spheres, which first brings out the production price equalizing the rates of profit in the different spheres. The latter process requires a higher development of capitalist production than the previous one.

In the stage of *laissez-faire* capitalism, there is a constant flow of capital. This is because producers don't much care about the use value of a commodity. What they really care about is the surplus value a commodity may yield, or at least the amount of profit that can be obtained from a given amount of capital advanced. Similarly capitalists do not care about the particular type of labor they employ. Furthermore, as the labor in all departments becomes transformed into simple labor it can be switched from one department or place to another. The free flow of capital between high- and low-profit departments and places then leads to the equalization of the rate of profit, and value is transformed into production price. As a result, "it is quite appropriate to regard the values of commodities as not only theoretically but also historically *prius* to the prices of production." (Marx 1894, 178)

To sum up, there is a necessary relationship between the value of commodities and production price. And there are some 'short moments' during the transition from value to production price in history, typified by the transition from the first to the second mode of production articulated by Sraffa (1960) and from the third mode of production to the fourth mode of production by Meek (1975). The 'short moments' are illustrated in Table 4.4.

Table 4.4

Capital	Rate of surplus value	Surplus value	Commodity value	Rate of profit	General rate of profit	Production price	Difference between production
	s/v	s	$c+v+s$	$\dfrac{s}{c+v}$	$r = \dfrac{\Sigma s_i}{\Sigma(c_i+v_i)}$	$(c+v) \times (1+r)$	
I: 80c+20v	100%	20	120	20%	22%	122	2
II: 70c+30v	100%	30	130	30%	22%	122	-8
III: 60c+40v	100%	40	140	40%	22%	122	-18
IV: 85c+15v	100%	15	115	15%	22%	122	7
V: 95c+5v	100%	5	105	5%	22%	122	17

Clearly, a series of assumptions are involved in this table:

1. there are five departments with the amount of capital input in each departments equal to 100;
2. there is just one type of means of production and one type of means of consumption respectively
3. the organic composition of capital across departments is the same;
4. the rate of surplus value in each department is 100%;
5. the constant capital of each department is completely consumed
6. the cost-price of commodities of each department is computed in the accordance with the values of the means of production consumed;
7. the turnover time of capital of each department is the same.

82

Under simple commodity-based economy, each department would sell its commodities based on their values of 120, 130, 140, 115 and 105. Though the rate of profit is different, it cannot induce capital flows. However, in the stage of laissez-faire capitalism, the same amount of capital demands the same amount of profits:

$$r = \frac{\Sigma s_i}{\Sigma(c_i + v_i)}$$

$$(20 + 30 + 40 + 15 + 5) / (100 + 100 + 100 + 100 + 100) \tag{2}$$

$$= 22\% \tag{3}$$

Therefore, all departments yield the same amount of profit (22) and the production price of the output of each department is 122.

Once value is transformed into production price, the commodities are sold in accordance with this production price instead of their value. It should be noted that the input data in this table is still calculated on the basis of value. The reason this static transformation is confined to this 'short moment' of history is that once static transformation crosses the threshold of simple commodity-based economy and laissez-faire capitalism, all the inputs and outputs will be calculated on the basis of prices of production. However, calculating inputs on the basis of production price is tantamount to denying a simple commodity-based economy stage. We would then lapse into the logical error of allowing production price to determine production price, a kind of circular reasoning.

As Table 4.4 shows, if a commodity is sold in accordance with its production price, and if the organic composition of capital is smaller than the average organic composition of social capital, its value will be greater than its production price. Department II and Department III are a case in point. Conversely, if the organic composition of capital is greater than the average organic composition of social capital, its value will be smaller than its production price, as with Department I, IV and V. As a result, when value is transformed into production price, production price normally deviates from value when commodities are exchanged. However, the law of value still plays a major role in the exchange.

First, the production price is deduced from value. Marx (1894, 157 believed

> They have as their prerequisite the existence of a general rate of profit, and this, again, presupposes that the rates of profit in every individual sphere of production taken by itself have previously been reduced to just as many average rates. These particular rates of profits = m / (c + v) in every sphere of production, and must, as occurs in Part I of this book, be deduced out of the values of the commodities.

Next, the sum of average profits is still equal to the sum of surplus values, which is

$$\Sigma p_i = \Sigma s_i \qquad (4)$$

As Table 4.4 shows,

$$\Sigma p_i = 22 \times 5 = 110 \qquad (5)$$

and

$$\Sigma s_i = 20 + 30 + 40 + 15 + 5 = 110 = \Sigma p_i \qquad (6)$$

The sum of production prices is also equal to the sum of values, which is

$$\Sigma(k_i + p_i) = \Sigma(c_i + v_i + s_i) \qquad (7)$$

As Table 4.4 shows,

$$\Sigma(k_i + p_i) = (100 + 22) \times 5 \qquad (8)$$

and

$$\Sigma(c_i + v_i + s_i) = 120 + 130 + 140 + 115 + 105 = 610$$

$$= \Sigma(k_i + p_i) \qquad (9)$$

As inputs are calculated on the basis of value, and average profit is redistributed in accordance with total surplus value being in proportion to the capital advanced, the two equalities can both be valid.

Finally, value still plays a major part in the variation of prices of production, which coincide with changes in labor productivity and commodity values. If cost prices are still calculated on the basis of value, regardless of the implied assumptions of Table 4.4, then only cost price, surplus value, value and the absolute magnitude of production price can be affected, while the formation of the average profit rate and the validity of the equalities cannot be impacted.

To make these conclusions more representative, we now generalize the mathematical example of Table 4.4.

Generalization of the transformation model

If c_i and v_i ($i = 1, 2, ..., n$) are used to denote the constant capital and variable capital calculated on the basis of value consumed by Department i of n departments, s_i is used to denote the surplus value generated by Department, i and p_i denote the ratio between the production price and the value of commodity i, and r denotes the general rate of profit, then the n department static transformation model can be expressed as follows:

$$\begin{cases} (c_1 + v_1)(1 + r) = (c_1 + v_1 + s_1)p_1 \\ (c_2 + v_2)(1 + r) = (c_2 + v_2 + s_2)p_2 \\ \qquad \cdots \cdots \cdots \\ \qquad \cdots \cdots \cdots \\ (c_n + v_n)(1 + r) = (c_n + v_n + s_n)p_n \end{cases} \tag{10}$$

$$r = \frac{\Sigma s_i}{\Sigma(c_i + v_i)} \tag{11}$$

In this group of equations,, c_i, v_i and m_i are the known variables and p_i and r the unknown variables. We have $n + 1$ equations and consequently $n + 1$ unknown variables, so the equations can be solved. The left side of equation group (10) is the average profit rate derived from the input values of the means of production and capital advanced, and is expressed as $(c_i + v_i)(1 + r)$. Clearly they equal the right side, the only difference being the method of calculation.

Based on equation group (10), we have:

$$\Sigma p_i = (c_1 + v_1)r + (c_2 + v_2)r + ... + (c_n + v_n)r = r\Sigma(c_i + v_i) \tag{12}$$

From (13) it follows that

$$\Sigma p_i = \Sigma s_i \qquad (14)$$

and then total profit is equal to total surplus value. Therefore:

$$\Sigma(k_i + p_i) = (1 + r)\,\Sigma(c_i + v_i) \qquad (15)$$

$$= \left[1 + \frac{\Sigma s_i}{\Sigma(c_i + v_i)}\right] \sum (c_i + v_i) \qquad (16)$$

$$= \sum (c_i + v_i + s_i)\frac{\Sigma(c_i + v_i)}{\Sigma(c_i + v_i)} \qquad (17)$$

$$= \Sigma(c_i + v_i + s_i) \qquad (18)$$

So total price of production is equal to total value, and the two equalities can be both be valid.

Based on this analysis, Marx employed the same method to deal with the transformation problem. His basic conclusions were hence not mistaken. However, when the economy crossed the threshold of simple commodity-based economy and laissez-faire capitalism, not only are commodities sold in accordance with their production price, but also inputs are purchased in accordance with their production price. As Marx (1894, 160) pointed out:

> This statement seems to conflict with the fact that under capitalist production the elements of productive capital are, as a rule, bought on the market, and that for this reason their prices include profit which has already been realized, hence, include the production price of the respective branch of industry together with the profit contained in it, so that the profit of one branch of industry goes into the cost-price of another.

In other words, the prices of inputs, just like the prices of outputs, can deviate from their values. If inputs are calculated on the basis of prices of production, the static transformation model and its attendant conclusions should be reevaluated.

The dynamic transformation model

Analysis of dynamic transformation

Before constructing the dynamic transformation model, we will look at a mathematical example (Ding Baojun 1995).[1] This is shown in Table 4.5. We assume the magnitude of values input into the constant capital of Departments I-V to be 70, 62, 54, 81 and 93 respectively (column C_i in the table) and these values are purchased in accordance with production prices of 80, 70, 60, 85 and 95 (the first entry in the first column of the table). The value of labor-power used by the five departments is assumed to be 18, 27, 36, 14 and 3 (not shown in the table), bought at production prices of 20, 30, 40, 15 and 5 (V_i, also the second entry in the first column of the table).

Table 4.5

Capital	e	S_i	r_i	C_i	V_i	Y_i =C+V+S	Π_i	P_i	$P_i - V_i$
I: 80c+20v	100	20	20	70	20	110	22	122	12
II: 70c+30v	100	30	30	62	30	122	22	122	0
III: 60c+40v	100	40	40	54	40	134	22	122	-12
IV: 85c+15v	100	15	15	81	15	111	22	122	11
V: 95c+5v	100	5	5	93	5	103	22	122	19
Total	—	110	—	360	110	580	110	610	30

e= Rate of surplus value
S_i= Surplus value
r_i= Departmental rate of profit
C_i= Value of constant capital
V_i = Reproduced variable capital
Y_i= Commodity value $(C+V+S)$
Π_i= Average profit
P_i= Production price
The general rate of profit is 22%

1   Editor: I have annotated the table for easier reading. The content of the table is unchanged from the original.

For the capitalists, the capital advanced is composed of means of production and the production price of labor (which is the production price of the means of subsistence). Clearly, the production price of the means of production then deviates from their values. 'The constant capital, or the raw and auxiliary materials, machinery, all of which it comprised, whatever their cost-price may be, could be greater or smaller than its value.' (Marx and Engels 1974, 181)

Marx (1894, 161) further argued that:

> *The price of a particular product, let us say that of capital B, differs from its value because the surplus-value realized in B may be greater or smaller than the profit added to the price of the products of B, the same circumstance applies also to those commodities which form the constant part of capital B, and indirectly also its variable part, as the laborers' necessities of life*

As regards labor-power, a very particular type of commodity, the capitalists would normally demand that the workers reproduce their variable capital in accordance with the value of labor-power, which they would do. To take Department III in Table 4.5 for example, the production price of labor-power is 40 and the value is 36 (40 and 36 being the production price and value of the worker's means of subsistence).

As regards the magnitude of the variable capital reproduced, it is equal to the value of labor-power, 36. Surplus value is also 36. The income the workers received is 40, which can be used to buy back means of subsistence valued at 36. So, the value of labor-power, 36, can be compensated. As Marx (Marx and Engels 1974, 181) argued: "variable capital, regardless of the gap between the value of variable capital and cost-price, would be compensated by a certain amount of labor-power which formed part of the new commodity's value."

Otherwise, if the workers do not reproduce variable capital in accordance with the value of labor-power but in accordance with the production price of labor-power, then the general rate of profit would not be static. Seen from another perspective, if the workers reproduce variable capital in accordance with the production price of labor-power, then they cannot compensate the value of their own labor-power by means of purchases made from their income.

In summary, as suggested by Table 4.5, the values of constant and variable capital both deviate from prices of production.

As Table 4.5 suggests,

$$\Sigma \Pi_i = 110 = \Sigma S_i \qquad (19)$$

which means that total profit equals total value. The gap between total production price [column 9] and total value [column 7] is +30, which means total production price is not equal to total value. It should be noted that the gap between the production price of inputs and the value transformed and the sum of reproduced variable capital is also +30. In the following sections, we will generalize this dynamic transformation model and in doing so, we hope to see if our conclusion is general.

The dynamic transformation model for an economic system of n departments is:

$$(\alpha_1 c_1 + \beta_1 v_1)(1 + r) = (c_1 + v_1 + s_1)p_1$$
$$(\alpha_2 c_2 + \beta_2 v_2)(1 + r) = (c_2 + v_2 + s_2)p_2$$
$$\text{... ... ...} \qquad (20)$$
$$\text{... ... ...}$$
$$(\alpha_n c_n + \beta_n v_n)(1 + r) = (c_n + v_n + s_n)p_n$$

$$r = \frac{\Sigma s_i}{\Sigma(a_i c_i + \beta_i v_i)} \qquad (21)$$

where c_i, v_i and s_i $(i = 1, 2, ..., n)$ denote the values of constant and variable capital and the surplus value of Department i respectively. α_i and β_i denote the production price-value coefficients of the constant and variable capital inputs of Department i respectively. r represents the general rate of profit and p_i represent the production price-value coefficient of the commodities of Department i.

In this equation group c_i, v_i, s_i and α_i, β_i, r are known variables, and p_i is the target variable.

The left side of Equation group 4.14 is the aggregate of cost-price and average profit. Clearly, the left side of this equation group is equal to the production price of the right side. Based on this equation group:

$$\Sigma p_i = r\Sigma(\alpha_i c_i + \beta_i v_i) \tag{21}$$

$$r = \frac{\Sigma s_i}{\Sigma(a_i c_i + \beta_i v_i)} \tag{22}$$

Since $\quad r = \dfrac{\Sigma s_i}{\Sigma(a_i c_i + \beta_i v_i)} \tag{23}$

Therefore $\quad \displaystyle\sum p_i = \sum \frac{(a_i c_i + \beta_i v_i)\,\Sigma s_i}{\Sigma(a_i c_i + \beta_i v_i)}$

So the sum of profits is equal to the sum of values and the gap between the sum of prices of production and the sum of values is:

$$\Sigma(k_i + p_i) - \Sigma(c_i + v_i + s_i) \tag{25}$$

$$(1 + r)\,\Sigma(\alpha_i c_i + \beta_i v_i) - \Sigma(c_i + v_i + s_i) \tag{26}$$

$$\Sigma(\alpha_i c_i + \beta_i v_i) + r\,\Sigma(\alpha_i c_i + \beta_i v_i) - \Sigma(c_i + v_i + s_i) \tag{27}$$

Since $\quad r\,\Sigma(\alpha_i c_i + \beta_i v_i) = \Sigma p_i = \Sigma s_i \tag{28}$

(27) yields $\quad \Sigma(\alpha_i c_i + \beta_i v_i) = \Sigma(c_i + v_i) \tag{29}$

It can be seen that total profit is equal to total value but total price of production is not in general equal to total value.

Interpretation of the equalities

According to the above model,

$$\Sigma p_i = \Sigma s_i \tag{30}$$

This is because the general rate of profit

$$r = \frac{\Sigma s_i}{\Sigma(a_i c_i + \beta_i v_i)}$$

enters the equation group as a known variable. Since

$$\Sigma p_i = r\,\Sigma(\alpha_i c_i + \beta_i v_i) = \Sigma s, \tag{32}$$

once the variable of average profit enters the equation group as a given, total profit necessarily equals total surplus value; it is hence a law requiring no further proof. We believe that the assumption that total profits are equal to total surplus values is a logical conclusion based on Marx's labor theory of value of production price.

The gap between the sum of production prices and the sum of values is just equal to the gap between the sum of production price of the means of production serving as inputs and the sum of their values. This is a straightforward conclusion, because the production price of outputs is composed of two parts. One is the cost-price and the other part is average profit. The result follows from equation (30)

As Marx (1894, 205) argued:

> *there are just two causes that can change the production price of a commodity: First, a change in the general rate of profit. This can solely be due to a change in the average rate of surplus-value, or, if the average rate of surplus-value remains the same, to a change in the ratio of the sum of the appropriated surplus-values to the sum of the advanced total social capital.*

But when it comes to the total of all social commodities, since $\Sigma p_i = \Sigma s_i$, there can only be one reason for the gap between total production price and total value, which is the gap between the total price of production of inputs and their total value.

To elaborate on the root cause of this gap, we will write down an iterative equation which indicates the gap between the sum of the production price of all social commodities and the sum of values in period t:

$$\sum_{i=1}^{n} F^t(k_i + p_i) - \sum_{i=1}^{n} F^t(c_i + v_i + m_s) \tag{31}$$

$$\sum_{i=1}^{m} F^{t-1}(k_i + p_i) - \sum_{i=1}^{m} F^{t-1}(c_i + v_i + s_i) \tag{32}$$

Here $\sum_{i=1}^{n} F^t(k_i + p_i)$ indicates the sum of prices of production of n departments in period t, and $\sum_{i=1}^{n} F^t(c_i + v_i + s_i)$ is the sum of the values of commodities produced by n departments in period t. $\sum_{i=1}^{m} F^{t-1}(k_i + p_i)$ is the sum of the production prices of commodities of m departments produced in period $t-1$ and consumed in period t and $\sum_{i=1}^{m} F^{t-1}(c_i + v_i + s_i)$ is the sum of the values of commodities of m departments produced in period and consumed in period t.

Equation (31) argues that total production price of commodities of n departments is not equal to the total value during period t. This isbecause the sum of the production prices of commodities of m departments consumed in period t and produced in period $t-1$ is not equal to the sum of their values.

There are two reasons for this. First, not all those departments whose inputs are means of production in period t are production-oriented departments in period $t-1$. Therefore, not all the means of production input in period t are outputs of period $t-1$, nor is there any way to ensure that the sum of profits of commodities entering production in period t is equal to the sum of surplus values. The gap between the two depends on the organic composition of capital in the departments that produce the inputs, and the level of cost-price. Second, it depends on the gap between the sum of prices of production of the means of production that are used as inputs in period t and the sum of their values. Similarly, the sum of the production prices of period $t-2$ that are used as inputs in period $t-1$ is not equal to the sum of their values because the putput of period $t-2$ will only partly become the raw materials of the next period, and so on.

Assuming the inputs of means of production in any period t are the total outputs of period $t-1$, in other words, all the outputs of period t enter the production stage of period $t+1$, we believe that the gap between the sum of the production prices of all social commodities and the sum of their values should be constant in any period after production commences.

This is because in the sum of production prices of inputs in any period $\Sigma p_i = \Sigma s_i$, the inputs of the current period is just the sum of the outputs of the previous period. In the static transformation model, the two equalities can be valid in the transformation from value to production price after production commences. We conclude that if the inputs of the production stage in any period t are the total outputs of the previous period, then $\Sigma p_i = s$ for the commodities of period t and the sum of production price is equal to the sum of values.

Clearly, the sum of production price of total social commodities is not equal to the sum of values generally and the gap between the two is

$$\Sigma(\alpha_i - 1)c_i + \Sigma(\beta_i - 1)v_i. \tag{33}$$

Does this gap suggest that the law of production price contradicts the law of value? Clearly not. The dynamic analysis shows that there was no increase or decrease in any production price without the presence of value. In other words, the gap between total production price and total value is based on real labor. Let us take the economic system of n departments as an example. The inequality between the sum of production price of all social commodities in period t and the sum of their values rests on the assumption that the sum of production price of inputs is not equal to the sum of their values.

The inequality between the sum of production price of inputs in period t and the sum of their values rests on the assumption that the sum of production price of commodities produced in period $t-1$ did not enter the reproduction process of period t, and so on. This means the portions of outputs produced in period $t-1$ but not used as inputs in period t. As in the previous analyses, if no commodity is withdrawn from social reproduction, which proceeds continuously, then total profit is equal to total surplus value in any period, and then total price of production is also equal total value. Thus, the two equalities are both valid.

To sum up, the law of price of production is no more than a reflection of the law of value in a more complex form. The validity of the two equalities is also reflected in a different form. Therefore, to better capture the essence of the two equalities, we should combine static with dynamic analysis. In other words, to pass judgment on whether or not total profit is equal to total surplus value, we should examine closely whether or not the target departments represented all departments in society. If so, total profit is equal to total surplus value, otherwise, this is not so. As for whether or not total production price equals total value, a dynamic analysis is needed. Social reproduction has to be understood as a continuous process, because the relationship between the sum of production prices and the sum of values of total outputs in any given period inevitably impacts the relationship between the sum of production price and the sum of values of total inputs in the next production period.

Ding Baojun (1995, 1999) made significant contributions to the study of transformation problem theoretically and methodologically. We will now conduct a comparative analysis of the transformation problem with reference to his work.

Analysis of Ding Baojun's solution

Ding Baojun (1995, 1999) proposed to extend Marx's model of value transformation. He employed linear and iterative equations to prove that total profits were equal to total surplus value, and total production price was equal to total value. At the same time he pointed out that under the guidance of dialectics and on the basis of the scientific abstract method, comprising both logical and historical analytical methods, though mathematical methods can play a major role in economic analysis, scholars of transformation in Western academia had "severed the economic connections between the production price system and the value system. Instead, they spared no effort to establish pure mathematical connections between the two, thus playing a mathematical game in the palace of economics." (Ding Baojun 1999)

Ding Baojun made Marx's labor theory of value the theoretical foundation of the study of transformation. He constructed a mathematical model to examine the relationship between variables during the transformation from value to production price.

Ding Baojun used the term 'simple Marx value transformation model' to describe a system in which inputs are measured in value. To illustrate, suppose c_i and v_i ($i = 1, 2, ..., n$) denote the constant and variable capital measured in terms of value consumed by department i and let s_i denote the surplus value and ρ_i the production price-value coefficient of commodity i. Let r denote the general rate of profit. The simple Marx transformation model then can be expressed by equations 4.34-4.35:

$$
\left\{
\begin{array}{l}
P_1(c_1+v_1+s_1) = (1+r)(c_1+v_1) \\
P_2(c_2+v_2+s_2) = (1+r)(c_2+v_2) \\
\qquad ... ... \\
\qquad ... ... \\
P_n(c_n+v_n+s_n) = (1+r)(c_n+v_n)
\end{array}
\right.
\tag{34}
$$

$$
r = \frac{\Sigma s_i}{\Sigma(c_i + v_i)}
\tag{35}
$$

94

In Equation group 34, c_i, v_i and s_i are known variables and the remaining $n + 1$ variables ($p_1, p_2, \dots p_n$ and r) are unknown. According to the mathematical formula computing the general rate of profit in (26), Ding Baojun correctly argued that the average profit was redistributed in accordance with total surplus values divided in proportion to the capital advanced and made it a prerequisite of the solution to the equations. This was important in seeking a solution to the transformation problem. Much like the static transformation model we constructed earlier, the two equalities held in this model.

Ding Baojun then constructed what he termed the 'extended Marx value transformation model' in which inputs are measured by their production price. He classified the transformation of inputs into production price under three headings: the transformation of constant capital into production price, the transformation of variable capital into production price, and the transformation of both constant and variable capital into production price.

We will now offer a detailed analysis of the third category as this category boasts a high level of generality. this allows us to analyze Ding Baojun's transformation theory.

Ding Baojun used the following equations to illustrate the extended Marx value transformation model:

$$
\begin{cases}
p_1(c_1 + \beta_1 v_1 + s_1) = (1 + r)(a_1 c_1 + \beta_1 v_1) \\
p_2(c_2 + \beta_2 v_2 + s_2) = (1 + r)(a_2 c_2 + \beta_2 v_2) \\
\quad \dots \dots \dots \\
\quad \dots \dots \dots \\
p_n(c_n + \beta_n v_n + s_n) = (1 + r)(a_n c_n + \beta_n v_n)
\end{cases}
\tag{36}
$$

$$
r = \frac{\sum s_i}{\sum(a_i c_i + \beta_i v_i)}
\tag{37}
$$

Here, α_1 and β_1 were used to denote the production price-value coefficients of the constant and variable capital inputs of department i.

The gap between the cost-price and value of the capital inputs would be transferred to the value of new commodities as a prerequisite. There is no issue concerning Ding Baojun's treatment of constant capital. The real question was his treatment of variable capital. Ding argued that regardless of the value of the labor-power the capitalists purchased at production price, $\beta_i v_i$, they would require the laborers to reproduce their variable capital in the course of production according to this price, $\beta_i v_i$. He based his argument on what Marx says

Variable capital, regardless of the deviation of its value from cost price, would always be compensated by a certain amount of labor-power which formed part of value of new commodities. As for whether or not the value of new commodities could find its expression in the price of new commodities, either higher or lower than price, it was not that important. (Marx and Engels 1974, 181)

Our view is the opposite. We read Marx as saying that the capitalists did not require laborers to reproduce their variable capital in accordance with $\beta_i v_i$. The inequality of value and cost price of variable capital can find its fullest expression in this argument.

As we have already noted Marx (1894, 61) argued:

The price of a particular product, let us say that of capital B, differs from its value because the surplus-value realized in B may be greater or smaller than the profit added to the price of the products B, the same circumstance applies also to those commodities which form the constant part of capital B, and indirectly also its variable part, as the laborers' necessities of life.

Here, Marx explicitly confirms that laborers do not reproduce variable capital in accordance with $\beta_i v_i$. This is because the general rate of profit, produced on the basis of the production price of labor-power and other variables, is not a stable general rate of profit. Moreover, Ding Baojun's assumption violates the principle of fair exchange. Therefore, we argue that laborers can only produce variable capital in accordance with v_i rather than $\beta_i v_i$. This point has been discussed in the preceding sections.

On this issue, Ding Baojun was perhaps influenced by the concept of the 'Monetary Expression of Labor Time' (MELT) proposed by Foley and Dumenil.[2] The MELT wielded considerable influence on the WCR model

2   Translating editor: the Monetary Expression of Labour Time or MELT was first proposed by the Costa Rican economist Alejandro Ramos (1995); its predecessors were the Monetary Expression of Value, due

and the TSSI school's approach to the transformation problem, both discussed later. It should however be noted that Ding Baojun's interpretation of
the theory of value was fundamentally different from that of Dumenil and
Foley.

In Ding Baojun's extended Marx value transformation model, total profit
equals total surplus value, because in Equation group 36, r is a prerequisite
of the solution. This suggests that average profit constitutes surplus value redistributed in accordance with capital advanced. The equality of total profit
and total surplus value is not in question. The relation between total production price and total value reduces to the difference between total production
price less total value on the one hand, and total constant capital measured in
production price less total constant capital measured in value on the other,
being the gap between total constant capital and total constant capital measured in value, that is:

$$(1 + r) \Sigma(\alpha_i c_i + \beta_i v_i) - \Sigma(c_i + \beta_i v_i + s_i) \tag{38}$$

$$\Sigma \alpha_i c_i - \Sigma c_i \tag{39}$$

This is somewhat different from the conclusion of our dynamic transformation model. Clearly, this difference arises from how we view the reproduction of variable capital by workers. Apart from this, Ding Baojun (1999)
offers an excellent interpretation on the causes of the deviation of total production price from total value. He argues that:

> If we integrate and examine these miscellaneous value systems char-
> acterized by complex interplay with each other, then some portions of
> social commodities studied by the extended Marx value transforma-
> tion would also impact the deviation of production price from value
> of the next value transformation system as the input factor.

to Aglietta (1979). Foley (1982) employs the concept of the 'value
of money', which may be thought of as the inverse of the MELT. New
Interpretation Scholars have since for the most part adopted Ramos's
terminology, though they do not generally acknowledge the origin of
the term.

Ding also conducted a qualitative analysis of the extent of deviation. As he pointed out, in the value transformation system in period $t-1$, the higher the organic composition of capital of Department I, the higher the production price of constant capital inputs compared to its value in period t, the higher the production price of outputs compared to their value, and vice versa. Ding also elaborated on the deviation of production price from value. As our analysis of the construction of dynamic transformation model is more or less the same, we do not discuss it here.

By insisting on making Marx's labor theory of value and production price the theoretical foundation of transformation study, Ding Baojun correctly grasped the essence of the transformation problem. He not only studied the relationship among many variables in the process of transformation by using mathematical models, but also conducted detailed analysis of the equalities. This was a significant contribution to the study of the transformation problem. However, there are some weak points in his work.

First, his theory lacked historical analysis, leading him to fail to distinguish between the simple Marx value transformation model from the extended Marx value transformation model. Furthermore, his analysis of the simple model and the extended model lacked theoretical foundations and proof.

Second, he made a mistake as on whether variable capital should be reproduced in accordance with the value of labor-power or its production price. Since the grounds for his argument were incorrect, his conclusions also erred.

Finally, in social reproduction, not all commodities of each department are basic commodities. He had actually noticed that this point could make the production price of inputs deviate from their value in some production periods. However, he failed to develop a deeper understanding of the root cause of the deviations of production price from value of commodities produced in period $t-1$, which serve as inputs in period t. This deviation is the result of two factors. First, there is a gap between the total profit and total surplus value of inputs; Second, there is a gap between the production price of inputs and their values. In his qualitative analysis of the deviation of total production price of total social commodities from their total value, Ding

Baojun attributed the deviation to the ratio between the organic composition of capital of Department I and the average organic composition of social capital in the value transformation system in period t–1. Thus he only took the first factor into consideration but did not consider the impact of the second.

Finally, Yue Hongzhi (2002) also proposed a solution to the transformation problem in 2002 and had a debate with Ding Baojun. Yue's solution also approached the transformation problem in two phases. In the first phase, inputs are calculated on the basis of value leading to the equations (40) and (41)

$$\begin{cases} c_1 + v_1 + r_1{}^1 s_1{}^1 = (1 + r_1)(c_1 + v_1) \\ c_2 + v_2 + r_2{}^1 s_2{}^1 = (1 + r_2)(c_2 + v_2) \\ \quad\quad \text{... ... ...} \\ \quad\quad \text{... ... ...} \\ c_n + v_n + r_n{}^1 s_n{}^1 = (1 + r_n)(c_1 + v_1) \end{cases} \tag{40}$$

$$r_1 = \frac{\Sigma s_i^1}{\Sigma(c_i + v_i)} \tag{41}$$

The coefficient of surplus values realized in Department I is the ratio of the average profit in this department to the surplus value generated by this department. Hence commodities in Department I are sold in accordance with their production price $(1 + r_1)(c_i + v_i)$. As is r_1 known, the coefficient of surplus values of this group of equations $r_1{}^1$ can be deduced from Equation group (40). $r_1{}^1 s_1{}^1$ represents the amount of profits realized in Department I.

By adding the first set of equations and including the final equation, Yue obtained:

$$\Sigma c_i + \Sigma v_i + \Sigma r_i{}^1 s_i{}^1 = \Sigma c_i + \Sigma v_i + \Sigma s_i{}^1 \tag{42}$$

And

$$\Sigma r_i{}^1 s_i{}^1 = \Sigma s_i{}^1 \tag{43}$$

Equations 4.42 and 4.43 proved that the two equalities are both valid. The result is essentially the same as our static transformation model. In the second stage, inputs are calculated in accordance with their production price, and included in the following equation group:

$$\begin{cases} c_1 + v_1 + r_1{}^2 s_1{}^2 = (1 + r_1)(c_1 + v_1) \\ c_2 + v_2 + r_2{}^2 s_2{}^2 = (1 + r_2)(c_2 + v_2) \\ \qquad \cdots \cdots \cdots \\ \qquad \cdots \cdots \cdots \\ c_n + v_n + r_n{}^2 s_n{}^2 = (1 + r_n)(c_1 + v_1) \end{cases} \tag{44}$$

$$r_2 = \frac{\Sigma s_i^2}{\Sigma(\alpha_i c_i + \beta_i v_i)} \tag{45}$$

Here, Yue Hongzhi uses $s_1{}^2$ to denote the surplus value generated by department when inputs are measured in production price, and α_i and β_i to denote the production price-value coefficients of constant and variable capital of department i. $r_i{}^2$ denotes the coefficient of surplus value realized in department i. $r_1{}^2 s_1{}^2$ denotes the profits realized in department i and r_2 represents the general rate of profit of the whole of society.

By adding the first set of equations and then including final equation, we get:

$$\Sigma\alpha_i c_i + \Sigma\beta_i v_i + \Sigma r_i{}^2 s_i{}^2 = \Sigma\alpha_i c_i + \Sigma\beta_i v_i + \Sigma s_i{}^2 \tag{46}$$

and $$\Sigma r_i{}^2 s_i{}^2 = \Sigma s_i{}^2 \tag{47}$$

Equation 4.46 suggests that total profit is equal to total surplus value. In approaching Equation 4.47, Yue Hongzhi argued that as the constant capital and variable capital in the second stage of production are the result of the first stage of production, based on Equation (42), we get:

$$\Sigma\alpha_i c_i + \Sigma\beta_i v_i = \Sigma c_i + \Sigma v_i + \Sigma s_i{}^1 \tag{48}$$

and by including Equation 39 in Equation 37, we get:

$$\Sigma\alpha_i c_i + \Sigma\beta_i v_i + \Sigma r_i{}^2 s_i{}^2 = \Sigma c_i + \Sigma v_i + \Sigma(s_i{}^1 + s_i{}^2) \tag{49}$$

Equation 13 proves that after inputs have been converted into prices of production, the total production price of outputs is still equal to total value and Marx's two equalities can both be valid at the same time. Yue Hongzhi further believed that the reasoning process could be applied to the production process of any period t. As long as this had been through a limited number of iterations, it could be transformed to the first stage.

Obviously, Yue Hongzhi's method overlooked the continuous production process between the first phase of production and the production process of period *t*. However, the two equalities could both be valid. However, not all inputs in the production process in one or many periods are outputs of the previous period. In this case, there is no way to ensure that total production price of commodities of period t is equal to total value. In this case, the equalities cannot be valid simultaneously as we have tried to show earlier. That is to say, Yue Hongzhi's solution was a very particular model at best and also lacked historical analysis.

Conclusion

According to the requirements of combining the historical and logical analytical method, we have approached the transformation problem by dividing it into two phases: static and dynamic. We then constructed a static transformation model and a dynamic one. Our intention was to elaborate the following points:

1. The labor theory of value is scientific and does not conflict with the theory of production price in terms of temporal sequence;
2. To develop a deeper understanding, it is necessary to adopt the historical analytical method. Only by a analyzing of the economic conditions in different historical periods can we capture the essence of the transformation problem and its evolution. The static and dynamic models were based on this principle;
3. The organic combination of logical analysis and dynamic analysis is the key to a better understanding of the two equalities after inputs have been transformed into production price;
4. After inputs have been transformed, the consistency of total production price with total value is reflected in a complex, indirect manner. However, this consistency does not conflict with the labor theory of value, nor does it contradict the conclusion of Volume III of Capital.

As the static transformation model deals with the historical 'short moments' of economic production — the transition from a simple commodity-based economy to *laissez-faire* capitalism, inputs are measured in accordance with their value and sold in accordance with their production price. Average profit is redistributed in accordance with total surplus value divided in proportion to the capital advanced. So total profit equals total surplus value and total price of production equals total value. Thus the two equalities can both be valid. In the dynamic transformation model, the total profit of all outputs in any period t is equal to total surplus value, as in the static transformation model. However, the total production price of inputs is not equal to total value. Therefore, total production price does not generally equal total value.

However, in any period during the transition from the simple commodity-based economy to laissez-faire capitalism, if total outputs are transformed into the inputs of period $t+1$, it is unrealistic to require that the two equalities be valid simultaneously. Therefore, we reach the conclusion that for some portions of commodities in any period t, total profits are generally not equal to total surplus value and total production price does not equal total value.

Therefore, to capture the essence of the equalities, we have to combine static analysis and dynamic analysis. In other words, to test whether total profits equal total surplus values, we must look at whether the target departments include all departments of the society. If so, total profits equal total surplus values. Otherwise, the two are not equal. As to whether total production price equals total value, we argue that dynamic analysis should be conducted and social reproduction should be viewed as a continuous process. Because the existence of social reproduction in any period of time in history is never independent of the previous period, the relationship between total production price and total value in any period impacts the relationship between the total production price of inputs and their total value. This will also impact the relationship between the total production price and total value of outputs.

Therefore only by combining static and dynamic analysis organically can we avoid jumping to the wrong conclusion that Marx was wrong and instead theorize that once inputs are transformed into prices of production, the two equalities cannot both be valid, and that the law of prices of production subverts the law of value. Actually, under the new conditions, the law of value can be expressed in the concrete form of the law of prices of production. Likewise, the validity of the equalities can be expressed in a different form.

Some scholars, Western scholars in particular, argue that the equalities cannot both hold when inputs are transformed into prices of production except under special conditions. They criticized, or claimed to have refuted, Marx's theory of transformation. In our next chapter, we will elaborate on some of their models, with reference to the static and dynamic transformation models of this chapter.

5
Classical solutions to the transformation problem

As early as the beginning of the 20th century, the German statistician von Bortkiewicz conducted meaningful research into the transformation problem from the standpoint of logic and mathematics. He divided the economy into three departments, producing means of production, means of subsistence for workers and means of subsistence for capitalists. He then wrote down a system of simultaneous equations which he solved with the further assumption that the ratio of price of production to value in the third department was equal to 1. This allowed him to analyze the two equalities.

Bortkiewicz's logical-mathematical method did in fact show that prices of production could be deduced from values. He also found a way to transform the value of total inputs and outputs into prices of production. As we shall see, the vast majority of subsequent models of transformation developed, modified or extended Bortkiewicz's solution; we shall refer to them as 'classical solutions'. They inherited both the strengths and the weaknesses of Bortkiewicz's solution. We will now analyze them with reference to the models constructed in Chapter Three.

Bortkiewicz's solution

In 1906 and 1907, Bortkiewicz published 'Value and Price in the Marxian System'[1] and 'On the Correction of Marx's Fundamental Theoretical Construction in the Third Volume of Capital'. These comprise the best-

---

1   Editor's note: the first of these was originally published in two parts, in 1906 and 1907. We refer to it as Bortkiewicz (1906) throughout.

known early systematic attempt to study the transformation problem from a mathematical standpoint and made a very significant impact on future studies. According to Bortkiewicz, the transformation problem should be divided into two distinct systems dealing with value and price respectively. He argued (Sweezy 1949, 27) that the peculiarity inherent in the Marxian system was its juxtaposition of value and price calculations, with price deduced from value and profits from surplus value. He considered the remaining points in the Marxist system less important.

He wanted to highlight whether the requirements (the two equalities articulated by Marx) for the transformation of value in each department of production of a national economic system could be expressed in the form of an equation system, and whether a solution to this system exists when both inputs and outputs are calculated on the basis of prices of production. He therefore supposed that all capital advanced turned over annually and was absorbed in the values or prices of products. Furthermore, all the various branches of production were subsumed in three departments. Finally, he assumed simple reproduction. He then first presented a value system, in which prices were determined by labor time:

$$c_1 + v_1 + s_1 = c_1 + c_2 + c_3 \tag{1}$$

$$c_2 + v_2 + s_2 = v_1 + v_2 + v_3 \tag{2}$$

$$c_3 + v_3 + s_3 = s_1 + s_2 + s_3 \tag{3}$$

If the ratio of surplus value $s' = s_1 / v_1 = s_2 / v_2 = s_3 / v_3$ then substituting into (1), (2) and (3) yields: $(1 + s)$

$$c_1 + (1 + s)\, v_1 = c_1 + c_2 + c_3 \tag{1'}$$

$$c_2 + (1 + s)\, v_2 = v_1 + v_2 + v_3 \tag{2'}$$

$$c_3 + (1 + s)\, v_3 = s_1 + s_2 + s_3 \tag{3'}$$

Bortkiewicz criticized Marx's solution to the transformation problem, arguing that constant and variable capital inputs could not be left untransformed, since the average profit rate was related to their transformed

106

magnitudes (Yan 2001, 300). Denoting the ratio of the price of production of the products of Departments I, II and Department III to their value by x, y and z respectively, he further supposed that this ratio was the same for inputs and outputs. Then, using ρ to represent the average profit rate in every department, he derived the following equations corresponding to (1'), (2') and (3'):

$$(1 + \rho)\, xc_1 + yv_1 = (c_1 + c_2 + c_3)x \tag{4}$$

$$(1 + \rho)\, xc_2 + yv_2 = (v_1 + v_2 + v_3)y \tag{5}$$

$$(1 + \rho)\, xc_3 + yv_3 = (s_1 + s_2 + s_3)z \tag{6}$$

This economic system meets the requirement of simple reproduction in either total values or total prices of production. Bortkiewicz then pointed out that in the three equations, there were four unknowns: x, y, z and ρ. Therefore, an additional equation is required to solve the three equations. He supposed that Department III produced gold and that the price of production of its output did not deviate from its value: that is to say $z = 1$. Three variables remained, being x, y, z and ρ. To simplify the calculation, he then wrote:

$$\frac{v_1}{c_1} = f_1 \tag{7}$$

$$\frac{v_2}{c_2} = f_2 \tag{8}$$

$$\frac{v_3}{c_3} = f_3 \tag{9}$$

$$\frac{c_1 + v_1 + s_1}{c_1} = g_1 \tag{10}$$

$$\frac{c_3 + v_3 + s_3}{c_3} = g_3 \tag{11}$$

$$1 + \rho = \sigma \tag{12}$$

From (1) and (10) we have

$$g_1 = \frac{c_1 + c_2 + c_3}{c_1} \tag{13}$$

107

With similar substitutions, (4), (5) and (6) can be rewritten

$$\sigma (x + yf_1) = xg_1 \tag{14}$$

$$\sigma (x + yf_2) = yg_2 \tag{15}$$

$$\sigma (x + yf_3) = xg_3 \tag{16}$$

It is noteworthy that Bortkiewicz declined to take into account the restrictive character of simple reproduction.

(7) now yields $x = \dfrac{\sigma y f_1}{g_1 - \sigma}$ \hfill (17)

Substituting into (8) yields

$$(f_1 - f_2)\, \sigma^2 + (f^2 g^1 + g^2)\sigma - g^1 g^2 = 0 \tag{18}$$

Bortkiewicz shows that whether $f_1 - f_2 > 0$ or $f_1 - f_2 < 0$, there is only one
relevant solution. In the first case

$$\sigma = -(f_2\, g_1 + g_2) + \frac{\left[(f_2\, g_1 + g_2)^2 + 4(f_1 - f_2)\, g_1\, g_2\right]^{\frac{1}{2}}}{[2(f_1 - f_2)]} \tag{19a}$$

And in the second

$$\sigma = \frac{\left\{ f_2\, g_1 + g_2 - [(g_2 - g_1\, f_2))^2 + 4 f_1\, g_1\, g_2]^{\frac{1}{2}} \right\}}{[2(f_2 - f_1)]} \tag{19b}$$

This yields:

$$y = \frac{g_3}{[\, g_2 + (f_3 - f_2)\sigma\,]} \tag{20}$$

$$x = f_1 \frac{g_3 \sigma}{[(g_1 - \sigma)g_2 + (g_1 - \sigma)(f_3 - f_2)\sigma]} \tag{21}$$

After this theoretical exercise, Bortkiewicz elaborated with numerical
examples.

108

Table 1: Value calculation

Departments of production	Constant capital	Variable capital	Surplus value	Product value
I	225	90	60	375
II	100	120	80	300
III	50	90	60	200
Total	375	300	200	875

This gives the following solution:

$$f_1 = 2/5; f_2 = 5/6; f_3 = 9/5$$
$$g_1 = 5/3; g_2 = 3; g_3 = 4; \sigma = 5/4$$

Whence

$$\rho = 1/4$$
$$x = 16/15$$
$$y = 32/25$$

This yields the system of prices of production:

Table 2: Price calculation

Departments of production	Constant capital	Variable capital	Average capital	Prices of production
I	288	96	96	480
II	128	128	64	320
III	64	96	40	200
Total	480	320	200	1000

Bortkiewicz then makes two points. First based on equations (10) and (11), the average profit rate bears little relationship to the composition of capital in Department III, but is determined by that in Departments I and II whose ultimate purpose is to produce consumption goods for workers. Second, we can conclude from tables 1 and 2 that total price of production is greater than total value. Bortkiewicz attributed this to the fact that the organic composition of capital of Department III, closely connected to price of production and value, was rather low. However, total profits did equal total surplus value. This was because the organic composition of capital calculated in the form of prices or value in Department III was low. In other words, Bortkiewicz claimed to have proved that the two equalities were not in general both valid.

Analysis of Bortkiewicz's solution

We argue that Bortkiewicz successfully deduced prices of production from values and showed how to transform capital input and output into prices of production. So he proved the validity of Marx's transformation theory in general. He also elaborated on some issues Marx failed to consider. However, there were serious flaws in his methodology.

Above all, he made simple reproduction a restrictive condition. We believe this to be a very mistaken idea. The conditions for simple reproduction concern whether the value or price of production can be realized, which bears little relationship to the transformation of values into prices of production. As Winternitz (1948, 277) notes:

> *Bortkiewicz and Sweezy base their analysis of the transformation problem on Marx's scheme of simple reproduction, i.e., such relations between the main departments of production as will make a continuation of production on the same scale possible. With Marx's method of transformation, the equilibrium of simple reproduction if it obtains with an exchange of equal values would not obtain with an exchange at prices of production. Sweezy finds this result logically unsatisfactory. This objection seems to me not justified. Every change in the price structure normally disturbs an existing equilibrium. A change of prices may necessitate a changed distribution of social labor to restore the equilibrium.*

Thus, Bortkiewicz in fact confuses price with price of production.

The second problem is that Bortkiewicz's solution involves only three productive departments This was done for ease of analysis, and for ease in imposing restrictive conditions such as simple reproduction. Although the restriction to three departments is acceptable, it makes it possible to reach

110

dramatically different conclusions than from pure economic analysis because of the particular internal structure of the equations, as we will show
in the following analysis. We cannot conclude that results based on three
departments can be generalized to many productive units.

Thirdly, Bortkiewicz was wrong to claim that the average profit rate can
be regarded as the target variable. This was because he failed to achieve
a deeper understanding of the essence of the transformation problem.
Actually, the average profit rate is the ratio of the capital advanced to the
sum of surplus values and should enter the equation as a known variable.
Instead, Bortkiewicz was obliged to add a fourth equation with the irrational
assertion that $z = 1$. This led to a series of wrong conclusions.

Last but not least, as Bortkiewicz believed that since equations (10)
and (11) did not include f_3 and g_3, the organic composition of capital of
Department III had no direct or indirect impact on the average profit rate.
He clearly tended to side with Ricardo rather than with Marx on this issue.

Let us therefore approach the issue from a number of different
perspectives.

First, Bortkiewicz concluded based on the first two equations of the following equation system:

$$\begin{cases} \sigma\,(x+y) = xg_1 \\ \sigma\,(x+y) = yg_2 \\ \sigma\,(x+yf_3) = xg_3 \end{cases} \tag{23}$$

The equation system (23) is equivalent to:

$$\begin{cases} (1+\rho)\,(xc_1 + yv_1) = (c_1 + c_2 + c_3)x \\ (1+\rho)\,(xc_2 + yv_2) = (c_1 + v_2 + s_3)y \\ (1+\rho)\,(xc_3 + yv_3) = (c_3 + m_2 + s_3) \end{cases} \tag{23'}$$

There are two hidden assumptions in the system (23') One is that there
is only one type of commodity in materials of production and of consumption respectively. The other is that the price of production-value coefficient
of the outputs of Department I and Department II is equal to the prices of
production-value coefficient of the inputs of constant and variable capital.

111

This is not true. The gap between price of production and value has two causes, namely the deviation of profit from surplus value and the deviation of prices of production of inputs from their values. Not surprisingly, Bortkiewicz's assumption addressed only the first cause. As a result, the structures of the first and the second equation in equation group (23') are the same, leading Bortkiewicz to the wrong conclusion that the average profit rate was related only to the organic composition of capital of Department I and Department II. He thus fell into the trap of mathematical formalism.

Second, If the inputs and outputs are understood as aggregates of commodities, for instance two types of means of production and two types of means of consumption, and if Bortkiewicz's other restrictive conditions are unchanged, then his system of prices of production can be formulated as follows:

$$\begin{cases} (1+\rho)(x_1c_1 + x_2c_1' + y_1v_1 + y_2v_1') = (c_1 + c_1' + v_1 + v_1' + s)x_1 \\ (1+\rho)(x_1c_2 + x_2c_2' + y_1v_2 + y_2v_2') = (c_2 + c_2' + v_2 + v_2' + s_2)x_2 \\ (1+\rho)(x_1c_3 + x_2c_3' + y_1v_3 + y_2v_3') = (c_3 + c_3' + v_3 + v_3' + s_3)y_1 \quad (24) \\ (1+\rho)(x_1c_4 + x_2c_4' + y_1v_4 + y_2v_4') = (c_4 + c_4' + v_4 + v_4' + s_4)y_2 \\ (1+\rho)(x_1c_5 + x_2c_5' + y_1v_5 + y_2v_5') = (c_5 + c_5' + v_5 + v_5' + s_5) \end{cases}$$

Clearly the average profit rate cannot be computed based on the first, second, third and fourth equations, which relate indirectly and directly to those departments that produce workers' daily necessities.

Third, Bortkiewicz maintained that the department producing luxuries did not contribute to the generation of average profit rate. Sweezy (1993) also argued that luxuries were a low proportion of production in a capitalist system and consequently had little or no impact on the formation of average profit rate. But actually, as long as profit rates differ between departments, every department inevitably gets involved in influencing the formation of an average profit rate. This tendency is determined by the nature of capital. Marx elaborated on the contribution of departments producing luxuries in his classic *Theories of Surplus Value*. Moreover, in today's national economies, departments producing luxuries and military products assume an increasingly important position even though their output is not necessarily related directly to workers' daily necessities. There is a strong case for saying

112

that the departments producing luxuries and military products wield enormous influence on the average profit rate.

Finally, let us examine Bortkiewicz's treatment of the two equalities. He argues that total profits equal total surplus values because the products used for measuring value and price are produced by Department III. Now, (4), (5) and (6) are valid under simple reproduction. Adding them yields:

$$(xc_1 + xc_2 + xc_3 + yv_1 + yv_2 + yv_3)\ (1 + \rho)$$

$$= (c_1 + c_2 + c_3)x + (v_1 + v_2 + v_3)y + (s_1 + s_2 + s_3)z$$

that is

$$\rho(xc_1 + yv_1) + \rho(xc_2 + yv_2) + \rho(xc_3 + yv_3) = (s_1 + s_2 + s_3)z \qquad (25)$$

The left side of this equation represents total values and right side of the equation is $z\ \Sigma s_i$. If total profit equals total surplus value, will be equal to 1. Thus, this fact is actually the result of the restrictive condition of simple reproduction. But in reality, since average profit is just the result of redistributing surplus value, the fact that total profit equals total surplus value bears little relation to $z = 1$. Moreover, Bortkiewicz assumed $z = 1$ for ease of finding a solution, artificially distorting the relationship between the total price of production and total value. This is because whether $z = 1$ or not largely determines the organic composition of capital of Department III and the average organic composition of social capital.

Tables 1 and 2 suggest that total price of production equals total value. Bortkiewicz attributed this to the low level of organic composition of capital of Department III, which determined the prices of production and values of products because, according to Bortkiewicz, it supplies gold, the money commodity. Sweezy further explained that since the organic composition of capital of Department III was lower than the average organic composition of social capital, the price of production of gold should be lower than its actual value. However, if it was assumed that $z = 1$ and the prices of the products of Department I and II were expressed in gold, their total price would certainly exceed their total value. The reason for this is that if z is assumed to equal 1, the price of production of gold will be exaggerated. If the prices of all products are expressed in gold, these will all be exaggerated.

If gold's transformed price of production is smaller than its value, suggesting that its purchasing power has shrunk, then its reduced purchasing power from a monetary perspective increases the prices of all products. Total price of production would then be always greater than total value. In general, total price of production is not always equal to total value in general. We hold they could be equal only if the organic composition of capital of Department III was exactly the same as the average organic composition of social capital.

Table 3: Value calculation

Dept	Constant capital	Variable capital	Surplus value	Value	Rate of surplus value (%)	Organic composition of capital (%)	Rate of profit (%)
I	250	75	400	200	100	77	23
II	50	75	200	100	100	40	60
III	100	50	200	100	100	66.6	33.3
Σ	400	200	800	400	—	—	—

Table 4: Price calculation

Departments of production	Constant capital	Variable capital	Average capital	Prices of production
I	1137/4	225/4	225/2	450
II	225/4	225/4	75/2	150
III	225/2	75/2	50	200
Total	450	150	200	800

Sweezy illustrated this point with a mathematical example. He assumed an economic system with three departments in which the value system and the price of production system were given by tables 3 and 4, in which total price of production equals total value. He pointed out that this was so because of the special case given in table 3, where the organic composition of capital of Department III was equal to the average organic composition of social capital.

Michael Howard and John King (1985) elaborated on this in their *The Political Economy of Marx*. They pointed out that the Bortkiewicz solution suggested two logical prerequisites for value to be transformed into prices of production from Marx's perspective: Department III must have the average organic composition of social capital and the prices of production of the products of all departments must be measured by the value of the products of Department III ($z = 1$). If these prerequisites were not both satisfied simultaneously, then either

1. Total profit would not equal total surplus value, although total price of production would equal total value; or
2. total price of production would not equal total value, although total profit would equal total surplus value; or
3. neither would total price of production equal total value, nor would total profit equal total surplus value.

We hold that there is actually no proof that the organic composition of capital of Department III must equal the average organic composition of social capital, nor that only the values of the products of Department III can be used to measure prices of production while those of the products of other departments could not.

Based on our dynamic transformation model in the previous chapter, we argue that whether or not the total price of production of outputs is equal to their total value depends largely on whether or not the total price of production of inputs is equal to their total value, and is unrelated to whether or not the organic composition of capital of Department III is equal to the average organic composition of social capital as in the Bortkiewicz model.

In other words, the organic composition of capital of Department III affects the equality of total price of production and total value but is not the only factor. In general, total price of production will not equal total value in our dynamic transformation model However, Bortkiewicz attributed this to Marx's transformation theory.

Impact of the Bortkiewicz tradition

An ardent admirer of Ricardo and Walras, Bortkiewicz for the first time attempted to revise Marx's transformation theory by relying on mathematical methods. He first deduced the price of production of inputs, then the relations between value and prices of production. However, he failed to develop a deeper understanding of transformation problem as he failed to capture the essence of transformation problem. Moreover, he was hamstrung by methodological flaws. Winternitz, May and others also criticized his solution. However, these criticisms lay in questioning the validity of his assumptions: simple reproduction, $z = 1$, and so on. However, Winternitz and others inherited Bortkiewicz's basic method, for instance, his simultaneous equation groups. Starting in the 1950s, the transformation problem began to attract increasing attention in academia, and Bortkiewicz's solution began to have a profound impact.

In commenting on this impact, Desai (1974, 54) argued that the Bortkiewicz solution clearly showed price and profit rate could be deduced from value. He also suggested price was not positively related to value under normal circumstances, but could be deduced from value. Indeed, he argued, Bortkiewicz corrected a deficiency in Marx by computing the average profit rate after converting inputs into prices of production, which Marx had failed to do. Bortkiewicz thus, he claimed, successfully showed how to deduce prices of production from values. This also suggested that Marx's transformation theory was valid, but regrettably, Marx had failed to explain this issue in full.

Bradley and Howard (1982, 21) then noted that although Marxists had made no progress in the transformation problem since Marx, non-Marxists like Bortkiewicz (1907) and Seton (1957) had done so. Bortkiewicz was not a Marxist. However, his contribution to Marx's economic theory, particularly Marx's transformation theory, could not be neglected. After Bortkiewicz, most transformation debates were conducted within the Bortkiewicz tradition.

The Winternitz solution

The Winternitz solution was developed on the basis of revisions of Bortkiewicz solution. Winternitz criticized this on three grounds (Hu Daiguang 1990, 154):

(1) Simple reproduction was not relevant to the transformation problem. A transformation which was valid only under this assumption would be insufficient. For the normal case is expanded reproduction, when there is some net investment;

(2) It made an arbitrary and unjustified assumption: gold, the money commodity, was one of the luxury goods so prices in the third department were unaffected by the changeover from values to prices of production;

116

(3) The Bortkiewicz solution made total price deviate from total value, which was non-Marxian.

Winternitz then provided his own solution. He denoted the coefficients of price of production-value of the products of three departments by x, y and z, the rate of profit by r, and the total value of department i by a_i. He then wrote:

$$c_1 + v_1 + s_1 = a_1 (xc_1 + yv_1)(1 + r) = x\, a_1 \qquad (25)$$

$$c_2 + v_2 + s_2 = a_2 (xc_2 + yv_2)(1 + r) = y\, a_2 \qquad (26)$$

$$c_3 + v_3 + s_3 = a_3 (xc_3 + yv_3)(1 + r) = z\, a_3 \qquad (27)$$

As the rate of profit of Department I and II were equal, he wrote:

$$1 + r = x \frac{a_1}{xc_1 + yv_1} = y \frac{a_2}{xc_2 + yv_2} \qquad (28)$$

Using m to represent x/y, (28) could be solved thus:

$$m = \frac{\left\{ a_2 c_1 - a_1 v_2 + [(\, a_2 c_1 - a_1 v_2)^2 + 4\, a_1\, a_2\, v_1\, c_2]^{\frac{1}{2}} \right\}}{2\, a_1\, c_2} \qquad (29)$$

Substituting this into (12) gave him:

$$r = m \frac{a_1}{m\, c_1 + v_1} - 1 \qquad (30)$$

He pointed out that the above equation suggested the rate of profit generated by Department III equaled the amount of capital invested in this department and the general rate of profit was unaffected. His solution was thus exactly the same as the Bortkiewicz solution.

Winternitz further pointed out that to determine prices of production, a further equation was needed. What should this equation be? Winternitz (1948, 279-80) argued that

the equalization of the rate of profit determines the prices relations between the three departments (x; y; z), the price level for the system as a whole has still to be determined. The obvious proposition in the spirit of the Marxian system is that the sum of prices is equal to the sum of values. This is not a tautological or meaningless thesis. It says that the sum of all prices changes only if and in so far as the number of hours necessary to produce the aggregate output or the value of the money commodity changes. As a matter of fact, the price level goes up and down in the trade cycle at variance with the total value and the equation holds true only in the average over a whole cycle.

It should be noted that Winternitz, wittingly or unwittingly, had confused prices of production with prices. He believed that the fourth equation should be:

$$x\,a_1 + ya_2 + za_3 = a_1 + a_2 + a_3 \tag{31}$$

The solution would then be:

$$x = \frac{am(mc_1 + v_1)}{[m\,a_1(mc_3 + v_3) + (ma_1 + a_2)(mc_1 + v_1)]} \tag{32}$$

$$y = \frac{a(mc_1 + v_1)}{[m\,a_1(mc_3 + v_3) + (ma_1 + a_2)(mc_1 + v_1)]} \tag{33}$$

$$z = \frac{xa_1(mc_3 + v_3)}{[(mc_1 + v_1)a_3]} \tag{34}$$

He argued (Winternitz 1948, 279-80) that

If we apply this transformation to the equation of simple reproduction, we find that they are invariant not only to this specific transformation, but to every transformation which affects the prices of input and output in the same way. This transformation is, however, equally applicable to the conditions of expanded reproduction. These are essentially functional relations between the rates of accumulation in the various departments. These relations do not remain unchanged by the transformation.

Winternitz's solution included all the three of Bortkiewicz's equations. The only difference was that Winternitz's solution included a fourth equation to determine prices of production. In other words, he used a different assumption to find a solution.

118

Analysis of the Winternitz solution

Winternitz's solution abandoned the requirement of simple reproduction and the assumption that $z = 1$ which he believed to be an irrational creation by Bortkiewicz for the purpose of finding a solution. This had significant implications. As May (1948, 596-7) pointed out:

> *The note by Winternitz is a step in the right direction. His equations show that if value and price of production are defined according to Marx, there exists a simple transformation connecting the two. The transformation is independent of any equilibrium conditions (which appear redundantly in Bortkiewicz) and preserves the total of values. The 'transformation problem' in the formal sense of linking value and price of production is seen to be practically trivial mathematically. Winternitz thus clears up an artificial confusion initiated by Bortkiewicz, whose pseudo mathematical mystifications bore little or no relation to the basic problem posed by Marx.*

Although a great step in the right direction, Winternitz's solution had serious flaws.

Above all, Winternitz and Bortkiewicz committed the same mistake by asserting that the deviation of prices from values affected input and output equally, and that the generation of the general rate of profit was irrelevant to the third department.

Winternitz made a further mistake by making a prerequisite of the equality of total price of production and total value. Once inputs were converted to prices of production, this equality ceased to be a conclusion. But this is the precise issue that transformation theory needed to elaborate, as is clear in the dynamic transformation model of the previous chapter.

Finally, Winternitz's assumption led him to the conclusion that total profits generally was not equal to total surplus value. If we put the four equations in Winternitz solution, we have:

$$\begin{cases} (xc_1 + yv_1)\,(1 + r) = x\,a_1 \\ (xc_2 + yv_2)\,(1 + r) = x\,a_2 \\ (xc_3 + yv_3)\,(1 + r) = x\,a_3 \\ x\,a_1 + y a_2 + z a_3 = a_1 + a_2 + a_3 \end{cases} \tag{35}$$

Adding the equations gives

$$(xc_1 + yv_1)(1 + r) + (xc_2 + yv_2)(1 + r) + (xc_3 + yv_3)(1 + r) = a_1 + a_2 + a_3 \quad (36)$$

Since

$$c_1 + v_1 + s_1 + c_2 + v_2 + s_2 + c_3 + v_3 + s_3 = a_1 + a_2 + a_3 \quad (37)$$

Equation (36) can be written:

$$xc_1 + yv_1 + xc_2 + yv_2 + xc_3 + yv_3 - (c_1 + v_1 + c_2 + v_2 + c_3 + v_3)$$
$$= s_1 + s_2 + s_3 - [(xc_1 + yv_1) r + (xc_2 + yv_2) r + (xc_3 + yv_3) r]$$

The left side of this equation represents the difference between the total price of production and the total value of the means of production, that is, the inputs. The right side represents the difference between total surplus value and total profits. However, according to the dynamic transformation model, the former is not in general equal to zero. Therefore, according to Winternitz'a solution, total profits are not actually equal to total surplus value in a general sense. This, he held, appeared to contradict the 'the spirit of the Marxian system.'

Meek's solutions A and B

Meek came up with two solutions in 1956 and 1977 respectively, both in the Bortkiewicz tradition. When he proposed his 1977 solution, he abandoned the labor theory of value and turned to the Sraffa system. According to Meek, the labor theory was no longer the right way to solve the transformation problem. We will elaborate on the two solutions in order of their appearance.

Solution A

In 1956, Meek (1956a) published *Some Notes on the Transformation Problem*, in which he summarized the basic points of Marx's transformation theory. According to Meek the transformation of values into prices resulted from the conversion of surplus value into profit. Now the volume and rate of surplus value were determined by the ratio $(\Sigma a_i) = (\Sigma v_i)$ (where a_i denotes the value of the commodity produced in Department i, and is the labor in Department i); and the volume and rate of profit are determined by the ratio $(\Sigma a_i v_i) / (\Sigma v_i p_i)$ (where the addition of p_i signifies that a_i and v_i have been converted to prices of production). If these two expressions were equal, it was possible to convert values into prices of production.[2]

"In effect," he argued "$(\Sigma a_i) = (\Sigma v_i) = (\Sigma a_i v_i)/(\Sigma v_i p_i)$ was what Marx had in mind when he said that total values equal total prices." (Meek 1956b, 96) Meek thus sought to give a new interpretation of Marx's belief that 'total values equal total prices.' Meek (1956b,96) further claimed that:

> If the ratio between the value of commodities in general and the value of the commodity labor power, upon which he had in Volume I conceived surplus value to depend, remains unchanged when it is expressed in terms of prices rather than values, so that profit can be said to be determined in accordance with the Volume I analysis. If this is so, it can be plausibly argued that the very degree to which individual prices of production diverge from values is ultimately determined according to the Volume I analysis.

Meek was clearly influenced by Maurice Dobb. In the latter's *Political Economy and Capitalism* (2014[1937]) he made the unreliable assertion that although the conversion of values to prices of production could change the division of social labor in each department, the actual level of wage and the size of labor should remain constant. The argument was, however, unfounded. Based on Table 4.5, we hypothesize whichever department produced consumer goods $(\Sigma a_i) = (\Sigma v_i)$ and $(\Sigma a_i v_i)/(\Sigma v_i p_i)$ were not equal. What Marx attempted to prove was that total value should be equal to total price of production and total surplus value should be equal to total profit. If the validity of these two equations could not be tested, how could he ensure that the transformed prices of production fell within the range of values and were the transformed form of value? Meek obviously misinterpreted Marx's theses; but this misinterpretation laid the foundation for him to propose his own transformation formula.

2 Editors' note: Meek has an idiosyncratic use of the terms 'Rate of surplus value' and 'rate of profit'. He writes (Meek 1956a,96): "I am using the expression 'rate of surplus value' here to mean the ratio of surplus value to total capital. Marx normally used it to mean the ratio of surplus value to variable capital." This does not entirely clarify his meaning but draws the readers' attention to a potential source of confusion.

Since both the Bortkiewicz and Winternitz solutions failed to make both the equalities valid at the same time, Meek set out to prove that $(\Sigma a_i) = (\Sigma v_i) = (\Sigma a_i v_i)/ (\Sigma v_i p_i)$. According to Meek, this equality meant that the law of value did exist. He elaborated on this using the three departments as examples. He assumed that the rate of profit in each department was equal. He further assumed that the organic composition of capital of Department II was equal to the composition of the average organic composition of social capital. He then obtained the system of prices of production:

$$xc_1 + yv_1 + p_1 = (c_1 + v_1 + s_1)x = x\,a_1 \qquad (38)$$

$$xc_2 + yv_2 + p_2 = (c_2 + v_2 + s_2)\,y = y\,a_2 \qquad (39)$$

$$xc_3 + yv_3 + p_3 = (c_3 + v_3 + s_3)\,z = z\,a_3 \qquad (40)$$

Clearly:

$$\frac{p_1}{xc_1 + yv_1} = \frac{p_2}{xc_2 + yv_2} = \frac{p_3}{xc_3 + yv_3} = 1 + r \qquad (41)$$

Meek then assumed that the gross profits were equal to total surplus value, then:

$$p_1 + p_2 + p_3 = s_1 + s_2 + s_3 \qquad (42)$$

Therefore
$$\frac{x\,a_1 + y a_2 + z a_3}{yv_1 + yv_2 + yv_3} \qquad (43)$$

$$= \frac{[(c_1 + v_1 + s_1)x + (c_2 + v_2 + s_2)y + (c_3 + v_3 + s_3)z]}{[y(v_1 + v_2 + v_3)]}$$

$$= \frac{\left[\frac{(c_1 + v_1 + s_1)x}{y} + (c_2 + v_2 + s_2) + \frac{(c_3 + v_3 + s_3)z}{y}\right]}{v_1 + v_2 + v_3}$$

$$= \frac{\left[\frac{(c_2 + v_2 + s_2)(xc_1 + yv_1)}{(xc_2 + yv_2)} + (c_2 + v_2 + s_2) + \frac{(c_2 + v_2 + s_2)(xc_3 + yv_3)}{(xc_2 + yv_2)}\right]}{(v_1 + v_2 + v_3)}$$

$$\frac{\left[\frac{c_2 + v_2 + s_2}{v_1 + v_2 + v_3}\right](xc_1 + yv_1 + xc_2 + yv_2 + xc_3 + yv_3)}{xc_2 + yv_2}$$

$$= \frac{\left[\frac{c_2 + v_2 + s_2}{v_1 + v_2 + v_3}\right]\left[\frac{(c_1 + c_2 + c_3)x}{v_1 + v_2 + v_3} + y\right](v_1 + v_2 + v_3)}{\left(\frac{xc_2}{v_2} + y\right)v_2}$$

Meek assumed that the organic composition of capital of Department II was equal to the average organic composition of social capital, so:

$$\frac{c_2}{v_2} = \frac{c_1 + c_2 + c_3}{v_1 + v_2 + v_3} \tag{44}$$

As a result, the above equation can be transformed into:

$$\frac{\left[\frac{c_2 + v_2 + s_2}{(v_1 + v_2 + v_3)}\right]\left(\frac{xc_2}{v_2} + y\right)(v_1 + v_2 + v_3)}{\left(\frac{xc_2}{v_2} + y\right)v_2}$$

$$= \frac{\left[\frac{c_2 + v_2 + s_2}{(v_1 + v_2 + v_3)}\right](v_1 + v_2 + v_3)}{v_2}$$

$$= \frac{c_2 + v_2 + s_2}{v_2} \tag{45}$$

Also

since

$$\frac{a_1 + a_2 + a_3}{v_1 + v_2 + v_3} = \frac{c_1 + v_1 + s_1 + c_2 + v_2 + s_2 + c_3 + v_3 + s_3}{(v_1 + v_2 + v_3)}$$

$$= \frac{c_1 + c_2 + c_3}{(v_1 + v_2 + v_3)} + 1 + \frac{s_1 + s_2 + s_3}{(v_1 + v_2 + v_3)} \tag{46}$$

and

$$\frac{c_1 + c_2 + c_3}{(v_1 + v_2 + v_3)} = \frac{c_2}{v_2} \tag{47}$$

and

$$\frac{s_1 + s_2 + s_3}{(v_1 + v_2 + v_3)} = \frac{s_2}{v_2} \tag{48}$$

Equation (44) becomes

$$\frac{c_2}{v_2} + 1 + \frac{s_2}{v_2} = \frac{c_2 + v_2 + s_2}{v_2} \tag{49}$$

(49) and (45) are the same, so:

$$\frac{x\,a_1 + y a_2 + z a_3}{y v_1 + y v_2 + y v_3} = \frac{x\,a_1 + y a_2 + z a_3}{v_1 + v_2 + v_3} \tag{50}$$

Meek's claim is thus proven.

We hold that Meek's conclusion rests on his mistaken assumptions. The first is that after value is transformed into prices of production $(\Sigma a_i) = (\Sigma v_i)$ should equal $(\Sigma a_i v_i)/(\Sigma v_i p_i)$. The second is that the organic composition of capital of Department II is equal to the average organic composition of social capital. Since the assumptions are mistaken, the conclusions are also mistaken.

Meek also believed that there was no way to guarantee that his solution could make total price always equal total value. For this reason, he argued (Meek 1956, 105) that:

[S]uch an illustration, however, would fill only part of the gap in Marx's analysis. To fill the rest of it, one must turn to economic history rather than to mathematics. The 'derivation of prices from values,' according to Marx's general economic method, must be regarded as a historical as well as a logical process. In 'deriving prices from values' we are really reproducing in our minds, in logical and simplified form, a process which has actually happened in history.

Meek clearly eschewed theoretical analysis, failing to elaborate on the formation of prices of production from historical and logical perspectives.

Solution B

Meek (1977) argued in *Smith, Marx and After* that Winternitz's fourth equation, added to secure the equality of total price of production with total value, made total profits deviate from total surplus value. This was even more inconsistent with Marx's original idea. Actually, the deviation of total price of production from total value had already contradicted Marx's original idea (Meek 1956a, 115). To prove that total profits and total surplus value remained constant in the transformation from values to prices of production, Meek proposed an input-output system with three departments, with value as the measure.

I. $k_{11} + k_{12} + k_{13} + s_1 = a_1$
II. $k_{21} + k_{22} + k_{23} + s_2 = a_2$
III. $k_{31} + k_{32} + k_{33} + s_3 = a_3$
$e_1 \ e_2 \ e_3$

The first three rows suggest that the value produced by each department is the sum of the values consumed in production, plus surplus value. The first three columns indicate that the value of outputs from each department is the sum of the use of the products of each department by the three departments and the values available for consumption and investment by capitalists. s represents surplus value, and e represents the values of the surplus products. Therefore

$$e_1 + e_2 + e_3 = s_1 + s_2 + s_3$$

If the above value system was to be transformed to prices of production, we have:

$$(k_{11}P_1 + k_{12}P_2 + k_{13}P_3)(1 + r) = a_1 P_1 \qquad (51)$$

$$(k_{21}P_1 + k_{22}P_2 + k_{23}P_3)(1 + r) = a_2 P_2 \qquad (52)$$

$$(k_{31}P_1 + k_{32}P_2 + k_{33}P_3)(1 + r) = a_3 P_3 \qquad (53)$$

Based on this system, regardless of the prices of production-value coefficients p_1, p_2 and p_3 total profit Σp_1 can be deduced:

$$\Sigma p_1 = a_1 P + a_2 P_2 + a_3 P_3$$

$$- (k_{11}P_1 + k_{12}P_2 + k_{13}P_3 + k_{21}P_1 + k_{22}P_2 + k_{23}P_3 \, k_{31} + P_1 + k_{32}P_2 + k_{33}P_3)$$

$$= a_1 P + a_2 P_2 + a_3 P_3 - [(a_1 - e_1) P_1 + (a_2 - e_2) P_2 + (a_3 - e_3) P_3]$$

$$= e_1 P_1 + e_2 P_2 + e_3 P_3 \qquad (54)$$

Therefore, the total profit of the capitalists enables them to purchase all the surplus goods, the value of which was equal to (and could determine) the total surplus value generated by society (Meek 1977, 118-9). Thus, there was no need to assume that the total profit was equal to total surplus value. However, a 'constant' assumption was still needed so as to determine the absolute price level rather than the price ratio. If one department is taken to be a standard of measure for which , a solution can be found, and the system is determinate.

Meek's solution rejected Bortkiewicz and Winternitz's inappropriate fourth equations. However, it repeated their error in supposing three departments and assuming that the price of production-value coefficients were the same for inputs and outputs. Furthermore Meek did not fully elaborate on the exact relationship between total price of production and total value after value had been transformed into prices of production. Instead, he argued that their equality was actually not a must for transformation but a possible outcome under particular circumstances which Marx would concede (Meek 1977, 118-9). Moreover, to find a solution to his equations, Meek made one department the basis for measurement. This misinterprets the transformation problem and manifests Sraffa's influence on Meek, implying that transformation is no more than a conversion problem.

In addition, Meek interpreted the equality of total profit and the total surplus value from the perspective of value distribution, while Marx's theory interprets it from the perspective of value production.

Meek had actually abandoned the labor theory of value when he proposed this solution, siding with Sraffa's system. He argued that to approach the transformation problem on the basis of Sraffa's production model could not only help scholars attain Marx's goals and reach his conclusions, but was also more effective than approaching transformation from a value perspective (Meek 1977, 118-9). What Meek stressed was the goal, not the process.

Makoto Itoh's view of the transformation problem

In approaching the transformation problem, Bortkiewicz, Winternitz, Meek and many others had been engaging in debates on what kinds of 'invariant assumptions' should be chosen and employed. However, they provided no rational explanation for the two equalities, regardless of which fourth equation they chose to add. Itoh (1980), however, put an interpretation on the invariant equations referring, in a philosophical tradition, to their content and form.

Itoh first pointed out that as a kind of concrete and developed form, price of production was computed on the basis of cost prices and the monetary value of average profit. But prices of production were also the result of adjustments in the prices of value-based material goods, which was in turn an effect of the law of value. In consequence, debates on the transformation problem overlooked the fact that the price of production was just a form of value. Once this was accepted, then the deviation of total price of production from total value, or of total profit from total surplus value, were acceptable. We have argued that this oversight was partly caused by Marx. However, Itoh held, Marx's vestigial ideas made him view price as a form of value in the first chapter of the first volume of *Capital*. As a result, subsequent scholars generally did not view price of production as a form of value. This criticism suggests that Itoh fail to develop a deeper understanding of the methodology of Marx's *Capital*. Actually, there are no such vestigial ideas.

126

Itoh argued that the assumption $z = 1$ made by Bortkiewicz and Sweezy, and other assumptions which did not set z equal to 1, would lead the form, which was prices of production, to deviate from the content, which was value. He illustrated this point with Bortkiewicz's mathematical example. He assumed that if a society is engaged in simple reproduction and the products generated in the first year are sold at their price of production, then the content is converted to the form. However, to engage in social reproduction on the same scale, society would have to buy back the products of this value and in so doing convert form back into content. Itoh provided three tables to illustrate this point. The numerical value and formula for computation are based on the Bortkiewicz model.

Table 5 : Value-based material goods a_i (millions of hours)

Departments of production	c_i	v_i	s_i	a_i
I	225	90	60	375
II	100	120	80	300
III	50	90	60	200
Total	375	300	200	875

$$a_i = c_i + v_i + s_i \; ; \; s_i/v_i = 2/3$$

Table 6: Prices of Production p_i (million/USD)

Departments of production	xc_i	yv_i	p_i	P_i
I	144	48	48	240
II	64	64	32	160
III	32	48	20	100
Total	240	160	100	500

$$p_i = r \, (xc_i + yv_i) \; ; \; r = \%25 \; ; \; x = 0{,}64 \; ; \; y = 0{,}533 \; ; \; z = 0{,}5$$

Table 7: Restored value-based material production a_i'
(Unit: millions of hours)

Departments of production	c_i	v_i	s_i'	a_i'
I	225	90	96	411
II	100	120	64	284
III	50	90	40	180
Total	375	300	200	875

$$s_i' = \frac{p_i}{z} = \sum s_i \left(\frac{p_i}{\sum p_i} \right) \; ; \; a_i' = c_i + v_i + s_i'$$

Tables 5 and 6 show that value has been transformed to prices of production, as in table 1 and 2 of Bortkiewicz. The only difference is that price of production is reduced by half as the assumption $z = 1/2$ is made in Table 6. The relationship is that the capitalists have to purchase a certain amount of monetary value based on prices of production, in order to acquire the necessary means for simple reproduction next year.

In this way, consumed constant and variable capital can be restored. That is to say, it must be possible to use xc_i to purchase the previous amount of productive material sc_i and yv_i must enable workers to purchase the same amount of v_i. The values of c_i, v_i, Σc_i and Σv_i in table 7 are the same as the corresponding values of table 5 on this basis, the only difference being that s_i in table 5 is redistributed in table 7 in proportion to the capital $(c_i + v_i)$.

Itoh put an interpretation on the philosophical category of content and form. Although the price of production indicated by table 6 and the value indicated by table 5 adopt different measures, and price of production is not equal to value, total prices and total profits are only the form of total value and total surplus value. The data in table 6, or the form, is ultimately determined by the data, being the content of table 5. The regression of the value-based material goods of each means of production in table 7 to the content of table 5 suggests that the deviation of form from content will have no significant impact on the reproduction of value-based material goods. Therefore, the theses that total value was equal to total prices and total profit equals total surplus value were not weakened, but strengthened, on account of the difference between value-based material goods and value (Itoh 1980, 77).

Finally, Itoh(1980, 77) emphasized that the basic logical structure in these three tables would remain constant when extended to n departments.

Based on Itoh's analysis of the equalities in the light of the traditional philosophical distinction between content and form, we find as follows:

First, Itoh correctly points out that the relationship between value and prices of production was a relationship between content and form. At the same time, he claims that this relationship holds regardless of the value of z. Outwardly, it seems that he has defended his argument, but actually, since the value system is determinate, the price system should also be determinate and with it the value of . This is because the value of z is determined by the organic composition of capital of departments. Otherwise, prices of production can be confused with values.

Next, Itoh failed to elaborate on the relationship between the different variables after value has been transformed to prices of production. If each price of production in table 6 is taken as the value variable, it too can explain the value compensation issue in the course of reproduction. However, this would confuse price of production with value.

Thirdly, in table 7, the first two columns are the compensated values of constant and variable capital. The third column represents the average profit each department receives after total surplus value is redistributed. However, a_i', the aggregate of c_i, v_i and s_i', is totally meaningless and $\Sigma a_i' = 875$ alone cannot prove that total price of production is equal to total value.

Fourthly, the mathematical formula Itoh employs rely heavily on the Bortkiewicz model, which is riddled with limitations.

We argue that although Itoh's study on the transformation problem is riddled with limitations, he points out that the connection between value and price of production is in essence the connection between content and form. This point was not well understood by many researchers specialized in the transformation study, but is the lynchpin of the solution to the transformation problem from the authors' perspective.

6
The Seton and Morishima models

The ultimate goal of the theories of Seton and Morishima was to investigate the validity of the two equalities, moving from the 'postulates of invariance' to the 'special model'. These postulates called for a set of stringent requirements, which in turn ruled out the possibility that they both held at the same time.

Both Seton and Morishima argued that it was unnecessary to approach transformation from the perspective of value theory, and that the labor theory of value was redundant. In effect, the purpose of studying transformation was to prove the need to abandon the labor theory of value. Their theories dealt not only with the controversies in a narrow sense but with transformation in a broader sense. This chapter provides an in-depth analysis of their models.

The Seton model

The *Transformation Problem*, published by Seton in 1957, was acclaimed by Paul Samuelson as one of the most representative research papers since Bortkiewicz. Mark Blaug (1979, 304) said Seton had said the final word on the issue. Whether or not we accept Blaug's comment, Seton's statement led economists to shift the focus of debate from the logic of transformation to the labor theory of value *per se*.

Seton, in his perspective on transformation, sympathized with Bortkiewicz, Sweezy, Winternitz and Meek. By means of a systematic examination of transformation problem relying on quantitative methods, Seton believed he had perfected or significantly improved the logic of transformation theories of the past five decades. He believed that the logical superstructure of transformation theory was nearly perfect and that was why he could rise above the debate on transformation as such and question the validity of the labor theory of value. He phrased it thus (Seton 1982, 149-160):

> *While the internal and consistency and determinacy of Marx's conception of the transformation process, and the formal inferences he drew from it, have been fully vindicated by this analysis, the same can certainly not be said of the body of the underlying doctrine, without which the whole problem loses much of its substance and raison d'être. The assumption of equal 'rate of exploitation' in all departments has never to my knowledge been justified. Neither has the notion that the 'organic composition of capital' must needs be higher in the capital goods industries than elsewhere in the economy. Above all, the denial of productive factor contributions other than those of labor, on which the whole doctrine of the surplus rests, is an act of fiat rather than of genuine cognition. It is these doctrinal preconceptions which must remain the centre of any reappraisal of Marxian economics, rather than the logical superstructure which our analysis has shown to be sound enough.*

Thus, it can be seen that Seton's interpretation of transformation problem was no more than a prelude to his criticism of labor theory of value.

Elaboration of transformation theory

Seton pointed out that previous scholars tended to subdivide the economy into three departments producing capital goods, wage goods and luxury goods respectively. They also hypothesized that the ultimate use of each of the physical commodity in the economy was invariable and predetermined by its department of origin. It could be shown that the most general n-fold subdivision of the economy, in which each product may be distributed among several or all possible uses, was equally acceptable. Flawed as it was, it was more reasonable than the 'three department' hypothesis.

Therefore, Seton proposed a system of prices of production for n departments, similar to Leontief Input-Output Models and based on prices of production.

$$(k_{11}p_1 + k_{12}p_2 + \ldots + k_{1n}p_n) + \Pi\,(a_1 p_1) = a_1 p_1$$
$$(k_{21}p_1 + k_{22}p_2 + \ldots + k_{2n}p_n) + \Pi\,(a_2 p_2) = a_2 p_2$$
$$\ldots\ldots\ldots \tag{1}$$
$$\ldots\ldots\ldots$$
$$(k_{n1}p_1 + k_{n2}p_2 + \ldots + k_{nn}p_n) + \Pi\,(a_n p_n) = a_n p_n$$

k_{ij} represents the input cost of industry j's product into industry i (reckoned in terms of labor value) – where the term input cost is taken to cover the portion used for further processing, and, in the case of labor, the quantity that the workers of industry i buy out of wages for their own consumption. p_i represents the price-value coefficient, a_i the total commodity value of department i, being $a_i = c_i + v_i + s_i$. Π represents the profit-ratio of all departments.

From equation (1), we can obtain solutions for Π and the $n-1$ ratios p_1/p_2 , $p_2/p_3, \ldots, p_{n-1}/p_n$ etc. Seton thus outlined the prerequisites for transforming values into prices of production (relative prices) in a more general way and demonstrated that a solution could be obtained using quantitative methods.

Seton's solutions

Seton argued that to determine the absolute levels of prices of production of commodities, we should select a definite aggregate of the value system which was to remain invariant under transformation. He argued that the references in the Marxian texts support a number of mutually incompatible invariants.

He then reviewed the three postulates of invariance made by previous scholars. The first such proposed invariance for the unit-value of goods. Thus the Bortkiewicz-Sweezy analysis claimed invariance for the luxury products of department III in the traditional three-sector analysis, in the postulate $z = 1$. This aimed at ensuring prices would be expressed in terms of the value of gold (a product of department III) which brought the solution into line with Marxian monetary theory. An alternative was the invariance of the unit value of wage goods, and this was clearly supported by the notion that under capitalism "the worker was paid the full value of his labor" as suggested by Meek's solution A.

The second type of postulate proposed invariance for the value aggregate suggested by "total value equals total price" as manifested in Winternitz's approach. This was noteworthy for its symmetry, claiming no special status for any particular department. It is a weighted average of all prices, rather than a single price equated to unity. However, some prices would exceed values and others would fall short. Bortkiewicz, Sweezy and Meek's solutions contradicted this postulate.

The third type of postulate proposed invariance for the surplus rather than for aggregate output, equating total profit (in price terms) to total surplus (in value terms). Meek's (1973 & 1977) solutions employed this postulate. It was consistent with the Marxian notion that capitalists could redistribute the surplus among themselves in proportion to their capital.

On these three alternatives Seton (1982, 66) opined:

> No doubt the three alternative postulates do not exhaust all the possibilities. There may be other aggregates or relationships with perfectly reasonable claims to invariance whose candidacy has not so far been pressed. But the point which concerns us here is that the principle of equal profitability in conjunction with any one invariance postulate will completely determine all prices $(p_1, p_2, \ldots, p_n)$ and thereby solve the transformation problem. However, there does not seem to be an objective basis for choosing any particular invariance postulate in preference to all the others, and to that extent the transformation problem may be said to fall short of complete determinacy.

Seton further pointed out that since he based himself on the most general model of value flows amenable to mathematical treatment, generality should be abandoned in assessing the determinacy of the transformation problem. Scholars therefore recast the basic scheme employing the Marxian approach of making simplifying assumptions. He reduced the n industries to three departments. Department I produced goods used in further processing. Department II produced wage goods consumed by workers. The third department produced luxury goods consumed by capitalists. The equations could then be simplified to:

$$c_1 p_1 + v_1 p_1 = \rho \, a_1 p_1$$
$$c_2 p_2 + v_2 p_2 = \rho \, a_2 p_2 \qquad (2)$$
$$c_3 p_3 + v_3 p_3 = \rho \, a_3 p_3$$

where p_i stands for the coefficient of the prices of production-value of goods from department i, $\rho = 1 - \Pi$ stands for the average cost ratio, and a_i stands for the value of the goods produced by department I, being $a_i = c_i + v_i + s_i$.

Writing $r_i = c_i / a_i$ for the ratio of constant capital to value output, and $\mu_i = v_i / a_i$ for the ratio of variable capital to value output, we obtain

$$(r_1 - \rho) \, p_1 + \mu_1 p_2 = 0$$
$$(r_2 p_1 + (\mu_2 - \rho) \, p_2 = 0 \qquad (3)$$
$$r_3 p_1 + \mu_3 p_2 - \rho p_3 = 0$$

which we can write in matrix notation as

$$\begin{vmatrix} r_1 - \rho & \mu_1 & 0 \\ r_2 & \mu_2 - \rho & 0 \\ r_3 & \mu_3 & -\rho \end{vmatrix} = -\rho \begin{vmatrix} r_1 - \rho & \mu_1 \\ r_2 & \mu_2 - \rho \end{vmatrix} = 0 \qquad (4)$$

and we can calculate ρ, the average profit rate, which is $r = (1-\rho)/\rho$, and the ratios of p_1 to p_2 and p_3. But to obtain the absolute value of p_1, p_2 and p_3, it was desirable to look for special assumptions concerning a particular department. Before making his own assumptions, Seton assessed the special assumptions made by other scholars.

For example, Meek had assumed that the organic composition of capital in the wage goods industry was equal to the national average. At the same time, he assumed that that the rates of exploitation in all departments were equal. As a result, the department II became a simple scale model of the total economy $(c_2 : v_2 : a_2 = \Sigma c_i : \Sigma v_i : \Sigma a_i$ and $a_i = c_i + v_i + s_i)$. Meek however argued that though this equation could be justified, the determination of the absolute price level required a further postulate.

Meek further supposed that the capital goods industry was department I, rather than the wage goods industry, which was to be a scale model of the whole economy ($c_1{:}v_1{:}a_1 = \Sigma c_i{:}\Sigma v_i{:}\Sigma a_i$). At the same time, the ratio of total goods to constant capital was the same, being $\Sigma a_i/\Sigma c_i = \Sigma a p_i/\Sigma c p_i$ (where p_i represents a_i and c_i has been transformed into prices of production).

As Seton pointed out, the assumption of representativeness could equally well be applied to the luxury goods department ($c_3{:}v_3{:}a_3 = \Sigma c_i{:}\Sigma v_i{:}\Sigma a_i$). So in (2), $p_3 = 1$ and $\Sigma a_i = \Sigma a p_i$. If simple reproduction was also assumed, since total profit is $\Sigma s_i = a_3$, the three invariances could be postulated:

$$\frac{\Sigma\, a_i}{\Sigma\, s_i} = \frac{\Sigma\, a_i p_i}{\Sigma\, s_i p_i} \tag{4}$$

This was the fourth equation proposed by Seton. To some extent, this was the most satisfactory model since it allows us to postulate all three invariances at the same time. In other words we can achieve all three of $p_3{=}1$, $\Sigma a_i{=}\Sigma a p_i$, $\Sigma s_i{=}\Sigma s p_i$ suggesting that the postulate of invariance made by Bortkiewicz, Winternitz and Meek were all included.

Seton gave a simple illustration as follows. The value system was
$$80\ c_1 + 20\ v_1 + 20\ s_1 = 120\ a_1$$
$$10\ c_2 + 25\ v_2 + 25\ s_2 = 60\ a_2 \tag{6}$$
$$30\ c_3 + 15\ v_3 + 15\ s_3 = 60\ a_2$$

The requirement for simple reproduction could now be satisfied: the sum of the elements of row i must equal to the sum of the elements of column i.

Equation (2) combined with the postulate of invariance, yields the following solution:
$$p_1 = 6/5$$
$$p_1 = 3/5 \tag{7}$$
$$p_3 = 1$$

This yielded the system of prices of production:
$$96\ cp + 12\ vp + 36\ sp = 144\ ap$$
$$12\ cp + 15\ vp + 9\ sp = 36\ ap \tag{6}$$
$$36\ cp + 9\ vp + 15\ sp = 60\ ap$$

In these equations, the qualifier p implies that the item concerned has been transformed into prices of production. The profit ratio is equalized in all departments. Total production costs (144+36+60) equaled total value (120+60+60). Total profits (36+9+15) equaled total surplus value (20+25+15). The coefficient of prices of production-value of department III was 60/60=1.

Comments on the Seton model

Seton undoubtedly generalized the Bortkiewicz solution from three to n departments, and obtained a general mathematical expression for value transformation in an input-output matrix-like formalism. Moreover, the Seton solution offers a unique way of calculating the relative and absolute price, helping future research. However, Seton failed to overcome the limitations of Bortkiewicz, Winternitz and Meek.

First, his general model failed to designate the average profit rate as an exogenous variable, leading to a failure to obtain a general solution. For this reason, Seton simplified the general model and imposed a particular postulate for a particular productive department. The root cause of his recourse to simplification was his lack of understanding of the theoretical foundation of transformation, namely that average profit is just the result of redistributing total surplus value in accordance with the capital advanced by each investor. The average profit rate should therefore be input into the model as a known variable. As a result, Seton's model failed to prove the relationship between value, prices of production, profit and surplus value after value had been transformed into prices of production.

Next, the validity of his model depended upon three particular postulates: (1) the n industries could be reduced to the familiar three departments; (2) simple reproduction; (3) the organic composition of capital of Department III was the same as the average organic composition of social capital. This special model, meeting the three requirements, does have the potential to realize $z = 1$ and the invariance equations. Bortkiewicz had already mentioned the three requirements for $z = 1$ when exploring the incompatibility between total price of production and total value. Sweezy had also elaborated this point. The Seton model thus made no progress compared with the Bortkiewicz-Sweezy solution.

Thirdly, although Seton's invariance postulate subsumed the requirements necessary for Bortkiewicz, Winternitz and Meek's invariance postulates, the three requirements of Seton's special model were illogical as they lacked theoretical foundation. Al three requirements are rarely if ever met at the same time in real life. The solution therefore has many limitations. Seton acknowledged this as Hu Daiguang (1990, 162) notes:

> this model could thus impart complete determinacy to the transformation problem while satisfying all the Marxian preconceptions as to the characteristics of the solution. It is, however, a very restrictive model and may not commend itself in view of its radical departure from generality.

Last, although the invariance postulate $\Sigma a_i / \Sigma s_i = \Sigma a_i p_i / \Sigma s_i p_i$ might be the most satisfactory model from the standpoint of realizing all three invariances at one and the same time, Seton was wrong to make this the starting point for developing further postulates. The postulate $z = 1$ per se is irrational; we have no reason to believe that the prices of production of the products of Department III are consistent with their values, as we noted when commenting on Bortkiewicz. As for the equality of total prices of production to total value, we showed that according to the dynamic transformation model, this occurs only if the total prices of production of inputs equals their total value. Thus the total prices of production of outputs do not equal their total value in general. Seton hence failed to integrate history and logic with dynamic analysis.

Seton labored over the circumstances in which Marx's two invariance postulates could both hold. But for this very reason, he failed prove the validity of the labor theory of value under general circumstances. In fact this was not his intention. His conclusion was that Marx's labor theory of value had a negative impact on the solution to the transformation problem. Hence, we will later see, the starting point and conclusion of his research were the same as Morishima's.

Seton's 'historical transformation problem'

In Seton's (1982) *Transformation Problem*, he conducted a series of empirical studies to test the transformation problem. He found that according to Marxist thinking, the transformation of values into prices is not merely a logical, but also a historical progress (Seton 1982, 65):

> *in the early stages of capitalism, when this transformation has hardly begun, the rate of profit obtainable in capital goods industries will not as yet have reached equality with that of consumer goods industries. Capitalists will therefore prefer to invest their resources in the latter until the transformation has gone far enough to equalize the rate of profit everywhere. In Marxist ideology, therefore, the process of capitalist industrialization is bound to begin with the development of light industry and to delay the take-off of heavy industry until a comparatively advanced stage has been reached. This is held to be an obstacle to the realization of the fastest rate of growth attainable on technological grounds and to discourage the fullest use of labor-saving methods even when capitalism has reached maturity. Thus, in the Marxist view, society is cheated of the fruits of technological advance by the capitalist requirement of equal profitability, and the claims of socialism as a speedier engine of industrialization and greater liberator from human toil can be more plausibly advanced to the extent that it can dispense with this requirement and start the process from the opposite end of heavy industry.*

However, he argued, while Marx's transformation theory supported these conclusions, the theory itself was defective. It considered only the transformation of outputs, but failed to consider the transformation of inputs. Seton had shown that prices would exceed values in industries with a higher than average organic composition of capital and vice versa, so they would inevitably deviate from values. His purpose, however, was not to prove that Marx's transformation theory was correct but that his argument for two types of industrialization was valid. This is because Seton had serious doubts about the validity of premises. These premises include whether the rate of profit was equal; whether the organic composition of capital was sufficiently high in capital goods-producing departments, and whether labor was the only source of value *per se*.

Seton threw some light on the historical transformation problem from the perspective of the development of capitalism. However, his doubts about the premise of Marx's theory of industrialization lacked theoretical support and proof. And his elaboration of the historical transformation problem contradicted his abandonment of labor theory of value. From this perspective, his analyses of transformation problem turned out to be meaningless.

The Morishima model

Morishima's reinterpretation of Marxist economics

Morishima, in his 1973 book *Marx's Economics: a Dual Theory of Growth*, argued that the purpose of studying Marxist economics was not to reinvent it, but to provide a precise conceptualization of it using modern economic methods such as Leontief's input-output analysis and Walrasian general equilibrium theory. He argued that general equilibrium theory was the core of Marxist theory, which was composed of two parts: value theory and re-production theory.

According to Morishima, Marx and Walras proposed general equilibrium theory simultaneously and independently. In contrast with Walras, Marx proposed a two-step general equilibrium theory. It is generally believed that Walras' micro equilibrium theory was too general and complex to help scholars draw definite conclusions. To remedy this deficiency, Hicks proposed the aggregation theorem. He used fewer variables and equations in order to translate the micro equilibrium system to the macro economic system.

However, Marx was satisfied neither with the 'Hicksian' method of taking relative prices as weights of aggregation, nor the 'Keynes' approach of measuring aggregate output, aggregate consumption and so on in terms of wage units, because the weights used in these methods of aggregation would fluctuate, depending on market conditions. Marx sought to establish economic laws of a very long-run nature, such as the law of the tendency of the rate of profit to fall, the law of population peculiar to the capitalist mode of production, the general law of capitalist accumulation, and so forth, so he had to base his macro model on more stable and more solid aggregates.

In summary Marx sought to identify definite laws of motion for capitalist society; he therefore needed a method of aggregation. This avoided the pure, general but powerless Walrasian conclusion that everything depends on everything else. Morishima (1973, 2-3) argued that in Marx's economics, the importance of the labor theory of value was to provide a system of constants, in terms of which a microeconomic model may be aggregated into a two-departmental macroeconomic model, under a number of assumptions.

Morishima also held that Marx's theory of reproduction was very similar to Leontief's input-output analysis. It could even be argued that Leontief reproduced Marx as well as Walras in a pragmatic way.

Morishima elaborated on, and emphasized, Marx's idea of a 'double duality', which referred to the dualities between physical and value systems and between physical and price systems. For Marx, exploitation was necessary for the continued existence of any capitalist economy. Without it, value and price would be the same. But because of it, the law of value did not present itself in its pure and simple form. This led to a gap between value and price. Therefore, the transformation problem concerned the conversion of accounts in terms of value into accounts in terms of price.

Morishima thus lacked a deeper understanding of the implications of value and price. He failed to acknowledge that the transformation problem was actually the problem of the distribution of surplus value and the equalization of rate of profit, by no means a matter of mere accounting.

Morishima noted that he shared Samuelson's methodology. However, "I intend to sympathize more with Marx's theory than Samuelson did." (Morishima 1973, 6) In addition to his research findings on transformation, Morishima had another important finding: various elementary sectors (or industries) with identical value compositions of capital could be aggregated into two major departments, producing consumption and capital goods respectively. Morishima believed that this aggregation condition was a necessary result of transformation problem and provided a basis for Marx's formulation of the growth theory of the two departments. The implications of this were even more far-reaching than his major research findings even though Marx was probably not aware of these implications.

In this sense, we argue that Morishima's idea of transformation is rather impractical. It suggests that he had not achieved a deeper understanding of Marx's reproduction theory.

It could be argued that Morishima's reformulation of Marxist economics included many of his own interpretations. These were quite subjective and far-fetched or even biased.

Morishima in 1973 and 1978 (Morishima and Catephores 1978) also studied the labor theory of value in its relation to (1) the heterogeneity of labor; (2) joint production and (3) the problem of choice of techniques. He argued that if any one of these three were admitted, the labor theory of value would run into trouble. This is a contradictory conclusion: he argued that his own model could not admit Marx's method unless the labor theory of value was abandoned. The paradox is that Marxian economics without the labor theory of value is Walrasian economics without utility theory, for the following reasons:

(1) Morishima understands the labor theory of value as a theory of aggregation, reducing the number of sectors to a manageably small number;

(2) we are now richer in the techniques of dynamic analysis than Marx was. It is even possible for us to derive fruitful conclusions from a Marxian multi-sectoral growth model by using these techniques. Aggregation can then be avoided, and the role of labor theory of value would diminish as a result.=

Morishima wanted to reinterpret Marxian economics from the perspectives of value analysis and material goods by relying on Leontief and Walrasian analytical methods. In other words, he believed that Marxian economics was a dual economics. He also understood the labor theory of value in this way.

Marx's dual labor theory of value

Because of his sympathy with Marx's points of view, Morishima intended to strengthen the logic of Marx's labor theory of value. He argued that Marx's interpretations of value included a conceptualization of both value analysis and input-output analysis. The first is what Marx meant when he said:

142

All that these things now tell us is, that human labour power has been expended in their production, that human labour is embodied in them. When looked at as crystals of this social substance, common to them all, they are — Values.(Marx 1867, 46).

The second is why he wrote

We see then that that which determines the magnitude of the value of any article is the amount of labour socially necessary, or the labour time socially necessary for its production. (Marx 1867, 47)

Evidently, these are not two definitions of 'value' in that one refers to the characteristics of value and another refers to their quantitative determination. But from Marx's perspective there was only one definition of value.

It is possible that Morishima failed to distinguish between value inherent in the fruits of abstract human labor and value in the form of socially necessary labor time. In other words, He should have distinguished the value inherent in physical commodities from the magnitude of value. This misinterpretation of Marx's definition of value was probably intentional: its purpose was to pave the way for introducing input-output analysis.

According to the dual definition of value, Morishima presented Marx's definition of value as follows. Assume a society producing only grain and fertilizer. To produce one unit of grain needs a_{11} units of grain, a_{21} unit of fertilizer and l_1 hours labor. Morishima used λ_1 to denote the value of grain and λ_2 to denote the value of fertilizer. According to the first definition of value, the value of grain is determined by the total labor embodied in the grain commodity. This gives

$$\lambda_1 = a_{11}\lambda_1 + a_{21}\lambda_2 + l_1 \qquad (9)$$

In this equation, $a_{11}\lambda_1$ represents the labor contribution of grain consumed in production and $a_{21}\lambda_2$ that of fertilizer. l_1 represents the contribution of direct labor. This equation is to be computed on the basis of hours of labor.

Using Leontief's input-output analysis, Morishima arrived at another equation. To produce one unit of net output of grain, l_1 units of labor are per unit of grain, of which q_1 are consumed as inputs, and l_2 units of labor are required per unit of fertilizer, of which q_2 units are consumed as inputs. Therefore, $l_1 q_1$ and $l_2 q_2$ denote the total labor used by the department producing grain and the total labor used by the department producing fertilizer. The computation is in labor hours. As a result, the labor time socially necessary for producing one unit of grain is:

$$u_1 = l_1 q_1 + l_2 q_2 \qquad (10)$$

Morishima argued that this equation is actually based on the second definition of value. Thus the mathematical expressions of λ_1 and u_1 are different. As for whether or not $\lambda_1 = u_1$, Morishima proved this would be so given the following conditions:

1. Each industry uses one and only one technique of production. As a result, there is no choice of technique;
2. Each industry produces one and only one commodity. Without joint production, industries correspond one-to-one with commodities;
3. There are no primary factors of production except homogeneous, unskilled labor;
4. There are no fixed capital commodities: all inputs are entirely used up in one production period;
5. All commodities have the same period of production;
6. Production processes are all point-input-point-output processes: inputs are all bought on one day and outputs are all realized on one day, a year later.

Morishima went on to study the production process and quantitative determination. Assuming a unit of commodity i is produced by a_{ji} units of capital goods j ($j = 1, 2, 3, \ldots, n$) and l_i units of labor. a_{ji} is measured in natural physical units and l_i is the duration of labor, that is, labor-time. The production process of commodity i is given by the vector $(a_{1i}, a_{2i}, \ldots, a_{ni}, l_i)$. Evidently, such an equation embodying the input-output relationship can be transformed into a value equation. Assuming a unit of input commodity j includes labor input λ_j, the total labor input for a unit of commodity i should be:

$$\lambda_i = a_{1i} \lambda_1 + a_{2i} \lambda_2 + \ldots + a_{ni} \lambda_n + l_i \qquad (11)$$

144

This gives us a value-determination equation for each commodity. Assuming there are two capital goods and one wage good, an equation system can be rewritten as

$$\lambda_1 = a_{11}\lambda_1 + a_{21}\lambda_2 + l_1 \tag{12}$$

$$\lambda_2 = a_{12}\lambda_1 + a_{22}\lambda_2 + l_2 \tag{13}$$

for capital goods, and

$$\lambda_3 = a_{13}\lambda_1 + a_{23}\lambda_2 + l_3 \tag{14}$$

for the wage good.

The two equations for capital goods together determine the unknown values of two capital goods, say λ_1 and λ_2. At the same time, they determine the value of the wage good λ_3:

> It is seen that no single sector can independently determine the value of its product, except in the trivial case of the system being completely decomposable into sectors (i.e. the case of $a_{ji}=0$ for all i, j such that i ≠ j). Values are thus determined socially. But it must be noted that they are determined only by technological coefficients, they are independent of the market, the class-structure of the society, taxes and so on. Marx wanted to explain economic phenomena by using this materialistic concept. 'It becomes plain, that it is not the exchange of commodities which regulates the magnitude of their value; but, on the contrary, that it is the magnitude of their value which controls their exchange proportions' (Morishima 1973, 14-15).

What Morishima clearly refers to is that value is composed of two aspects: materialized labor and living labor. He just expresses it differently.

Assuming n capital goods and $m - n$ wage or luxury goods, the above equations can be rewritten in a more convenient way in matrix form:

$$\Lambda_I = \Lambda_I A_I + L_I \tag{15}$$

$$\Lambda_{II} = \Lambda_{II} A_{II} + L_{II} \tag{16}$$

Where

$$A_I = \begin{bmatrix} a_{11} & \cdots & a_{1n} \\ \vdots & & \vdots \\ a_{n1} & \cdots & a_{nn} \end{bmatrix} \quad A_{II} = \begin{bmatrix} a_{1n+1} & \cdots & a_{1m} \\ \cdots & & \cdots \\ a_{nn+1} & \cdots & a_{nm} \end{bmatrix} \quad (17)$$

$$L_I = (l_1, \cdots, l_n) \quad L_{II} = (l_{n+1}, \cdots, l_m) \quad (18)$$

$$\Lambda_I = (\lambda_1, \cdots, \lambda_n) \quad \Lambda_{II} = (\lambda_{n+1}, \cdots, \lambda_m) \quad (19)$$

Where and are capital coefficient matrices, and are labor input coefficient vectors and and are value vectors. , , and are all row vectors.

According to Morishima, based on the second definition, the value of a commodity is the total amount of labor required to produce a unit of product with the method of production prevailing in the society. To produce a unit of capital good i, $(a_{11}, a_{21}, \cdots, a_{n1})$ units of capital goods (1 ... n) are required. Therefore, an increase of one unit of output of the capital good i brings about multiplier effects on the outputs of capital goods 1, 2, $\cdots$, n. Morishima tested and proved that $\lambda_1 = u_1$ on the basis of the six assumptions listed above.

He pointed out that, although under certain circumstances the two value definitions would be identical, people can still criticize the value-determining concept on the grounds that it is more difficult to understand and handle than the price-determining concept. The fact that the two value definitions are identical helps avoid this criticism. Value by itself was not a mysterious thing and should occupy a position in today's precision economics. Seen from the standpoint of its second definition, value could mean the employment multiplier debated by Kahn and Keynes. Its magnitude could be computed using Leontief's input-output analysis. From the standpoint of the first definition, the increase in employment could be attributed to the increase in inputs to the factors of production. There thus existed a quite sophisticated concept behind the classical labor theory of value. It could be argued that there was a hypothesis of a duality between the 'interdependence of goods' and 'value' which united the two aspects of the economy.

Morishima hence provided two alternative systems of determination of values. But he argued there was a hidden assumption, which was that

146

all values were positive or at least non-negative. People normally took this for granted. because value could not be created in the absence of the non-negativity of material and labor inputs. However, Morishima argued that it was perfectly possible for the value-determining equations to give negative solutions unless additional conditions were satisfied. He gave an example to illustrate this point.

Assume an economy producing only two goods A and B. To produce 10 units of A, we suppose 5 units of A and 6 units of B and 1 unit of labor are required. To produce 10 units of B, we suppose 4 units of A and 7 units of B and 1 unit of labor are needed. The value equations are:

$$\lambda_1 = 0,5\ \lambda_1 + 0,6\ \lambda_2 + 0,1$$
$$\lambda_1 = 0,4\ \lambda_1 + 0,7\ \lambda_2 + 0,1 \tag{20}$$

and the solutions are

$$\lambda_1 = 1, \quad \lambda_2 = -1 \tag{21}$$

In this example, the two value equations are mutually independent regardless of how much of A or B is produced. As a result, the values of good A and good B should be determined independently and cannot be arrived at by jointly solving the two value equations. However, Morishima offered solutions for λ_1 and λ_2, which were both negative, in the second way.

He argued(Morishima 1973, 22) that the reason Marx failed to provide an explicit explanation of this issue was that he believed that the productiveness of the capital-good industries were implicit in the labor theory of value:

> It will be seen that, given other unrestrictive assumptions, the produc-
> tiveness of the capital-good industries is necessary and sufficient for
> any sort of products. One of Marx's basic assumptions must be like
> this: Since productive techniques had been well above this level, the
> productive process of capital goods at this level should be productive.

The 'productiveness' characteristic just refers to the ability to produce surplus goods or value. This is the circumstance under which value can be positive. Morishima further pointed out that in a self-contained society, the productiveness of capital-goods industries was not only a necessary but also a sufficient requirement, but for a capitalist society, it was necessary but not sufficient. To make it a sufficient requirement, the wage level must be such that exploitation took place.

After thorough empirical tests, Morishima (1973, 27) concluded that the requirements for positive values were

1. the coefficient of matrix A_I giving the inputs of the capital-goods industries should be non-negative and could not be further decomposed, and the coefficient of vector L_I giving labor inputs should be positive and non-zero;

2. the coefficient of the matrix $[A_{II} \ L_{II}]^T$ of the capital and labor inputs in each column of the wage and luxuries departments should be non-negative and non-zero.

The first assumption suggested that in addition to the decomposability and productiveness characteristics of the capital-goods industries, labor should be indispensable. The second assumption suggests that the wage and the luxury departments did not necessarily need labor. However, it was possible for industries in the two departments to use either some capital goods or some labor input or both.

But the productiveness of capital was actually the thesis that Marx always opposed. For Marx, capital was the product of labor and served as an instrument of labor. Capital by itself did not create value. Morishima's positivity requirements were actually a reformulation of Say's production factor theory of value. According to Say, this had to be incorporated into the labor theory of value to prove the compatibility of the value and price systems.

This was obviously impossible. Morishima, however, insisted that the two systems were identical and claimed that the compatibility of the value and price systems was implied by Marx's labor theory of value.

After a long-winded analysis in *Marx's Economics*, Morishima thus believed he had proved the duality in Marx's labor theory of value. He then elaborated on Marx's transformation theory.

Marx's transformation theory

Morishima argued that Marx's transformation theory comprised two aspects. One concerned the transformation from surplus value into average profit, the other the transformation from commodity values into prices of production.

On the first point, Morishima held that the Marxist equations were irrational, but the outcomes were correct. Marx had confused price and value: the profit rate should be the ratio of profit to the price of used capital but for Marx, it was the ratio of surplus value to fixed and circulating constant capital. Morishima pointed out that Marx was fully aware that value differed from price, but still developed the equations. The claimed irrationality could hardly affect Marx's basic viewpoint, which theorized that surplus value was the source of profits. We find Morishima's argument absurd. In computing the average profit rate, Marx simply computed the ratio of surplus value to fixed and circulating constant capital without transforming inputs into prices of production, but this was determined by the assumptions he made in order to study transformation. Morishima regrettably failed to develop a proper understanding of this point.

On the second point, Morishima argued that the equations developed by Marx were by no means incapable of attaining his conclusion even under conditions of balanced growth. To justify these conclusions the value composition of capital must be equal and the internal value composition of capital must also be equal. In addition, a very particular relationship termed the 'linear dependence of industries" (Morishima 1973, 77-78) must hold. This was so specific that Marx's equations were in fact, he argued, incapable of transforming value into prices of production.

But the fact that value could be transformed into prices of production had been proved not only by Marx, but also by the Bortkiewicz, Winternitz and Meek models. The relationship between total value and total prices of production after inputs had been converted to prices of production was a different matter. Morishima's argument was hence unfounded.

To examine Marx's transformation theory, Morishima isolated five points:

1. The total prices of production of commodities and their total value are always identical;

2. The cost of a commodity is always smaller than its value;

3. "Surplus-value and profit are identical from the standpoint of their mass";

4. "Aside from possible differences in the periods of turnover, the production price of the commodities would then equal their value only in spheres, in which the composition [of capital] would happen to be [the same];"

5. "The value of the commodities produced by capital [of higher value composition] would, therefore, be smaller than their production price, the production price of the commodities [produced by capital of lower composition] smaller than their value."

Morishima accepted that Marx was fully aware that under the capitalist system of production, the 'law of value' was not in force in its pure and simple form, and that the prices of commodities could deviate from their values. On the other hand, he argued, Marx always confused value with price. Marx had pointed out that value and price were dimensionally different, but the two could be identical at times. This would occur when the rate of exploitation and the profit rate were identical and zero; in other words, when there was neither exploitation nor profit and value was proportional to price. This was what Adam Smith had once argued that under the ideal circumstances, the value of a commodity was determined only by labor. Morishima argued that under the capitalist mode of production, the rate of profit would normally always be positive. His first and the third point could therefore never be realized.

We believe Morishima actually abandoned Marx's transformation theory, since he made the two invariance equations the basis for testing it.

Although Morishima considered it irrational to confuse an account in terms of values with the corresponding account of price it was he who actually did this. he did not understand that production price was the actual expression of value under capitalist economic conditions characterized by free competitions, nor that average profit was the result of reallocating total surplus value in accordance with capital advanced. The two equalities have

150

been elaborated thoroughly in the third chapter in the second part of this book.

Morishima further pointed out that profit could be proportional to surplus value provided the value compositions of capital in each industry were identical. But this differs from normal circumstances in which profit as determined by the general cost-price equation is not equal to surplus value. Therefore the equations and data used for computation should be overhauled so as to make the transformation of value into production price possible. He correctly pointed out that after inputs had been converted to prices of production, all advanced capital should be calculated in production prices in order to determine the average profit rate. But regrettably, he failed to incorporate the average profit rate as an exogenous variable into his solutions to the transformation problem.

He (Morishima 1973, 84-85) finally concluded:

> *Many of Marx's propositions are found to be correct with some revisions and under some additional assumptions. But as these assumptions are rather restrictive, one might think that Marx was unsuccessful in solving the transformation problem... However, the purpose of Marx's transformation theory is not to show that individual exploitation and individual profit are disproportional unless some restrictive conditions are imposed.*

Morishima thus accepted Marx's transformation theory with significant reservations. In Morishima and Catephores (1978) he then further examined the 'restrictive conditions' and provided his own solution to the transformation problem.

Morishima's solutions to the transformation problem

In 1978, Morishima and Catephores published a book titled *Value, Exploitation and Growth*. Morishima elaborated on the logical and mathematical aspects of transformation. They proposed a solution based on Markov process theory. Production price, on the basis of this theory, be deduced after multiple iterations starting from value. They (Morishima and Catephores 1978, 160-1) argued that:

*Marx was aware that both inputs and outputs had to be transformed
from those in terms of values into the ones in terms of prices. But he
did not transform them simultaneously; instead, he used an alternative approach transforming inputs and outputs in a successive way.*

To transform the value of commodities into the production price, Marx
employed the following equation:

$$p_i = (1 + \pi)\,(c_i + v_i) \quad i = 1, 2, ..., n \tag{22}$$

Morishima cited Marx's (1894, 125) comment that

*It is necessary to remember this modified significance of the cost-price,
and to bear in mind that there is always the possibility of an error if
the cost-price of a commodity in any particular sphere is identified
with the value of the means of production consumed by it.*

In this passage, Marx provided a detailed explanation for the following
points:

(1) The prices deduced from his formula were different from the values;

(2) Since value has been transformed into prices of production, the original
costs of production $(c + v)$ must be recalculated at production prices $(c^p + v^p)$;

(3) Applying the same algorithm to $(c^p + v^p)$, we have to correct p_i to

$$p_i' = (1 + \pi)\,(c^p + v^p)$$

(4) In so far as p' differs from p, cost prices need to be further recalculated
on the basis of new prices. The process of correction and recalculation can
then continue until exact prices are attained. Further correction was then
unnecessary. "Marx's prices are no more than a first approximation to the
true production-prices and he was not concerned with a closer examination
of them." (Morishima and Catephores 1978, 160-1)

Morishima pointed out that in Marx's system, the scale of each sector had
already been adjusted appropriately, though Marx never stated this explicitly.
This is an implicit prerequisite. To find the specific units employed by Marx to
measure quantities of commodities when he approached the transformation
problem, Morishima first measured the outputs and inputs in conventional, or
natural units such as a pound of tea, a quarter of corn or a ton of iron. Using

A and *DL* to denote matrices of input and labor coefficients respectively, and *y* the column vector of outputs, $(A+DL)y_0$ in natural units would be required to produce y_0 as output. We can then calculate the surplus outputs $y_0 - My_0$, where $M = A+DL$. Total surplus value is then $\Lambda y_0 - \Lambda My_0$ (Λ represents the unit value of the given commodity) and total constant and variable capital is ΛMy_0. The rate of surplus value is $(\Lambda y_0 - \Lambda My_0)/\Lambda My_0$.

Clearly some industries would produce surplus outputs at a greater or smaller rate. To dispel this disproportionality, the output vector had to be re-adjusted to make the rate of surplus output production tend to be the same. The adjustment formula proposed was:

$$y_1 = (\Lambda y_0 - \Lambda My_0) \, My_0 \qquad (23)$$

Here is the output vector after readjustment. This formula implied that commodities were produced, after readjustment, in amounts equal to the necessary outputs. uniformly expanded at the average rate of surplus outputs. Should not produce surplus outputs at an equal rate, a similar adjustment would be made, so Morishima and Catephores obtained a sequence of output vectors generated recursively, generated by:

$$y_{t+1} = (\Lambda y_t - \Lambda My_t) \, My_t \quad t = 0, \dots, 1, 2 \qquad (24)$$

y represented the eigenvector of *M*, which was associated with the characteristic root with the largest absolute value, ρ, that is (Morishima and Catephores 1978, 163):

$$\lim_{x \to \infty} y_t = y \qquad (25)$$

where

$$\rho \, y = M \, y \qquad (26)$$

We can also show that 1 plus the average rate of surplus value converges to the reciprocal of ρ, namely

$$\lim_{x \to \infty} y \, (\Lambda y_t - \Lambda My_t) = 1 / \rho \qquad (27)$$

They believed that *y* constituted the output vector that equalized the rate of surplus goods produced by each sector. This created the appropriate scale of production.

On the basis of this appropriate scale of production, the authors obtained the production price iteratively (Bai 1999, 136-8). Λ was used to multiply equation (26), and then divided by ρ, to give

$$1 / \rho = \Lambda y - \Lambda M y \qquad (28)$$

Since equaled $C + V + S$ and $\Lambda M y$ equaled $C + V$, where C, V and S are the vectors of constant and variable capitals and surplus value. This yields:

$$1 / \rho = 1 + S (C + V) \qquad (29)$$

Now let $\qquad\qquad \pi = 1 / \rho - 1 = S (C + V)$

represent the average profit rate. this then yields the following iterative sequence:

$$P_{t+1} = (1 + \pi) \, p_t M \qquad (30)$$

This was an infinite sequence. In 9, M is given and π was determined, so the matrix $M^* = (1 + \pi) M$ could be regarded as given. Now M^* is a Markov matrix, that is, a non-negative matrix whose largest positive characteristic root was unity. So Suppose

$$p = \lim_{t \to \infty} p_t \qquad (31)$$

then we have

$$p = (1 + \pi) \, p M = p M^* \qquad (32)$$

From (10) it can be seen that the limit vector is the production-price vector and is the average rate of surplus value, that is, the equilibrium rate of profit.

Morishima and Catephores argued that if the initial point p_0 was close to p, the iteration method would be the most effective. They further pointed out that Marx started the sequence at $p_0 = \Lambda$ as he was fully aware that under simple commodity production, values would give long-run equilibrium prices. As a result, although there would inevitably some deviations of equilibrium prices from values, they would not be very far from the corresponding equilibrium prices in a capitalist society unless each and every sector in the economy had the same organic composition of capital. Therefore, for Marx, the iteration process was actually a process that transformed the initial Λ into the ergodic p.

154

They showed that Marx's two invariance postulates between the value and price accounting hold for prices calculated according to the above algorithm.

First, post-multiply Equation (30) by y:

$$p_{t+1}y = (1 + \pi)\, p_t My \tag{33}$$

Now since

$$1/\rho = 1 + \pi$$

from Equation (26), we have:

$$y = (1 + \pi)\, My \tag{34}$$

From (33) and (34), we have:

$$p_{t+1}y = p_t y \tag{35}$$

Since p_0 is an arbitrary non-negative vector, the authors assumed:

$$\Lambda = p_0 \tag{36}$$

giving

$$\Lambda y = p_1 y = p_2 y = \dots = p\, y \tag{37}$$

Since Λy represents the value magnitude of total products, $p\, y$ represents the production price magnitude of total products, so the first invariance postulate, total value = total price, was valid.

$$\Lambda My = p_t My \tag{38}$$

Subtracting (14) from the respective terms of (13) yields

$$S = \pi_1 y = \pi_2 y = \dots = \pi y \tag{39}$$

where

$$S = \Lambda y - \Lambda My$$

represents total surplus value and

$$\pi_t = p_t - p_t M \text{ and } \pi y = py - pMy$$

represent the average profit rate. Equation (39) suggests that the second invariance postulate, total surplus value = total profit, is also valid.

They (Morishima and Catephores 1978 165-6) noted that:

Obviously, these results were very favorable to Marx. The iteration process (6) assured that, as long as the sequence {y$_t$} starts from $p_0 = \Lambda$ it converges to the long-run equilibrium price vector at that particular absolute level at which both conditions, 'total value equals total price' and 'total surplus value equals total profit' are consistently satisfied.

Analysis of the Morishima model

By distinguishing between value as the crystallization of abstract labor from value as the socially necessary labor time needed to produce a certain commodity, given the wage level and the rate of exploitation, Morishima proved that Marx's value and price systems were not incompatible. Although he was ridiculed by Samuelson as an 'antiquarian', Morishima insisted that his mathematical deduction did not make Marx's theory of value acceptable as a theory of price. From Marx's point of view, price as determined by competition was fundamentally different from value calculated by technicians on the basis of general production coefficients. He emphasized on the contrary that it was in a society characterized by simple commodity production rather than under a developed capitalist economy that value equations would determine prices.

To reinterpret Marxist theory so as not to confuse value with price, we too have had to be antiquarians, which means we must distinguish between the value of commodity *i* (the labor embodied in each unit of commodity *i*) and its exchange value (or exchange price). The latter is regulated by the former, but apart for very particular conditions, value and price are different both in the short- and long-run. Morishima argued that he understood that in Volume I of *Capital*, Marx implied that each sector of the economy could be aggregated into a single sector (each sector had equal capital composition) so that value and price, surplus value and profit were proportional to each other. Therefore, once Marx denied this aggregation and started working on composition in Volume 1 and Volume 3 of *Capital*, the proportionality would no longer hold. for Marx (Hu 1990, 186) this was quite normal.

Morishima correctly pointed out that the concept of time in relation to the process of transformation became more abstract when Marx was dealing with the two invariance postulates. Therefore, once input had been converted to prices of production, it was hard to prove the validity of the two invariance postulates by mathematical deduction. Morishima, however, relying on Markov process analysis, achieved the transformation of input and output into prices of production and finally proved the validity of the two invariance postulates. Setting the methodology and conclusion aside, Morishima's dynamic analytical method had important implications for scholars in determining the relationship between variables in the transformation process.

Like Seton, Morishima shifted the debate on transformation problem from the invariance postulates to the selection of a particular model. However, both Morishima and Seton committed a serious mistake.

First of all, in Marx's system, the scale of each sector had already been adjusted to an appropriate one. Morishima regarded such an adjustment as a prerequisite for solving the transformation problem. But actually, the solution bears little relation to the precise scale of each sector. According to Morishima's approach all sectors, including producing a saw, a sickle, a bulldozer, a lathe, a pen, or a pair of shoes, which he excluded from his analysis, contribute to the formation of an equal profit rate. As long as the rate of profit is unequal, transformation would take place in the context of competition and would be decided by the nature of capital. The scale of production of each such individual sector is by no means an obstacle to solving the transformation problem.

Secondly, when Morishima constructed equations whose purpose is to transform value into prices of production iteratively, he also transformed the old system into the new system so that S and $C + V$ could be aggregated and the average profit rate calculated. He excluded non-basic goods, for example, luxury-goods and held that the organic composition of capital in these sectors exerted little influence on the general rate of profit. As a result, the economic sectors in his model exclude luxury goods. In this he sympathized with Bortkiewicz, Winternitz and Sweezy. However, he provided no detailed explanation. We have already elaborated fully on this point in commenting on Bortkiewicz and Winternitz's solutions.

Thirdly, Morishima's formula for the general rate of profit is actually wrong. (27) implies that:

$$\pi = 1 / \rho - 1 = S (C + V) \qquad (40)$$

This is understandable, since in (7), input is still calculated in terms of value. Iteratively:

$$p_{t+1} = (1 + \pi) \, p_t M \qquad (41)$$

Here, the general rate of profit is arrived at on the basis of input measured in terms of value. Therefore, it is the general rate of profit on pre-paid capital. After inputs have been transformed into prices of production, $C + V$ should also be measured in terms of prices of production when the general rate of profit is calculated. However although this calculation was not remedied, it does not impact Morishima's mathematical deduction, because the latter bears little relation to the general rate of profit.

Fourthly, the Morishima model calls for strict prerequisites for the validity of the two invariance postulates. Equation (38) suggests that when the output vector converges to y, the total value of inputs equals their total price of production. Now, our dynamic transformation model, we argue, can ensure that total price of production equals total value. However, the validity of Equation (38) depends on the validity of equation (31), that $p = \lim\limits_{t \to \infty} p_t$ and on the presence of appropriate scale of production. However, the latter rests on the very special prerequisite that production techniques remain constant and all surplus value is devoted to expanded reproduction (Bai 1999, 140).

As for the invariance postulate that total value equals total surplus value, Morishima excludes all non-basic goods-producing sectors. This is what gives him the result that total profit is always equal to total surplus value.

Therefore, the Morishima model is still a special one. Since he failed to develop a proper understanding of the transformation problem, he set his mind on proving the validity of two invariance postulates as soon as he constructed his model. However, proving the validity of these are not the core issue for transformation theory research.

Finally, although Morishima provided a thorough interpretation of transformation problem, he did not set out to defend the labor theory of value. He even believed that there was no need to deduce prices of production from

158

value when studying the issues of joint production, choice of technique and the heterogeneity of labor.

On the historical transformation problem

After a thorough elaboration on the transformation problem from a mathematical and logical perspective, Morishima argued there was no need to make the labor theory of value the starting point. In further asserted that the transformation of value into production price was not an actual historical fact.

He further asserted that as early as 1894, Werner Sombart and Conrad Schmidt proved that the transformation problem was one of logical analysis, in which values and prices of production play the role of alternative logical tools. In other words, "Value constituted a mental, logical, fact; according to Sombart, a pure fiction, although a theoretically necessary fiction as Schmidt put the matter."(Morishima and Catephores 1978, 179)

Engels refuted Sombart and Schmidt's viewpoints, arguing that the transformation problem was not only a fact of life on the ideological level, but also a historical fact. The former was actually an abstract reflection of the latter:

In a word: the Marxian law of value holds generally, as far as economic laws are valid at all, for the whole period of simple commodity production, that is, up to the time when the latter suffers a modification through the appearance of the capitalist form of production. Up to that time prices gravitate towards the values fixed according to the Marxian law and oscillate around those values, so that the more fully simple commodity production develops, the more the average prices over long periods uninterrupted by external violent disturbances coincide with values within a negligible margin. Thus the Marxian law of value has general economic validity for a period lasting from the beginning of exchange, which transforms products into commodities, down to the 15th century of the present era. But the exchange of commodities dates from a time before all written history, which in Egypt goes back to at least 2500 B. C. , and perhaps 5000 B.C. , and in Babylon to 4000 B.C. , perhaps 6000 B.C. ; thus the law of value has prevailed during a period of from five to seven thousand years. (Engels, 'Supplement to Volume III' in Marx 1894:899)

Hilferding and Winternitz sympathized with Engels's argument while Bettelheim, Emmanuel and Althusser disputed it from the standpoint of methodology. Other scholars like Nell and Meek restated Engels's arguments in a modified form and Meek's elaboration had special implications.

According to Engels, this historical transformation should be divided into the pre-capitalist period (the simple commodity period) and the capitalist period. Meek argued that it should be further divided into three periods:

1. The value-epoch period of pre-capitalism (the simple commodity period). In this period, laborers retained the ownership of means of production and commodities were exchanged on the basis of value. Exploitation during this period did not exist;

2. The early period of capitalism: During this period, the means of production belonged to its owners and commodities were still exchanged in accordance with value. Different from the first period of capitalism, exploitation and surplus value began to exist. During this period, the profit rate of each sector was different;

3. The period of developed capitalism: During this period, the already uneven rate of profit tended to equalize and value started to be transformed into production price.

After a brief review of the previous scholars' viewpoints, Morishima offered a different criticism. His sought to show that in history, there was actually no period characterized by independent simple commodity production for exchange in accordance with values. He argued that the alleged 'simple commodity economy' had three unique features:

1. There was no uniform planned production;

2. Each owner had individual ownership over the means of production; and

3. There were no limits on the mobility of laborers, so that income per man-hour was equalized throughout society.

He believed that no economy with these characteristics had ever existed in history:

> Marx considered simple commodity production to be a distinct socioeconomic formation, on a par with feudalism and capitalism, and that he had even pinpointed three epochs, classical antiquity, late

feudalism and the early period of modern colonization, as the historical loci of appearance of that system...on the other hand, as we pointed out above, in the preface to A Contribution to the Critique of Political Economy, which is his main theoretical text on the evolution of socio-economic formations, or in any other part of his voluminous writings as far as we know, he reserved no place for a separate mode of simple commodity production in the key list of successive socio-economic formations (Asiatic, ancient, feudal and modern bourgeois) ... Marx believed that the scheme of transition from simple commodity production to capitalism was considered by Marx as applicable to some aspects only of historical evolution and not to others (Morishima and Catephores 1978, 184).

Actually, standards for defining socioeconomic state and simple commodity economy vary and depend on the focus of research. Morishima's criticisms are hence not well founded. He argues that in certain periods of history, undeveloped commodity production forms did exist. However, they were admixed with, or served as subsidiary elements of, other socioeconomic formations, whose structures remained predominant. Never had simple commodity production been realized in history in its full or pure form or even in some tolerably approximate form. The reason is the insufficient numbers of small independent producers and the limitations on their mobility between jobs in the pre-capitalist age.

Marx was fully aware of this: under capitalism, "all or a majority of products existed in the form of commodities." (Marx and Engels 1996, 179) He repeatedly emphasized that only under capitalism could the idea of abstract labor "achieve sufficient meaning" (Marx and Engels 1979b, 43) that the concept of value could exist in its "pure and general form." (Marx and Engels 1979b, 205). However, the law of value is the basic law of any commodity economy. The exchange of commodities in accordance with their values is unrelated to whether a simple commodity economy occupies a dominant position in the pre-capitalist age.

Morishima then argues that in pre-capitalist times, the increase of merchants' business activities and the growth in the quantity of commodities failed to promote commodity exchange in accordance with their values.

Marx (1894, 330) had once argued:

> *So long as merchant's capital promotes the exchange of products be-*
> *tween undeveloped societies, commercial profit not only appears as*
> *out-bargaining and cheating, but also largely originates from them.*
> *Aside from the fact that it exploits the difference between the prices*
> *of production of various countries (and in this respect it tends to level*
> *and fix the values of commodities), those modes of production bring*
> *it about that merchant's capital appropriates an overwhelming por-*
> *tion of the surplus-product partly as a mediator between commu-*
> *nities which still substantially produce for use-value, and for whose*
> *economic organization the sale of the portion of their product enter-*
> *ing circulation, or for that matter any sale of products at their value,*
> *is of secondary importance; and partly, because under those earlier*
> *modes of production the principal owners of the surplus-product with*
> *whom the merchant dealt, namely, the slave-owner, the feudal lord,*
> *and the state (for instance, the oriental despot) represent the consum-*
> *ing wealth and luxury which the merchant seeks to trap.*

We believe that historically, a simple commodity economy and competitive capitalism were not two separate phenomena at a single point in time.
In the simple commodity economy, the owners of surplus goods tended to
transfer a certain portion of them to merchants. This differs fundamentally
from the replacement of the law of value with the law of production price. As
for business 'trespass and fraud', these are not research topics of transformation theory. Therefore, the quotes Morishima extracted from Marx's works
do not serve as solid grounds for supporting his argument that "there existed
a particular period characterized by exchange in terms of value and [this]
involved no alienation of surplus value from the direct producers."

After his thorough criticism of the thesis that "there existed a particular
period characterized by exchange in terms of value and involving no alienation of surplus value from the direct producers," Morishima went on to criticize Meek's three-stage theory.

For Morishima, the periodization of the alleged historical process into
three epochs was inherently contradictory. By treating the pre-capitalist age

162

as a period in which exchange was made in terms of value and further re-garded it as the starting point for the transformation of value into produc-tion price, Meek removed this stage from the transformation process.

> *So the historical transformation problem would then consist of the need to explain the transition from a capitalist value-epoch to a capi-talist production price epoch without the need to assume a pre-capi-talist value epoch....*

The formulation suggested here would be equivalent with dropping his phase one and limiting the historical transformation problem to the transi-tion between his phases two and three. (Morishima and Catephores 1978, 193)

Morishima (Morishima and Catephores 1978, 194-195) also asserted that

> *in Engels's view, the early capitalism never dealt in values, but moved directly into a production price regime by adapting to the conditions created by merchant capital in the pre-capitalist era. If so, we must conclude that the second stage of Meek's historical-logical scheme of the transformation should also be struck off, like the first, as histori-cally invalid.*

By capitalizing on the conflict between Engels's two-stage thesis and Meek's three-stage thesis, Morishima criticized Meek's argument and denied the existence of the historical period characterized by exchange of commod-ities in terms of values. The criticism however lacked precision, because it did not provide substantial evidence for his argument. The apparent conflict between Engels' and Meek's theses arose from their different standards of definition of the historical period and did not exist in a fundamental sense.

Morishima also asserted that in Engels' view, prices of production were formed in sector after sector in a certain order. A general equilibrium meth-od employing simultaneous equations therefore had nothing to do with the historical process. In other words, since the transformation of value into prices of production did not happen simultaneously in each sector but took place in one sector after another, then theoretically a simultaneous transfor-mation should be regarded as the product of abstract logical thinking rather

163

than the recording of historical process *per se*. Transformation as explained by Meek was not therefore an actual historical fact.

This illustrates Morishima's lack of a deeper understanding of the organic combination of abstract and concrete thinking employed by the Marxian system. The movement from abstract to concrete should reflect historical transformation in its logical structure. However, in studying historical transformation, the movement from concrete to abstract is essential for understanding the transformation of value into prices of production. This is no different from the gap which necessarily appears between the postulates of a model and actual economic conditions, on which it appears rather absurd to lay blame. Morishima's criticism of Marx's historical transformation and of Meek's three-stage formulation therefore lacked theoretical foundation and proof.

To prove value was only an abstract logical tool, Morishima cites two of Marx's arguments:

> *Although it, value, is an abstraction, it is an historical abstraction, which only on the basis of a given economic evolution of society can be derived. (Marx to Engels 2 April 1858)*

> *The example of labor strikingly demonstrates how even the most abstract categories despite their validity in all epochs – precisely because they are abstractions – are equally a product of historical conditions even in the specific form of abstractions and they retain their full validity only for and within the framework of these conditions. (Marx 1857, 108)*

There are two layers to the implication of these statements:
1. Value is a historical abstraction rather than a conceptual abstraction;
2. Labor is a combination of natural and social features and the nature of labor cannot be fully understood unless its social features are also thoroughly understood.

164

Morishima (Morishima and Catephores 1978, 198) nevertheless concluded:

We may now construe Marx's simple commodity production model as a hypothetical abstract model for explaining phenomena of exploitation in the capitalist economy. The model is so constructed that it is similar to the capitalist economy in allowing labor to move freely from job to job, but dissimilar to the same in making exploitation impossible in it, as all necessary means of production are owned by each member of the economy. In this economy, values prevail as equilibrium exchange ratios which may be compared, as Marx compared them, with the equilibrium production prices in the actual capitalist economy, provided that both economies, fictitious and actual, adopt the same techniques of production. This is the problem of transformation of values into prices.

He further believed that "It follows from the above that the transformation problem consists in developing, choosing and relating between themselves analytical tools appropriate for the analysis of capitalism." (Morishima and Catephores 1978, 199)

In sum, he argued that the transformation of value into prices of production was not an actual transformation of value into capitalist prices of production. Rather, it was a logical analytical device for transforming values in a virtual simple commodity economy into prices of production in a real capitalist economy. The virtual simple commodity economy, in logic, was a virtual quasi-capitalist economy in which there was no exploitation and exchanges were made in terms of values. Values, however, were extracted from the real capitalist economies. Value, just like the virtual simple commodity economy, by no means existed in the pre-capitalist age. Value was simply an abstract logical tool which could be used to deduce prices of production and then reveal the exploitation inherent in capitalism.

Morishima further elaborated on these viewpoints from a methodological perspective. He argued that transformation was not an actual existing reality in history, but a conceptual reality in our subjective world. He believed that Marx's research method already suggested that Marx did not actually view the transformation problem as a true reflection of the historical process, nor did he view the transformation problem as a historical reality *per se*.

Whilst he stated this as a viewpoint, he did not provide any actual proof. He simply believed that this was what Marx's originally thought.

He further asserted that in terms of logic and history, Engels took the former as a generalization of the latter and regarded the unfolding of the abstract concept as the reflection of historical development. However, Morishima held, this was wrong because it converted the presentation of reality by theory into a passive reflection of that reality.

The correct position was that of Max Weber's *Methodology of the Social Sciences*:

> *Thus far we have been dealing with ideal-types only as abstract concepts of relationships which are conceived by us as a stable in the flux of events, as historically individual complexes in which developments are realized....Developmental sequences too can be constructed into ideal types and these constructs can have quite considerable heuristic value. But this quite particularly gives rise to the danger that the ideal type and reality will be confused with one another. (Morishima and Catephores 1978, 204)*

Marx's system never made the unfolding of an abstract concept a passive reflection of history. For example, Marx emphasized that it was mistaken to rank economic sectors in accordance with their contribution to the history. Their ranking was determined by their inter-relations in the modern capitalist societies and this was the opposite of their rank in historical development (Marx 1962, 758). But Weber's argument that "it particularly gives rise to the danger that the ideal type and reality will be confused with one another" bears little relation to Marx's transformation problem. Marx believed that the logical construction must employ historical method. The use of logical constructs which deviated from the historical process was the method which capitalist political economy employed to construct its system. They thought that

> *Man's reflections on the forms of social life, and consequently, also, his scientific analysis of those forms, take a course directly opposite*

to that of their actual historical development. He begins, post festum
with the results of the process of development ready to hand before
him. (Marx and Engels 1996, 86)

According to Morishima, value and prices of production along with the
transformation of one into the other were only an abstract reflection of capitalist economies. In the pre-capitalist age, there was neither value nor production price, let alone transformation as defined above. How then can we
interpret pre-capitalist economies and their inner laws of development?

To Morishima, pre-capitalist economies were such a mess that during the
thousands and thousands of years before capitalism appeared on the stage,
the distribution of the means of production, wealth, and products, were per-
formed not on the basis of any economic law. It was only after human history
entered the age of capitalism that we human beings constructed the relationships of exchange revealed by the transformation problem.

Marx provided a conclusive comment in this regard:

> Apart from the domination of prices and price movement by the law
> of value, it is quite appropriate to regard the values of commodities as
> not only theoretically but also historically antecedent (prius) to the
> prices of production. This applies to conditions in which the laborer
> owns his own means of production, and this is the condition of the
> land-owning working farmer and the craftsman, in the ancient as
> well as in the modern world. This agrees also with the view we ex-
> pressed previously, that the evolution of products into commodities
> arises through exchange between different communities, not between
> the members of the same community. It holds not only for this primi-
> tive condition, but also for subsequent conditions, based on slavery
> and serfdom, and for the guild organization of handicrafts, so long as
> the means of production involved in each branch of production can
> be transferred from one sphere to another only with difficulty and
> therefore the various spheres of production are related to one another,
> within certain limits, as foreign countries or communist communities.
> (Engels, 'Supplement to Volume III' in Marx 1894:896)

Conclusion

To seek a solution to transformation problem, both the Seton and the Morishima models abandoned the 'postulate of invariance' of the Bortkiewicz tradition, which led them to turn to special models. We find that both the Seton and the Morishima model took their ultimate goal to be proving the validity of the two invariance postulates. However, neither model recognized average profit and prices of production as expressions of surplus value and value. As a result, they failed to identify the precise relationships between different variables in the transformation process. Both concluded that for the two invariance postulates to hold, a set of conditions dramatically opposed to real-life economic situations would have to hold. Actually, in real life conditions, both models invalidate the two invariance postulates.

Both Seton and Morishima also believed from their special models that it was unnecessary to approach transformation from the standpoint of value, and as a result they abandoned the labor theory of value. Seton argued that the transformation problem was more a historical transformation problem than a logic problem and therefore elaborated further on the historical transformation problem, which evidently contradicted his abandonment of Marx's labor theory of value. Morishima, however, was more absolute than Seton and believed that value was no more than an instrument for abstract logical analytical purposes. He viewed transformation as a set of theoretical concepts expressed in the form of a notional fact; the historical process of transformation from value to prices of production did not exist.

The weak points in Morishima's argument were that he neither stated how the transformation issue came to be, nor did he state the relationship between the logical aspect of the transformation problem and the history of transformation.

In sum, both the Seton and the Morishima models failed to provide a scientific explanation of the transformation issue.

7
Price behavior and transformation

After Seton articulated his solution in 1957, debates on transformation changed significantly. Until then, they had focused on the alleged conflict between Volumes I and III of Capital. They then shifted to whether the labor theory of value provided the theoretical foundation for the study of transformation.

There were two reasons for this shift. First, there were by now many studies of the problem's logical structure and it was felt there was no need for more. The second reason was the influence of Leontief's input-output analytical method and Sraffa's physical analytical method. Scholars like Paul Samuelson were clearly influenced by Leontief and preferred his input-output analysis to value analysis and the labor theory of value which they regarded as an 'unnecessary detour'. Others like Steedman and Meek adopted Sraffa's method to study Marx's transformation theory, believing it more effective and that it could save scholars trouble.

Both tendencies preferred to replace value analysis with price analysis in approaching the transformation problem.

Samuelson's 'reverse transformation'

The Labor theory of value as an 'unnecessary detour'

In 1957, Samuelson published *Wages and Interest: A Modern Dissection of Marxian Economic Models* in which he proposed that analyzing the labor theory of value by Leontief's input-output method was an 'unnecessary detour'.

He first converted Marx's model of simple reproduction in two major departments to the input-output table shown in table 1

Table 1

Departments	I	II	Total demand	Total output
I	q_1Q_{11}	q_1Q_{12}	0	$q_1Q_1 = M_1'$
II	0	0	q_2Q_2	$q_2Q_2 = M_2'$
Wage	wL_1	wL_2	–	–
Profit	$p(wL_1 + q_1Q_{11})$	$p(wL_2 + q_1Q_{12})$	–	–
Total costs	M_1'	M_2'	–	–

In this Table, I is the capital goods department and II the wage goods department. wL_i stands for variable capital with w being the money wage and L_i the labor power consumed by department i. The monetary cost of inputs stands for constant capital so that each item in the table reflects monetary capital circulation. Q_{ij} stands for the commodities of department i consumed by department j, q_i for the unit price of Q_i and p for the rate of profit (interest). M_I' stands for the gross product of department i. q_1Q_{1j} stands for constant capital (C). wL_i stands for variable capital (V), $p\,(wL_i + q_1Q_{1j})$ represents profit (which is also surplus value). The aggregates corresponding to each row and column were equal.

Simple reproduction is expressed in money terms. The hidden equilibrium conditions are therefore:

$$q_2Q_2 = w\,(L_1 + L_2) + p\,(wL_1 + q_1Q_{11}) + p\,(wL_2 + q_1Q_{12})$$
$$= w\,(L_1 + L_2) + pw\,(L_1 + L_2) + p\,(q_1Q_{11} + q_1Q_{12})$$
$$= w\,(1 + p)\,(L_1 + L_2) + pM_I' \tag{1}$$

To derive , Samuelson used the technical coefficients to indicate the commodities of department and to represent the living labor power consumed respectively in producing each unit of the output of department.

Samuelson further expressed the productive capital circulation with the following two equations:

$$\begin{cases} a_{01} Q_1 + a_{02} Q_2 = L \\ a_{11} Q_1 + a_{12} Q_2 = Q_1 \end{cases}$$

Therefore

$$q_i = (a_{0i} w + a_{1i} q_1)(1 + p), \quad i = 1, 2 \tag{2}$$

giving

$$\frac{q_1}{w} = \frac{a_{01}(1 + p)}{\left[1 - (1 + p) a_{11} \right]} \tag{3}$$

and

$$\frac{q_2}{w} = a_{02}(1 + p) + \frac{\left[a_{01}(1 + p)^2 a_{12} \right]}{\left[1 - (1 + p) a_{11} \right]} \tag{4}$$

Clearly, if p and w are known, we can derive the values of q_1 and q_2. And a_{01}, a_{02}, a_{11} and a_{12} are all exogenous input-output coefficients generated by statistical computation.

According to Samuelson, neither (1) nor (2) nor their quotient are proportional to the labor power embodied in the commodities concerned. This mathematical fact refuted the inference that the labor theory of value could be the theoretical foundation of exploitation. He further argued that if the wage rate is known, the profit rate p can be deduced from (2).

Moreover, the circulation of productive capital could be derived from the circulation of commodity capital. For example, suppose Department I needs a_{11} units of capital goods and a_{01} units of labor power to produce a unit of Q. Then for every a_{01} units of labor power, $1 - a_{11}$ units of pure capital goods are produced. In other words, one unit of capital goods /contains $a_{01} / (1 - a_{11})$ units of labor power including direct and indirect labor. Similarly to produce one unit of wage goods, units of labor and unit of capital goods need to be consumed while to produce units of capital goods, the labor consumed is . So the total labor power that needs to be consumed in producing each unit of wage goods is:

$$a_{02} + a_{12} \frac{a_{01}}{1 - a_{11}} = \frac{\left[a_{02}(1 - a_{11}) + a_{12} a_{01} \right]}{(1 - a_{11})} \tag{5}$$

Therefore

$$l_1 = \frac{a_{01}}{1 - a_{11}} \tag{6}$$

and

$$l_2 = \frac{\left[a_{02}(1 - a_{11}) + a_{12} a_{01} \right]}{(1 - a_{11})} \tag{7}$$

where l_1 and l_2 stand for the labor power consumed by the production of every single unit of capital goods or wage goods.

Assuming each unit of labor power creates λ, units of value, then in the second department, the variable capital contained in the gross social product is:

$$\left(\frac{wL_2}{q_2Q_2}\right)Q_2l_2\lambda = \frac{wL_2l_2\lambda}{q_2} \tag{8}$$

and the surplus value is
$$l_2\lambda - \frac{wL_2l_2\lambda}{q_2} \tag{9}$$

so the rate of surplus value is

$$s_2' = \frac{1 - \frac{wL_2}{q_2}}{\frac{wL_2}{q_2}} \tag{10}$$

Accordingly, the rate of surplus value of department I is

$$s_1' = \frac{\left[L_1\lambda - wL_1\frac{Q_1l_1\lambda}{q_1Q_1}\right]}{\left[wL_1\frac{Q_1l_1\lambda}{q_1Q_1}\right]} \tag{11}$$

$$= \frac{q1 - wL_1}{wl_1} \tag{12}$$

Based on (11) and (12) Samuelson believed that the rates of surplus value across different departments were different and Marx's assumption was hence wrong. Exploitation could be expressed in price terms. In department II

$$r = q_2 - wl_2 = q_2 - \frac{w[a_{02}(1 - a_{11}) + a_{12}\,a_{01}]}{(1 - a_{11})} \tag{13}$$

If $r > 0$ then we need $q_2 - wL_2$. From (4) it follows that only when $\rho=0$ is $q_2 = wl_2$ so that a positive r is a sufficient and necessary condition for a positive ρ. Therefore, a positive rate of profit coincides with the existence of exploitation.

Samuelson further believed that since the rate of profit was indicative of the rate of exploitation, there was no need to approach the transformation problem by starting from value. In other words, it could exploitation could equally well be proven to exist without recourse to a theory based on the transformation from value into price.

172

By labeling the labor theory of value a 'redundant theory' and extending its implications, Samuelson concluded that it was unrealistic for value to be transformed into production price. Rather, price could be 'transformed back' into value.

Reverse transformation

Before Samuelson articulated his concept of 'reverse transformation', he analyzed what he saw as the flaws inherent in the labor theory of value and then restated Marx's model of exploitation.

According to Samuelson, the labor theory of value was dogged by three inherent flaws. First, factors other than labor which contributed to value formation and transformation outside labor were overlooked. Like Ricardo, Marx believed that labor was the only factor determining value and consequently the only source determining income, regardless of the stage of social development. Both Marx and Ricardo overlooked non-labor factors entering into the formation of value, which Smith had once identified. Furthermore, Walras' conditions for equilibrium in value determination had been overlooked.

Second, Samuelson contended that socially necessary labor was an inadequate measure of the magnitude of value because of heterogeneous labor. For this reason, it could not clarify income distribution. Thirdly, the effects of time other than labor time had not been taken into consideration. Time is money, and interest can never be zero. Only by taking previous time-governed factors, including interest, into consideration could we obtain the actual competitive cost and production price.

Samuelson then restated Marx's model of exploitation. His first conclusion was that since the labor theory of value applied only to what Smith termed "early primitive societies", exploitation theory based on it applied only to the earnings of owners in such societies. It could not therefore explain earnings in societies characterized by free labor. Marx was therefore wrong to apply it to exploitation in capitalist societies.

Samuelson's (1971, 113) second conclusion was that under competitive capitalism

> The equilibrium profit rate will be between zero and the exploitation rate r*, at a level just large enough to coax out the balanced capital formation needed for the growing labor force to work with. The work force grows because the real wage exceeds the minimum cost of subsistence and of reproduction of labor power.

Samuelson further believed that Marx's inference that the function of the wage was to maintain a minimum standard of living was wrong. Therefore, surplus value could not be precisely conceptualized, so its existence had not been proved and exploitation was unexplained.

Samuelson then went on to argue that it was unrealistic for value to be transformed into production price because Marx's mathematical account was valid only for the special case in which the organic composition of capital of the whole of society was equal. Under normal circumstances, value was not equal to price.

Samuelson articulated his view that while it was unrealistic to transform value into production price, it was realistic to transform price to value, which he termed 'reverse transformation'. By adding the differentials between production price and cost, transformation scholars could obtain total profits. Since the volume of each type of capital was the same as in Marx's example, the rate of profit of each department was the same. Based on the volume of variable capital, transformation scholars could then obtain the magnitude of surplus value. If this was added to cost, the magnitude of value could be obtained. The implication of reverse transformation was that the starting point for studying the transformation problem was price, not value.

Analysis of reverse transformation

The following statement by Marx (1894,197) is the best comment on reverse transformation:

> The production price includes the average profit. We call it production price. It is really what Adam Smith calls natural price, Ricardo calls production price, or cost of production, and the physiocrats call prix

174

necessaire, because in the long run it is a prerequisite of supply, of the reproduction of commodities in every individual sphere. But none of them has revealed the difference between production price and value. We can well understand why the same economists who oppose determining the value of commodities by labor time, i.e., by the quantity of labor contained in them, why they always speak of prices of production as centers around which market-prices fluctuate. They can afford to do it because the production price is an utterly external and prima facie meaningless form of the value of commodities, a form as it appears in competition, therefore in the mind of the vulgar capitalist, and consequently in that of the vulgar economist.

Samuelson realized that market competition reflected the value of commodities in the form of price but concluded that the transformation of value to price was an 'unnecessary detour.' But by arguing that the value system conflicts with the price system, he distorted the issues at stake.

Marx's value theory begins from the standpoint of social relationships, asking how they determine prices, the wage, and profit. This was the diametric opposite of the neo-classical and neo-Ricardian approach, which deduces the magnitudes of price, wage and profits from the technical requirements of supply and demand. Marx's theory uncovered what lay beneath these phenomena. He thus spoke of the 'mystification' of surplus value: "Disguised as profit, surplus value actually denies its origin, loses its character, and becomes unrecognisable." (Marx and Engels 1998, 166)

But this is a process which occurs behind his back, one he does not see, nor understand, and which indeed does not interest him. The actual difference of magnitude between profit and surplus-value-not merely between the rate of profit and the rate of surplus value-in the various spheres of production now completely conceals the true nature and origin of profit not only from the capitalist, who has a special interest in deceiving himself on this score, but also from the laborer. The transformation of values into prices of production serves to obscure the basis for determining value itself. (Marx 1894, 167)

175

For Marx price and profit act as the direct regulators of reproduction, and social labor time as the inner regulator of price, profit, and social reproduction. The relationship between these two tiers is the dialectical unity of content and form, nature and phenomenon.

Now, Samuelson believed that approaching production price by starting with value was an 'unnecessary detour'. His reasoning was that

1. price was not proportional to the wage and relative price was not proportional to the labor embodied in commodities;
2. in terms of magnitudes, value was inconsistent with production price;
3. outwardly, value was not observable, and capitalists were only concerned with price and the money rate of profit. But this could be deduced directly.

Samuelson's first reason is incorrect. As table 1 shows, he sought to prove the Marxian equations by relying on input-output methods. He made variable capital the wage payment, arguing that the Marxian equations could be expressed by multiplying labor input by the money wage. He further identified constant capital with the physical magnitude of capital, being the commodities of department I multiplied by their price. But in so doing, he unwittingly identified price with the value category when studying Marx's equations. Wages, input costs, and miscellaneous fees he mentions are all expressed in monetary units: as a result, they are treated separately as price and as physical magnitudes. Price is then deduced from input-output relationships.

Now, if $q_1 Q_{1i}$ and wl_i in table 1 are treated as the production price of constant and variable capital, and if the general rate of profit is deduced from values, then other value calculations are possible. However, Samuelson instead made the magnitudes of q_p, w and ρ exogenous and unrelated to labor. Equation (2) thus took on a different character. Relative prices based on (3), (4) and (3)/(4) actually change in response to changes in a_{01}, a_{02} and ρ. But to Samuelson, the direction of determination is the opposite.

Samuelson likewise concluded that rates of surplus value in the two major departments were equal, based on (3) and (4). He calculated the value of variable capital from $(wL_i + q_i Q_i) Q_i l_i \lambda$. However, $Q_i l_i \lambda$ is the sum of values of the outputs of department i and $wL_i + q_i Q_i$ represents the proportion of

176

wage income in the output of department I, calculated on the basis of price. The result was not the value of variable capital. The calculation of surplus value was likewise incorrect, making the rates of surplus value unequal in the two departments.

Actually, the rate of surplus value arises from the severity with which the capitalists exploit the workers, derived from value. Alternatively, it could be argued that the rate of surplus value is determined this severity, but should still be derived from value. The rates of surplus value can be equal even if the organic composition of capital is different across departments.

Samuelson's argument that the validity of labor theory of value is hamstrung by three inherent flaws is also erroneous. Not least, he himself expressed serious reservations about factors other than labor determining value. He clearly confused the production of value with the production of use value. Marx never denied the contribution of non-labor factors to the production of use value but argued that labor was the only source of value. In a commodity-based economy, only through the embodiment of abstract human labor can different commodities be compared and traded on the basis of a single price. But there was is no special relationship between value and use value. Thus Marx emphasized that labor was not the only source of all wealth. Nature, just like labor, is also a source of use value. (Marx 1875, 7)

Next, Samuelson argued that because labor was heterogeneous, socially necessary labor failed to determine the magnitude of value and explain income distribution. However, concrete labor is heterogeneous but abstract labor is homogeneous. Samuelson's understanding of the duality of Marx's labor theory fell short.

Finally, Samuelson argued that Marx overlooked the implications of time other than labor time. Marx however discussed labor and non-labor time in production, circulation and in social reproduction. Samuelson ignored this discussion, attributing non-zero interest to a non-labor time factor. This made it more difficult to understand the nature of interest.

Samuelson's second reason was based on a misunderstanding of Marx's transformation theory. He believed that the transformation process should establish a correspondence between value and production price. But what Marx tried to demonstrate was not a proportionality between value and production price but the deviation of production price from value. As Morishima (1973, 85-86) notes:

> [I]n the transformation problem Marx did not intend to establish a proportionality between values and prices. On the contrary, he just wanted to show that except under rigorous conditions, there was a disproportionality between individual exploitation and individual profit....

> Thus it is clear that the transformation problem has the aim of showing how the aggregate exploitation of labor on the part of the total social capital is, in a capitalist economy, obscured by the distortion of prices from values.

William Baumol (1974, 86) also maintained:

> Marx did not intend his transformation analysis to show how prices can be deduced from values....Rather, the two sets of magnitudes which are derived more or less independently were recognized by Marx to differ in a substantial and a systematic manner. A subsidiary purpose of the transformation calculation was to determine the nature of these deviations. But this objective and, indeed, any explanation of pricing as an end in itself, was of very little consequence to Marx, for the primary transformation was not from values into prices but, as Marx and Engels repeatedly emphasize, from surplus values into the non-labor income categories that are recognized by vulgar economists, i.e., profit, interest, and rent.

Although we cannot accept Baumol's idea that Marx' purpose was not to derive price of production, he however thus argued that transformation was just a process of redistributing surplus value, refuting Samuelson's hypothesis.

Samuelson responded to Baumol's claim, saying he accepted Baumol's challenge. He pointed out that his treatment applied not only to the transformation of value into price but also to the transformation of surplus value into profit. He wrote (Literature on Economics 1974, 75).

Baumol, however, sympathized with my treatment of value-price trans-formation but objected to the surplus value-profit transformation. Clearly, Baumol's claim was untenable. Samuelson believed that the two analyses of the transformation were actually based on the same logic.

Baumol further pointed out that Marx never claimed scholars could obtain more statistical data on actual prices wages, profits, rent and interest from Volume 1 of Capital than from Volume 3. He argued that to end the dispute, Samuelson must recognize that Marx himself showed minimal concerns with data determination. According to Marx, the data were a superficial phenomenon; what made it important is that it concealed fundamental social relationships. Samuelson, who insisted on price analysis, felt it impossible to reveal the inner relationships behind economic phenomena.

Samuelson's third reason was also erroneous as Shaikh (cited by Hu Daiguang 1990, 174) points out:

Capitalists know that capitalism is an unplanned society, in which they are free to take their chances in producing commodities in the hope of profit. And they certainly know that there is no guarantee they will receive this profit, or any profit at all...they therefore know that prices and profits fluctuate constantly, and that there is never at any moment a uniform rate of profit, so that prices of production never exist as such. It follows from this that the prices, the individual profit rates, and even the general rate of profit, on which capitalists base their actual decisions are never equal to prices of production and the uniform profit rate on which Steedman apparently bases his decisions.

P. N. Junankar (1982,64) also points out:

[T]hese prices are also non-observable. Capitalists react to variables at market prices, or to non-observable expected prices. Unless they have rational expectations and their expected prices are the long-run equilibrium prices, prices of production and rates of profit at prices of production are also not observed by capitalists. Thus we have to choose between two sets of abstractions: one that uses value analysis and one that does not.

Junankar further pointed out that although the production price and the uniform rate of profit had never existed in circulation, they constantly regulated market prices and the rate of profit. In this sense, value and the rate of profit of value appeared to be even more important, since they regulated production price and the uniform rate of profit. This was what Marx had tried to prove.

Many Western Marxist economists leveled forceful criticism at Samuelson's 'reverse transformation'. D. Laibman (1973) pointed out that Samuelson denied the validity of labor theory of value and viewed the rate of exploitation as the result of social net income. This obscured the exploitation relationship, which should be viewed as the ratio of paid to unpaid labor. Its function was to reveal the underlying social relationship between value and production price: revealing social relationships behind class phenomena was a basic requirement Marx's value theory and of transformation.

Desai (1974) also strongly criticized Samuelson's 'reverse transformation'. He pointed out that Marx's value theory was fundamentally different from classical and neo-classical theories. It did not just aim to study relative price the distribution of resources by means of relative prices, but also to study the particularity of capitalist society and the economic foundations of its class relationships. He criticized Samuelson for confusing Marx's labor theory of value with the classical school's labor theory of value.

Desai further used Samuelson's price theory to analyze and refute the argument that value theory was unnecessary, setting out to prove that Samuelson had either failed to develop a deeper understanding of Marxian economic theory or distorted it. On the one hand, based on the Bortkiewicz solution, Desai acknowledged that through transformation in a narrow sense, values could always be transformed into production price. He proposed an equation including the organic composition of each department and the rate of surplus value so that the production price and rate of profit could be obtained. On the other hand, Desai's analysis of the extended form of value and production price, and the relationship between the two were substantively different from Bortkiewicz's solution. He argued that commodity fetishism, the value relationship and the price relationship belonged different theoretical levels.

180

Although the value relationship was aimed at dissecting the production relationship between capital and labor, it did not directly observe or measure the social relationships inherent in the magnitude of value. Desai thus brought the issue back to the way price relationships conceal value relationships. Thus, production price could be viewed as a form of value. The transformation problem could then be understood by relating it to a society characterized by commodity value based on the capital- labor relationship. This was what Samuelson's 'reverse transformation' lacked.

Samuelson argued that value and price, surplus value and profit were mutually replaceable but dramatically different systems. It was necessary to reverse the historical and logical order of these categories. We however argue that Samuelson's model misunderstood Marx's analytical method in integrating history and logic. It failed to identify the source and determinations of market parameters like price, wage and profit, and lapsed into the circular reasoning of price analysis.

Analysis of Sraffa's solution: Meek and Steedman

In 1960, Sraffa studied the state and characteristics of a production system in which the ratio of the scale of production to its elements was stable, in his *Production of Commodities by Means of Commodities*. Assuming proportionality between the wage, the rate of profit and commodity prices, Sraffa examined the relationship between wage, profit and price, the relative share of wage and its fluctuations, along with its the impact on the rate of profit and prices of production. Sraffa's method clearly involved a return to the classical tradition with its emphasis on the relationship between physical goods in production and on the relationship between wage and profit. At the same time, Sraffa's method represented a return to the neo-classical school by emphasizing the role of production and demand in contrast with marginal analysis, in equilibrium analysis.

The Sraffa system provided a new theoretical weapon for the debate between the two 'Cambridge Schools'. It did not explicitly involve value transformation, but some Western economists argued that it provided a new way of thinking about it. Meek and Steedman were two representatives of this approach to Sraffa's system.

As we have noted, Meek (1975, 1977) articulated his second solution with Sraffa's system as the guiding principle, after which he compared the Marxian system with the Sraffa system. Meek believed Sraffa's method was more effective than Marx's value-based method. It approached the relationship between production price and distribution by studying production conditions and physical goods.

Steedman (1977) then argued that the Sraffa system was in fact a replacement for Marx's theory. He suggested that Sraffa's method could establish the opposed relationship between wage and profit and so developing a theory of exploitation without recourse to the labor theory of value.

Seton, Morishima and Samuelson had already attempted this, and we have elaborated on this point in previous chapters. Although the theoretical foundations and analytical instruments of the 'neo-Cambridge' school differed, they also concluded that the labor theory of value was redundant in connection with the transformation problem.

Meek's 'second solution'

Meek vigorously championed the Sraffa system. After it was published in 1960, he tried to relate it to Marx's theories and synthesize the thoughts of the two scholars. In the introduction to the second edition of *Studies in the Labor Theory of Value* in 1975, Meek elaborated on this, arguing that the basic elements of the Sraffa system could be amended and employed by modern Marxists. He further believed that the basic points of the Sraffa system were what Marx had tried to express in his labor theory. For example, the latter argued that price and income were ultimately determined by the relationships of production, but the Sraffa system was more explicit and effective in this respect. Later, in his 1975 article *From Value to Price: Is It Necessary to Take Marx's Road?* (See Meek 1982) he completely sided with the Sraffa system and argued that to deal with the transformation problem, it was necessary to abandon the labor theory of value.

The Sraffa procedure which Meek referred to deduced production price from physical quantities, that is to say use-values, rather than values. Meek assumed a capitalist economy with two industries (wheat and cloth) and that 100 workers were employed by the capitalist economy. The input-output

182

diagram was as follows:

10 units of wheat + 20 units of cloth + 50 units of labor power → 100 units of wheat

20 units of wheat + 30 units of cloth + 50 units of labor power → 100 units of cloth

Here, all inputs and outputs are calculated in terms of physical goods. Meek assumed the unit wage was 2/5 units of wheat and 2/5 units of cloth, and that the total wage was 40 units of wheat and 40 units of cloth. Since total inputs to production were 30 units of wheat and 50 units of cloth, from the total output of 100 units of wheat and 100 units of cloth, the capitalists would take 30 units of wheat and 10 units of cloth as surplus goods.

Meek assumed that p_w and p_c were the prices of wheat and cloth respectively and r was the general rate of profit, so the unit wage was $(p_w+p_c) \times 2/5$. Then the model could be expressed in the following equation system:

$$\begin{cases} [10\,p_w + 20\,p_c + 50\,(p_w+p_c)2/5]\,(1+r) = 100\,p_w \\ [20\,p_w + 30\,p_c + 50\,(p_w+p_c)2/5]\,(1+r) = 100\,p_c \end{cases} \tag{14}$$

To obtain absolute prices, he assumed that $=1$, giving
$$p_w = 0.781; \ =0.231$$

Meek (1979, 34) argued that in deducing price from quantities, his method bore strong similarities to Marx's model. This had two implications: first, both models deduced production price from production conditions rather than demand conditions; Second, both could be used to explain the income levels of different social classes.

Meek argued that within the framework of the Sraffa model, he could determine both profit and price using the data on the production of physical goods and the wage. The value of labor played little role in determining either the general rate of profit or production price. Value thus became redundant in the exchange relationship. But what factors determined the structure of physical production? Marx had provided an explicit answer which was the labor process. It was human labor that determined input and output of various sorts. The labor process also materializes value in use values. Therefore, it is value that determines the proportions and output of physical goods in production. Meek instead saw production as a technical process rather than a labor process, emphasizing the social process of distribution over that of production.

Value was absent from Meek's solution. He tried to relate the Sraffa system to Marx's theories and synthesize elements of the two systems, arguing that it could solve the transformation problem more effectively. We maintain to the contrary that Meek's solution did not actually solve the transformation problem but avoided it. Although like Sraffa, he argued that a commodity price could be expressed in terms of labor, he wrote (Meek 1979, 131-132):

> But certain grim realities have to be faced. First, if the technical dif-
> ficulties standing in the way of the reduction of inputs to quantities
> of (dated) labor are really as serious as what Sraffa had argued, then
> we would have no choice but to replace the materialized labor with
> the commodity production models; Second, the notion that profit is
> produced exclusively by living labor, or that it is a deduction from the
> produce of labor, does not possess a great deal of scientific substance. If
> you define input and output as products of labor (or, to put it another
> way, if you decide to measure input and output in terms of labor),
> then obviously whenever there is a surplus of output over input its
> exclusive source will appear to be labor.

Meek thus clearly maintained that the labor theory of value could be dispensed with when approaching the transformation problem. He adopted Sraffa's physical production model and replaced value analysis with price analysis, in so doing avoiding the transformation problem. To show that Sraffa's model could prove Marx's theories of income and production price, Meek proposed a five-model sequence similar to Marx's 'logical and histori-cal analysis'. But in this Marx's labor theory was reduced to a negligible posi-tion. Its quantitative results were just a by-product of the analysis.

Of the five production models proposed by Meek, three were those de-veloped by Sraffa and introduced in Chapter Two of this book. Meek added two similar models between Sraffa's second and the third model and related them to each other via Marx's 'historical-logical analysis'.

The first model was very similar to Sraffa's first model, but Meek desig-nated it 'pre-capitalist commodity economic life.' He argued that it could represent the initial form of Marx's simple commodity production in which commodity prices were positively related to the direct and indirect input of

184

labor-power. Their cost was the wage, and profit did not exist. Meek also raised doubts about the Sraffa's assumptions which assumed that the scale of production would remain constant. Meek pointed out that in vigorous economies whose scale changed constantly, the change in scale would be influenced by the proportions of their various inputs, so demand could not be excluded. He thus suggested that supply analysis applied only to a limited extent.

In Meek's second model, surplus goods begin to emerge but there is no capitalist at this point, so all surplus goods belong to laborers. Meek believed that this represent the more advanced form of simple commodity production championed by Marx. Under this model, the wage was more than was needed for subsistence, and the rate of profit could differ between departments. All surplus goods still belonged to laborers. The rate of profit would not equalize across different departments.

In the third model capitalists have emerged and the surplus belongs to them. However, the rate of profit has not been equalized. in this model, the wage is negatively related to profit and the rates of profit differ across departments . Meek argued that this is like the second stage of Marx's analysis, in which commodities sell at their value. The rate of exploitation is the same in every department but rates of profit will only equalize if organic compositions are identical.

The fourth model is also Sraffa's second. Competition between capitalists leads to capital flows and the formation of a general rate of profit. The transition to this model was similar to that from the law of value to the law of production price in Marx's treatment.

The fifth model is just Sraffa's third. In it, workers unite and force the capitalists to give them some surplus. They can not only buy necessities with the wage, but command some of the surplus.

Meek intended to incorporate Marx's historical analysis into his logical analysis based on the Sraffa system. However, his historical analysis differed from Marx's, in that he began with the use-value quantities rather than values.

Meek maintained that the Sraffa model boasted commendable strengths compared with Marx's. Sraffa's 'standard commodities' and 'standard departments' replaced the departments with average social organic composition of capital in Marx's model. Sraffa could therefore better elaborate on the issue Marx had attempted to resolve. When the wage was determined, the relation of the profit rate and prices to labor inputs would change and the deviation would be affected by the relation between direct and indirect labor inputs in the 'general' departments. However, Marx's conclusion was only approximately correct, because he excluded the effect of changes in the wage on the prices of the elements of production in these departments. in contrast, Sraffa's method could deal with this issue without recourse to Marx's abstraction.

In his discussion of departments with intermediate capital composition, Marx, Meek asserted, excluded the impact of wage changes on the production price of the means of production used in that department. His conclusion that production price was ultimately determined by commodity value was therefore only roughly correct.

However, this did not affect the problem because value is content and production price is form, and the two are not consistent with each other. Furthermore, the extent of competition between capital and labor and the nature of the two also varied from time to time. The actual rate of profit was not always consistent with the ideal general rate of profit (the ratio of total surplus value to total social capital). The importance of Marx's departments of average composition is subordinate to the equality between total profit and total surplus value, and that between total production price and total value. The idea of an average organic composition of capital is only an atypical abstraction.

If these are replaced by 'standard departments', values and production prices would need a very high level of homogeneity, in which case conflicts within capitalist society will be obscured. As Shaikh (cited by Hu Daiguang 1990, 205) pointed out: "Once you replace the concept of tendential regulation with that of equilibrium, you have switched from abstraction as typification economy."

Outwardly, within departments producing 'standard commodities', the distribution of wage and profit will not affect the relation between net output and the elements of production and ultimately value. However, when the wage is determined, the general rate of profit is determined by the ratio of direct to indirect labor within the department producing 'standard commodities'. This makes it seem that the production price of commodities is based, within such a concept, on the labor theory of value. But this argument distorts the relationship between value and production price and is more consistent with Ricardo's method, which focuses primarily on directly proving the relationship between different economic categories whilst skipping necessary intermediate stages (Marx and Engels 1972, 181). The essence of Meek's argument was an attempt to generalize from departments with average organic composition.

Meek next argued that though Marx made every effort to examine the determination of the wage, profit and prices and their variations by starting from his labor theory of value, he relied on input-output relationships to prove that the former were actually transformed forms of the latter. If Marx had approached the problems of price and income by examining the quantity of physical goods, he would not have run into difficulties. Obviously, Meek was focused on the outcome rather than the process.

In 1972, Alfredo Medio (Hunt 1972, 325-26) published *Profit and Surplus-Value: Appearance and Reality in Capitalist Production*. Here he refuted Meek's argument, pointing out that:

> *The derivation of prices from values, the solution of the transformation problem is only subsidiary and a formal proof of consistency of Marx's theory of value. Even when this is worked out it remains to be explained how it is that profit exists at all. In a sense, the neo-Ricardian theory has pushed economic analysis back to a pre-Marxian stage. In this respect, Marx's theory of surplus value is significant and still constitutes the only valid alternative to the neoclassical explanation of the origin and nature of capitalists' gains. But Sraffa's approach was to define as surplus all output in excess of the physical means of production used up in the production process and then to show how, given the technical conditions of production, changes in the rates of wages and profits affected prices. Therefore, Sraffa had no need for labor values in his analysis, and hence he had no transformation problem. If one accepts the view that the object of a proper theory of value is to study the quantitative relations between wages, rate of profit and*

relative prices, value analysis and the related concepts or value and surplus value become an unnecessary detour and all the discussion about the transformation problem is much ado about nothing.

However, there is a big difference between Marx's theory and Sraffa's analysis. Marx's focus on the transformation of value into production price is more general and deals with many more issues. Medio (Hunt and Schwartz 1972, 325-26) therefore concluded: "Sraffa's theory, while providing the analytical tools for a correct solution to the transformation problem, at the same time denies its relevance."

Finally, we should note that Sraffa assumed the wage may include some of the surplus and in so doing, he wanted to prove that the income of each social class was indeterminate. From Meek's perspective, this was one of the strong points of the Sraffa model as it was more consistent with reality. Sraffa's assumption may have positive implications in the new stage of capitalist development, since the degree of relative rarity of capital and labor had changed. However, it can only affect the determination of the magnitude of variable capital and the magnitude of surplus value and has no effect on their wider implications. Sraffa's assumption thus has no substantive consequences.

To summarize, given a set of input-output relationships, Meek adopted Sraffa's method to deduce production price from physical quantities. Meek sought to establish the historical and logical relationships of transformation by constructing five 'stages' being simple reproduction, the presence of surplus, a non-uniform rate of profit, a uniform rate of profit and the appropriation of a portion of the surplus in the wage. This method completely departed from the core of the transformation problem. It suggested that Meek's method had actually avoided the transformation problem. Meek's was actually a simplified study, which also misunderstood Marx's method and theory, and could not solve the transformation problem. The claim that the labour was redundant arose because the value created by labor and price of use-values do not consists of the same substance.

Steedman's *Marx after Sraffa*

If it could be argued that in Meek's second solution, he still cleaved to Sraffa's analytical model and that the influence of Marx's labor theory was still vaguely present, then Steedman went further. He explicitly pointed out that the Sraffa system was a replacement for the Marxist system. Only through Sraffa's treatment of the quantitative conditions of physical production could the rate of profit and production price be determined. Sraffa's system would help scholars develop a better understanding of the conflictual relationship between wage and profit along with that between surplus value and profit. Steedman argued these goals could not be achieved by Marx's value analysis, which moreover created the meaningless transformation problem. The Sraffa system would liberate scholars from the shackles of transformation. At the same time, they could still conclude that there was exploitation in capitalist system.

These views were enunciated in his 1977 book *Marx after Sraffa*. In it, he not only criticized Marx's transformation theory, but argued that his labor theory of value was uncalled-for. Its validity was also hamstrung by its inherent logical flaws.

Steedman's understanding of the transformation problem

The steps in Steedman's elaboration (Zhang 1988, 69) were as follows:
1. A physical goods production system is created;
2. The value system can be deduced from the quantitative structure of this production system and from the quantitative relations of distribution;
3. The value system cannot determine price and profit and demonstrates Marx's mistakes;
4. The Sraffa method can calculate price and profit from the physical system and distribution relationships alone.

We explain these points one by one.

Table 2

Department	Inputs		Outputs	
	Iron	Living labor	Iron	Gold
Iron	28	56	56	0
Gold	16	16	0	48
Grain	12	8	0	0

Steedman assumed a society with only three departments, producing iron (means of production), gold and grain. He also assumed that the inputs of each department include only iron and living labor. This is consumed completely in one year, that is, there is no fixed capital. This gives us table 2, in which each unit of physical goods and each unit of living labor are fixed arbitrarily. Since the input of iron equals the output, this is a simple reproduction system and net output includes 48 units of gold and 8 units of grain.

Steedman also assumed that 5 units of grain are paid for 80 units of labor. And like Marx, he assumed that the wage (in the form of grain) is paid at the beginning of a year. At the end of a year, the capitalists receive 48 units of gold and 3 units of grain. As a result, of the 8 units of grain produced in one year, 3 go to the capitalists as part of their profit and the remaining 5 go to the workers as the wages of next year.

The output of iron is controlled by the capitalists. It is first appropriated by the capitalists who produce it, then through market exchange, is distributed to the capitalists of all three departments.

The value system based on the physical goods production and distribution systems

Steedman assumed that the living labor of table 2 is converted to homogeneous, socially necessary labor. He denoted the magnitude of value of each unit of iron, gold and grain by l_i, l_g and l_c respectively. Based on table 2 he produced the equations:

$$\begin{cases} 28l_i + 56 = 56l_i \\ 16l_i + 16 = 48l_g \\ 12l_i + 8 = 8l_c \end{cases} \tag{15}$$

The values of l_i, l_g and l_c were then

$$\begin{cases} l_i = 2 \\ l_g = 1 \\ l_c = 4 \end{cases} \tag{16}$$

These were thus determined by the quantities of physical goods in table 2 and were completely independent of the wage, profit and price. In other words, as long as the quantities of the means of workers' subsistence were known (which meant that the relations of distribution were known), the whole value system could be deduced from the materials goods production system.

Since as noted he assumed that the wage was 5 units of grain, the value of labor power v was

$$v = 5\,l_c = 5 \times 4 = 20$$

And since living labor was $v + m = 80$, total surplus value should be

$$s = 80 - v = 80 - 20 = 60$$

It was therefore clear that the ratio of necessary to surplus labor was $20v:60s=1:3$. Steedman thus pointed out that if the physical goods production conditions and the actual wage were known, they determined value, the value of labor power and surplus value. Then, he revised table 2 to give table 3, the value system

Table 3

Department	c	v	s	w
Iron	56	14	42	112
Gold	32	4	12	48
Grain	24	2	6	32
Total	112	20	60	192

According to this table , total value was 192 and total surplus value was 60.

The inability of the value system to determine price and profit and Marx's mistakes

Steedman asserted that, based on the value system in table 3, Marx argued that the ratio of the sum of surplus values to the sum of constant and variable capital determined the rate of profit r. He therefore calculated $(c+v)(1+r)$ to determine output prices. He held that in accordance with Marx's method:

$$r = 60 / (112+20) = (45+5/11)\%$$
$$\text{Production price of iron} = (56+14)(1+r) = 101+9/11$$
$$\text{Production price of gold} = (32+4)(1+r) = 52+4/11$$
$$\text{Production price of grain} = (24+2)(1+r) = 37+9/11$$

Total price of production was 192 and total profits were 60. The two invariant equations were both satisfied. But Steedman then alleged that, though Marx transformed the value of outputs into prices of production, he failed to transform the value of iron as an input into its price of production (c was unchanged). Nor did he transform the value of grain, which made up the wage that the capitalists needed to advance, into prices of production (v was unchanged). Therefore when iron and grain were sold as products or purchased as inputs, their exchange values were different although sale and purchase were two aspects of a single exchange process. This, he argued, was not rational. The values of inputs, like outputs, should be transformed.

Steedman argued that if $s/(c + v)$ was treated as the rate of profit, as Marx did, then any effort to solve the transformation problem would end in failure. Writing k_i for the Price of iron/Value of iron and for the Price of grain/Value of grain, the rate of profit was $(45+5/11)\%$. From the first and third row of Table 3

$$(56k_i + 14k_c)(1+5/11) = 112k_i \tag{17}$$

$$(24k_i + 2k_c)(1+5/11) = 32k_c \tag{18}$$

From (14) and (15) he obtained

$$k_c = 3/2k_i \tag{19}$$

$$k_c = 6/5\ k_i \tag{20}$$

192

Equation (19) obviously contradicted Equation (20). Steedman argued that the root cause of the conflict was the claim that the rate of profit was equal to where the magnitudes concerned were measured in value terms. But it should be calculated as the difference between the total price of outputs and the total price of inputs, divided by the price of inputs. Therefore, when price diverged from value, the rate of profit could not be $s/(c + v)$.

Steedman further maintained that it was impossible to deduce the price system from the value system. Transformation scholars should turn to the quantity system.

Finding value, price and profit from the physical system and relations of distribution

Let r stand for the rate of profit, w for the money wage per unit of labor time, and p_i and p_c for the money price per unit of iron and grain respectively. Suppose the unit price of gold to be 1. Total wages in units of grain would then be 5. Steedman then deduced an equation group from table 2, with the aim of using the physical goods production system and relations of distribution to solve for price and profit.

$$\begin{cases} (28p_i + 56w)\,(1+r) = 56p_c \\ (16p_i + 16w)\,(1+r) = 48p_c \\ (12p_i + 8w)\,(1+r) = 8p_c \\ 80w = 56p_c \end{cases} \qquad (21)$$

The approximate solution of (21) is

$$\begin{cases} r = 52.08\% \\ w = 0.2685 \\ p_i = 1.7052 \\ p_c = 4.2960 \end{cases} \qquad (22)$$

From (22) we have

$$\begin{cases} Sum\ of\ prices = 178 \\ Sum\ of\ profits = 61 \end{cases} \qquad (23)$$

These diverge from the previous results which were 192 and 60. Steedman maintained that there were general implications. But under special circumstances, say if the workers obtained the whole net product (8 units of grain and 48 units of gold), so $80w = 5p_c$ in (21) was replaced by $80w = 8p_c + 48$, then:

$$\begin{cases} r = 0 \\ w = 1 \\ p_i = 2 = l_i \\ p_c = 4 = l_c \end{cases} \qquad (24)$$

Steedman argued that the conformity between value and price suggested by (24) was just a special case. He concluded that Marx's solution to the transformation problem was incorrect, and that transformation scholars should deduce price and profit directly from Sraffa's system. From the conditions of physical production and the wage, he could deduce values profit, and prices. This could not be done from within the value system.

Comment on Steedman's solution

Steedman in fact approached the transformation problem along the lines of the Bortkiewicz solution within Sraffa's system. Elaborating on the inner logic of the transformation problem by means of mathematical calculations derived from static input-output models, he concluded that Marx's transformation procedure was logically untenable and that his theories of value and surplus value contributed little to the study of price and rate of profit.

Let us consider the implications for Marx's theory.

First, Steedman (1981, 28) argued that if the magnitudes of physical production and the wage were known, producers could determine value, surplus value and the value of labor-power. In this regard, the value of the means of production was given in advance while the values of inputs were calculated after value had been determined, hence table 3. This gives little cause for criticism. However, the concepts of value and surplus value, and their implications, were different from Marx's.

Steedman had concluded that the creation of value and surplus value depended on the conditions of production including those of wage products. Therefore, any change in production conditions would immediately affect the value of labor-power and surplus value. This was mistaken. By clearly distinguishing concrete from abstract labor, and use value from value, Marx abstracts from technological relationships, replacing them with human social relationships. The magnitude of value thus embodied is labor time.

194

Thus, Marx determines the rate of surplus value by means of socially necessary labor time and surplus labor time. The value of constant capital is predetermined, because it is known at the start of production whilst variable capital and surplus value are determined by socially necessary labor time, and the technological level or production conditions of constant capital exert little influence on them. Therefore, Steedman's claim that value was determined by production conditions does not hold water. Next, Steedman held that equations based on physical goods can help calculate the money rate of profit and the money production price, eliminating the need to deduce profit and production price from value. Here, he made the same mistake as Morishima and Samuelson. He did not establish the nature of price: he failed to establish which factors determine commodity price and what is the common unit of measurement. In contrast, the labor theory of value theorizes that the thing which makes commodity prices homogeneous, with the same unit of measurement, is precisely the human abstract labor consumed in producing them - their value. although the price of production of an individual commodity may deviate quantitatively from its value, it remains the bearer of abstract labor time.

It was precisely production price, with value at its core, that determines the exchange ratio between one commodity and another as well as their monetary price. Steedman, in arguing that price was no more than the exchange ratio between one commodity and another, failed to clarify its nature.

The theory equally failed to establish the nature of profit and capitalist exploitation. According to Steedman, profit was no more than difference between the money magnitude of output and input. But this does not establish the origins of profit. As Bob Rowthorn (Bai 2002, 154) noted in his criticism of the Ricardian School, by locating profit and exploitation in the spheres of circulation and distribution, this school obscured the process of surplus value production and capital accumulation. They could not therefore explain the capitalist mode of production itself, within which exploitation existed. Steedman defended his position, arguing that since profit was the difference between the net output produced by laborers and the wage they received from capitalists, profit was legally owned by the capitalists due to their ownership of the means of production. But in saying this, he unwittingly used the labor theory of value and surplus value.

Thirdly, Steedman believed that when Marx approached the transformation of value into production price, it was wrong to calculate the rate of profit as $s/(c + v)$. Now, Marx emphasized that the rate of profit was a concept at the "level of price" rather than the "level of value", which was correct. However, he gave some prerequisites for calculating the rate of profit as $s/(c + v)$. Inputs were to be calculated in terms of value and outputs were to be transformed into production price. This was a fair description of transformation characteristics during a particular period of economic development. We clarified this point in our discussion of the static transformation model. In *laissez-faire* capitalism, where both inputs and outputs have been transformed into production price, both constant and variable capital should be calculated in terms of production price when calculating the rate of profit.

In the stage when commodities were traded in terms of value, price was equal to value; when commodities are traded in their prices of production, price is equal to the production price. Accordingly, the formulae of calculation are different. Thus, no special conflict arises. However, Steedman maintained that not only should the calculation based on value be abandoned but that the transformation problem should be approached purely in terms of the quantity of physical goods. He thus failed to develop any understanding of Marx's integration of logical with historical analysis.

As a result, he saw (19) and (20) as in conflict with each other, based on (17) and (18). But the conflict arose because he mechanically reproduced the formula for the rate of profit in terms of value, after inputs had been transformed into production price.

Finally, Steedman artificially pegged the price of gold at 1, making this the unit of measurement when determining price and profit from the conditions of material production and distribution. He clearly viewed price as the exchange ratio between one commodity and another; it was just a relative concept with no real implications. This is little cause for criticism if price is understood from the perspective of exchange ratio, but he then deduced total prices and profits from (18) and (19) and compared them with total values surplus values from table 3. He thus identified the results of (18) with Marx's production price. This makes the previous assumption quite absurd.

196

Production price is a definite amount of labor time. It cannot simply be viewed as the basis for exchange nor as a mere exchange ratio. If the price of gold is pegged at 1 and made the unit of measurement, then the production price bears little relationship to value and labor. The comparison between production price and value, and between profit and surplus value, then becomes meaningless. But Steedman insisted on this comparison and used it to claim Marx's methodology was flawed.

When Steedman conducted his logical analysis of the transformation problem, he believed that Marx's labor theory of value could be dispensed with in calculating the rate of profit and production price. He further argued that under 'joint production' and 'fixed capital', the labor theory of value became fraught with conflicts and should be abandoned. Not surprisingly, he saw eye to eye with Morishima in this respect.

Redundancy and the labor theory of value

Steedman argued that under 'joint production' labor values cease to be a determining factor, because in these circumstances, negative surplus value can arise.

To illustrate this he supposed two methods of production each creating two commodities. Physical input-output relationships are given in Table 4. L_1 and L_2 stand for the values of commodity 1 and commodity 2 respectively and the unit of value is the same as the unit of labor. Table 4 gives

$$25 L_1 + 5 = 30 L_1 + 5 L_2 \qquad (25)$$

$$10 L_2 + 5 = 3 L_1 + 12 L_2 \qquad (26)$$

Table 4

Method of production	Input			Output	
	Commodity 1	Commodity 2	Unit of Labor	Commodity 1	Commodity 2
I	25	0	5	30	5
II	0	10	1	3	12

Solving this gives $L_1 = -1$ and $L_2 = 2$.

Steedman believed that these results showed the labor theory of value not only contributed little to the analysis of price determination and exploitation but, under joint production, caused more trouble and should be dispensed with.

We believe Steedman's reasoning was flawed. The negative value arises from a particular condition. Suppose in table 4 that the second method of production is used more frequently so, for example, the 6 units of labor are redistributed and 1 unit of labor used by the first method of production is transferred to the second method. Table then becomes table 5

Table 5

Method of production	Input			Output	
	Commodity 1	Commodity 2	Unit of Labor	Commodity 1	Commodity 2
I	20	0	4	24	4
II	0	20	2	6	24

Compared with table 4, for the same labour input, net output has increased by 2 units of commodity 1 and 1 unit of commodity 2. The second method of production is more efficient; Steedman's result is not the effect of joint production but a particular choice of technique.

Consequently, the value of one of the two commodities must be different under the first method in comparison with the second method. Table 4 can be transformed into table 6

Table 6

Method of production	Input			Output		Net output	
	Commodity1	Commodity2	Unit of Labor	Commodity1	Commodity2	Commodity1	Commodity2
I	5	0	1	6	1	1	1
II	0	10	1	3	12	3	2

We assume that the labor power consumed by each type of method of production is 1 unit respectively. Let us assume that the individual value of commodity 1 (or commodity 2) is the same under the first and the second method of production. As Table 6 shows, the net output of commodity 1 under the second method of production outweighs that under the first method. Since we assumed that the individual value of commodity 1 and the labor power consumed were the same under the two methods of production, the labor power consumed in producing commodity 1 under the first method of production will be smaller than under the second, whilst the labor power consumed in producing commodity 2 under the first method of production will be greater than under the second method of production. Thus, the individual value of commodity 2 with the second method of production will be smaller than that produced by the first. In consequence (25) and (26) concerning individual value cannot both be true.

Hence, there must be at least one commodity whose individual value is not equal to that should the same commodity be produced by another method of production. Steedman's statement on negative values is logically flawed.

In *laissez-faire* capitalist societies, the production condition of each producer is different; this is a ubiquitous phenomenon. Competition between capitalists in the same line of trade imposes the exchange of commodities on the basis of social or market value. Therefore, the value of a given type of commodity is not simply determined by the labor power consumed by one producer. It is affected by the labor power consumed by other producers under different conditions. once we understand value determination from this perspective, negative values do not arise.

Steedman obtained negative values because of two mistakes. The first was his failure to distinguish individual from social or market value, which arose from his failure to elaborate on the social process of formation of market values through the equalization of individual value. The second was the absence, from his logic-mathematical method, of a fair description of real-life economic relationships. Having assumed that two commodities are produced using different methods, he should have recognized that they contain different individual values which are equalized. Steedman's method determines neither individual nor market value.

Steedman however went on to argue that not only was the labor theory of value incorrect under joint production, but that it was riddled with contradictions: in particular, negative value was possible under what he termed fixed capital.

Table 7

Year	Input				Output		
	Corn	New machinery	Old machinery	Labor	Corn	New machinery	Old machinery
First Year	1	0	0	5	0	5	0
Second Year	9	5	0	10	10	0	5
Third Year	15	0	5	25	25	0	0
Total	25	5	5	40	35	5	5

To show this, he assumed a simple social reproduction cycle of three years producing corn and machines. In the first year, this society produces new machines with corn and labor. In the second year, it produces the old machines and corn with new machines, corn and labor (in the first year, joint production takes place since the new machines produced both corn and 'old machines). In the third year corn, labor and old machines are used to produce corn. After having been used for three years, the machines are junked. However, in the second and the third year, the efficiency of the machines varies. Table 7 shows the input-output relationship between corn, new and old machines and labor during the each of the three years.

Steedman thus adopted the depreciation method for fixed capital proposed by von Neumann. From the data for the second and third year, corn output derived from each unit of labor input is the same ($10/10=25/25$). But during the second year, the corn and machines input employed to make one unit of corn will be smaller than in the first year ($15/25<9/10$, $5/25<5/10$), because the older machines are more efficient than the new ones. Steedman uses l_c, l_n and l_o to stand for the value of corn, new machines and old machines respectively. As the Total column shows, if the input labor is 40 and net output is 10 units of corn, then:

$$10\, l_c = 40$$

So, incorporating these values into the input-output equation of the first year

$$l_c = 4 \tag{27}$$

and

$$l_c + 5 = 5\, l_n \tag{28}$$

and

$$l_n = 1{,}8 \tag{29}$$

According to Marx's straight-line depreciation method, $l_0 = l_n/2 = 0,9$. By incorporating the values of , and into the second and the third line, he got:

$$l_c = 14.5 \tag{30}$$

$$l_c = 2.95 \tag{31}$$

Based on (27), (30) and (31), we find three values of corn which are all different. Steedman concluded that under 'fixed capital', Marx's method for calculating the magnitude of value was incorrect. He argued that if Marx's aggregate method was used to seek the values, and at the same time Marx's straight line depreciation method was abandoned, he would get:

$$\left\{ \begin{array}{l} l_c + 5 = 5\,l_n \\ 9l_c + 5\,l_n + 10 = 10\,l_c + 5\,l_0 \\ 15\,l_c + 5\,l_0 + 25 = 25\,l_c \end{array} \right. \tag{32}$$

Solving (32), Steedman obtained

$$\left\{ \begin{array}{l} l_c = 4 \\ l_n = 1,8 \\ l_0 = 3 \end{array} \right. \tag{33}$$

Thus l_c and l_n are the same as before, but $l_0 > l_n$. If the aggregate method is adopted, the results conflict with Marx's value theory, and make value indeterminate or negative whether or not the straight-line depreciation method is used.

Steedman drew the same conclusion when he assumed that the efficiency of machines decreased, and finally asserted that Marx's aggregate method of calculating value would necessarily run into trouble with fixed capital, a form of joint production. Therefore, Marx's aggregate method should be abandoned.

However, we believe Steedman's assumptions were incorrect. First of all, he argued that Marx's straight-line depreciation method failed to guarantee that in social reproduction, the money value accumulated for the purpose of updating machinery would be consistent with the value of the updated fixed capital. To overcome this 'particular difficulty', von Neumann's fixed capital depreciation method should be adopted. But the difference between fixed and working capital was not an assumption introduced by Marx. Rather, it was a solid reality. Inconsistencies naturally exist between the value of updated fixed capital and the sinking fund accumulated in money form. No matter what depreciation method is adopted, this 'particular difficulty' will exist.

According to von Neumann's method, fixed capital that remains at the end of a period should be treated as a 'by-product'. All inputs can then be treated as the same regardless of whether they are fixed or working capital. However, the remaining fixed capital, as a 'by-product' does not enter the market in circulation, while working capital is generally directly replaced from the market. The remaining 'by-product' could not make an impact, because when its value is transferred to new commodities, the capitalists must accumulate a certain amount of money and use the money to buy back in advance the physical goods corresponding to this 'by-product'. However, there may be inconsistencies between the physical goods purchased in advance and the 'by-product'. This depreciation method was not substantially different from Marx's and did not overcome Steedman's 'particular difficulty'.

Notwithstanding, based on table 7, Steedman concluded that there were three values for corn. This was a natural conclusion and arose because these values were created by different machines with different efficiencies. But Marx never denied that the efficiency of machines could impact the individual value of commodities, nor that changes in social productivity in different periods of history would cause fluctuations in commodity values. What he emphasized was that the social value of a particular period could be different from individual value, and that the social value *per se* could and did vary from time to time and from productivity to productivity. The fact that the corn can have three values is no basis for Steedman's criticism of Marx's value theory.

After Steedman dropped Marx's straight-line depreciation method, he adopted von Neumann's fixed capital depreciation method and obtained a negative value for depreciation. Obviously, in the production of corn in different years, the values of corn were different. In this sense, the three equations in Equation group (29) could not be verified simultaneously. The basic points criticizing Steedman's 'joint production' previously apply here also.

In summary Steedman's attempt to refute and drop the labor theory of value based on what he termed 'joint production' and 'fixed capital' was not well-grounded. He turned to the quantitative analysis of physical goods, which ultimately proved fruitless.

202

Nobuo Okishio's dynamic transformation analysis

Steedman and Meek sought, with the use of Sraffa's system, to obtain values and the rate of profit using simultaneous equations. This method did obtain the values of the variables concerned but failed to relate the different steps in transformation This was unscientific from a historical and logical perspective.

Nobuo Okishio (1974) argued that the best method was to revise the values of prices of production and the rate of average profit on a progressive basis in order of time. The transformation of value to production price was a dynamic process. His method made a profound impact on the solution to the transformation problem. We believe his solution bears strong similarities to the reverse process of the static and dynamic transformation that we propose. In this sense, it is be best understood as a strong criticism of Steedman and Meek's solution.

Okishio assumed three departments (means of production, means of consumption and luxuries). None of them used fixed capital. Capital, surplus value, commodity value and the rate of profit based on value in these departments are presented in table 8.

Table 8

Department	Capital	Surplus value	Commodity value	Rate of profit (%)
I	60c+40v	40	140	40
II	50c+50v	50	150	50
III	20c+30v	30	80	60

According to Marx's solution, Okishio had:

General rate of profit: 120/250=48%

Production price:

  I. $(60+40)(1+48\%) = 148$

  II. $(50+50)(1+48\%) = 148$

  III. $(20+30)(1+48\%) = 74$

After inputs are transformed to production price, cost-prices in the three departments should be revised as follows:

  I. $60\times148/140+40\times148/150=102.86$

  II. $50\times148/140+50\times148/150=102.15$

  III. $20\times148/140+30\times148/150=50.72$

203

These revised cost-prices makes the rate of profit of each department un-equal across each department:

I. (148−102.86)/102.86=43.8%

II.(148−102.15)/102.15=44.8%

III. (74-50.72)/50.72=45.8%

It is then necessary to make a second revision to the general rate of profit and accordingly production prices. From the above, total profit is 114.27 and total capital is 255.73. The revised rate of profit is:

114.27/255.73=44.5%

Revised production prices in the second step are:

I. 102.86×(1＋44.5%)=148.63

II. 102.15×(1＋44.5%)=147.61

III. 50.72×(1＋44.5%)=73.29

Revised production prices in the next step are:

I. 60×148.63/140+40×147.61/150=103.056

II. 50×148.63/140+50×147.61/150=102.430

III. 20×148.63/140+30×147.61/150=50.752

However, the rate of profit of each department is still not equal:

I. (148.63−103.056）/103.056=44.22%

II. (147.61−102.430)/102.430=44.11%

III. (73.29−50.752)/50.752=44.4%

Therefore, successive revisions continue. Okishio showed that by using the mathematical method and progressive revisions, he could determine the value, price of production, and rate of profit on which the series converged, at which point the rates of profit were equal (Zhu 1991, 154-56).

Although Okishio did not approach the transformation problem by di-viding it into two phases of static and dynamic transformation, he treated it as a dynamic process. This was correct logically and historically. Okishio (1974) elaborated on value and price and drawing a distinction between them, which parted company with Sraffa's followers. In a sense, Okishio's solution should be treated in retrospect as a criticism of Sraffa's followers.

However, there were problems in Okishio's solution. While he made pro-gressive revisions to the production price and rate of profit, he used a wrong formula to calculate the rate of profit. In his second revision to profit, he rightly calculates the aggregate social capital using production price:

$$102.86+102.15+50.72=255.73$$
At this time, total profit should equal total surplus value, which is:
$$40+50+30=120$$
But Okishio believed that total profit was:
$$255.73×44.8\%=114.27$$
This method calculated total profit as that received if commodities are sold with at their original production price. But if the capital advanced by the three departments is taken into consideration, and the newly added value is 40, 50 and 30, then profit should be the result of the distribution of total surplus value divided in proportion to the percentage of capital advanced. The reason for this mistake was that Okishio failed to develop a better understanding of the relationship between surplus value and average profit. If Okishio's solution were adopted to solve the transformation problem, we would find that the two invariant equations could not both be valid.

Conclusion

The transformation problem in a broad sense outlined in this chapter essentially concerned the relationship between Volume I and Volume III of Capital. Samuelson regarded the ratio of value to price as the problem the transformation problem was supposed to solve. As a result, he failed to understand the real purpose of transformation study from the outset. He believed it was better to deduce the relative price of commodities more directly, by using input-output relationships to bypass the phase of value. However, this could only prove how price was calculated, but could not establish which factors determined the magnitude of value. The exploitation concept articulated by Samuelson adds nothing to Marx's viewpoint that profit derives from surplus value and exploitation from employing labor in production.

By relying on the neo-Ricardian analytical method created by Sraffa, Meek and Steedman sought to find a solution to relative price and average profit starting from the wage level and technological conditions. They believed that the analysis of value had become redundant in the study of price determination. From their perspectives, value was actually a concept related to production cost.

The statements on transformation offered by Samuelson, Meek and Steedman essentially proposed to replace value analysis by price analysis, viewing the wage level be viewed as an exogenous variable and then determining the rate of profit and price simultaneously. In doing so, they avoided the transformation problem. But we have found that price analysis is powerless to prove how prices are determined or to establish the nature of exploitation, or to integrate historical with logical analysis. In summary, Samuelson, Meek and Steedman failed to provide a solution to the transformation problem in a scientific way.

8
New developments in the study of transformation

Prior to the 1960s, many discussions on transformation focused on the logic of the transformation from value to production price. The 'Sraffa Revolution' then directed discussion to the relevance, consistency and possible redundancy of labor values. Since the 1980s, debates on transformation subsided somewhat. However, new interpretations continued to emerge. Most sympathized with Marx's economics. Generally, they do not aim to question the validity of the equalities but to transcend previous debates and find new approaches to establishing the validity of Marxist transformation theory. Some also set out to revise the concept of value *per se*, arguing that only thus could transformation theory be rendered consistent with Marx's transformation philosophy. All of them, however, took Marx's labor theory of value as their starting point.

The Shaikh solution

Extending Marx's transformation procedure

Anwar Shaikh (1977 & 1984) believed that prices of production could be correctly computed if Marxist transformation procedures were strictly followed and appropriately extended. He argued that the relationship between value and prices of production was so obvious that it could be simply ignored. Essentially, Marx's procedure was the first step of a transformation from 'direct price' (price positively related to direct labor inputs) to 'indirect price' (production price). Shaikh argued that Böhm-Bawerk and Samuelson were wrong and that the Bortkiewicz solution and the Seton model were unsatisfactory.

Shaikh argued that the computation of prices of production should be strictly based on the theoretical foundation and essence of transformation and not from a pure methodological point of view. Though there are differences between two methods, their importance lies not in the results of the computation, but in the extent to which, by making value theory their theoretical starting point, they yield a deeper understanding of Marx's value theory. There is much truth in this, and the argument is important.

Shaikh rightly stated that the factors which make up the structure of society as a whole are invisible to the masses. In dissecting this structure, Marx's starting point is the analysis of production. The capitalist mode of production is a unity of labor process and the growth of value. It could be argued that the theory of value can be developed by studying production alone. But it must also elaborate on the relationship of exchange on which production depends, and on the relations of production themselves.

Steedman *et al.* (1990, 264) argued, Shaikh noted, that prices of production were, as Marx had outlined, the outward form of value and its reflection in circulation. Marx may have introduced new factors and sources of change, but his methodology could not alter the mechanism of transformation. Therefore, these authors concluded, transformation is just the result of the redistribution of surplus value arising from the varying organic composition of capital.

From this perspective, no variation in value magnitudes can occur and the sum of value must be the same as the sum of prices of production. Shaikh argued that Marx's procedure was basically correct, and as long as scholars stuck to the first step of it, they should find that the sum of value equaled the sum of prices of production.

Shaikh adopted Bortkiewicz' three-division model to elaborate on Marx's transformation procedures as shown by tables 1 and 2 below:

Table 1

Department	Constant capital	Variable capital	Surplus value	Rate of profit (%)
I	225	90	60	19.5
II	100	120	80	36.36
III	50	90	60	42.85

In table 1, exchange based on values generates different rates of profit which competition averages to the rate of profit across departments as shown in table 2.

Table 2

Departments	Constant capital	Variable capital	Surplus value	General rate of profit	Production price
I	225	90	60	29.63%	408.3
II	100	120	80	29.63%	285.2
III	50	90	60	29.63%	181.5

Shaikh emphasized that Marx's theory only focused on the variation of prices rather than of value. Since Bortkiewicz, many scholars believed that Marx failed to transform inputs and that a thorough transformation should include both input and output. Shaikh argued instead that Marx's method disconnected value from price.

He pointed out that Marx was clearly aware of the fact that inputs should be converted. But Marx believed that there was no need to do so for the time being. Shaikh then (1977, 131) argued, "Let us extend Marx's procedure by progressively feeding back the effects of the initial price-value dispropor-tionalities and see what happens."

To show that transformation and its extension only affect money flows and not value flows, Shaikh included both. He argued that this made it clear that value and surplus value were distinct from price and profit, a distinction which arose precisely from the difference between the spheres of production and circulation. He then (Yan 2001, 405-407) extended the procedure.

In Table 3, Step 1 represents exchange at values. Total prices are 1750 and total profits, namely the sum of surplus value, are 400. Step 1B repre-sents Marx's transformation, which reallocates surplus value. Total prices of production and profits do not change. After the transformation, com-pared with before, the price in Department I has changed by a factor of $\varphi_1=816.67/750=1.089$, in Department II by $\varphi_2=570.37/600=0.951$ and in Department III by $\varphi_3=362.96/400=0.907$.

Table 3 The transformation from direct prices to prices of production

	Dept	Constant capital	Variable capital	Surplus value (profit)	Value (Price of production)	Rate of profit (%)	Change factor φ
Step 1A	I	450.00	180.00	120.00	750.00	19.05	—
Exchange at values	II	200.00	240.00	160.00	600.00	36.36	—
	III	100.00	180.00	120.00	400.00	42.85	—
Step 1B	I	450.00	180.00	120.00	816.67	29.63	1.09
Marx's transformation	II	200.00	240.00	160.00	570.37	29.63	0.95
	III	100.00	180.00	120.00	362.96	29.63	0.91
Step 2A	I	490.00	171.18	155.49	816.67	23.52	—
Cost-prices adjusted to reflect prices of production of step 1B	II	217.80	228.24	124.33	570.37	27.87	—
	III	108.90	171.18	82.88	362.96	29.59	—
Step 2B	I	490.00	171.18	172.83	834.01	26.14	1.02
Prices of production adjusted to equalize rates of profit in step 2A	II	217.80	228.24	116.59	562.63	26.14	0.99
	III	108.90	171.18	73.21	353.36	26.14	0.97
...							
Final Step		504.00	168.00	168.00	840.00	25.00	1.00
Correct prices of production		224.00	224.00	112.00	560.00	25.00	1.00
		112.00	168.00	70.00	350.00	25.00	1.00

In Step 2A, since Department I produces the means of production for all departments, its price multiplier $\varphi_1 = 1.089$ implies higher money prices for all means of production. Similarly, since Department II produces the means of subsistence, its price multiplier $\varphi_2 = 0.951$ implies that the money costs of labor power are falling. φ_3 affects neither component of cost-prices, since it produces on for capitalist consumption. Therefore, cost-prices differ from those in Step 1B. If commodities were sold on the basis of the prices in Step 1B, the rates of profit differ between departments. However, it should be noted that in Step 2A, total profits are 362.7, slightly lower than total surplus value, which was 400.

Therefore, each department has to readjust prices to adjust the rate of profit to the average and, at the same time, general prices of production stay at 1750. This is step 2B. Compared with 2A, $\varphi_1 = 834.01/816.67 = 1.02$ and $\varphi_2 = 0.986$; $\varphi_3 = 0.974$ and total profit is 362.63.

Shaikh held that if the procedure was repeated until the changes from one step to the next were negligibly small, then the correct prices of production would be obtained as shown in table 3.

Thus Shaikh championed extending Marx's procedure by progressively feeding back the effects of the initial price-value disproportionalities. He made it clear that the intention was not to replace Marx's theory but to apply it. He arrived at four conclusions: first of all, the issue was not transforming value to price but transforming one form of value into another – in this case prices of production.

Secondly, this is a pure change of form entailing no essential change in the system as a whole. The mass of commodities and the different portions of it going to each class remain the same as before, as did total value and total surplus value. The real effect of transformation is a division of the total pool of surplus value among individual capitalists.

Thirdly, Marx's procedure reflects the inherent nature of equalization. This is a continuous process. Marx's procedure changes the prices of individual commodities whilst leaving the total price of a given mass of commodities intact. This can be extended in a simple way to derive the 'correct' prices of production.

Lastly, with the correct prices of production, the money rate of profit differs from the value rate. However, like the deviations of prices of production from values, these deviations are systematic and determinate.

This summary suggests Shaikh's understanding of transformation and its theoretical foundations of this theory was correct. However, there were errors in his understanding of transformation procedure.

In the first place, he assumes that total prices of production always equal total value. However, this should not be the premise of the procedure but a goal when testing it. Based on the dynamic transformation model, the equation is not valid. To ensure total prices of production always equal total values, Shaikh adjusted the profit rate at each step without legitimate reasons.

Next, according to Shaikh's interpretation, total profits do not equal total surplus value. The average profit results from reallocating total surplus value in accordance with previous capital inputs. Therefore, total profit should always equal total surplus value.

Lastly, the correct prices of production as Shaikh alleges do not exist. As we know, economic development is a dynamic process, and the continuous advance in Science and Technology continues to impact the wage. Should Shaikh's procedure be repeated, the resulting changes are not negligible. Continued social reproduction prevents the transition from one step to another from returning to the correct prices of production.

Balanced growth and the invariant equations

Table 3 shows that Shaikh's procedure fails to make total profit equal total prices of production. He (Shaikh 1984) pointed out that in general, total profit could not equal total surplus value. The two could only be equal under balanced growth.

Shaikh explained capitalist reproduction with diagram 1, where C' and M' denote capitalist commodities and money respectively and LP denotes labor power. M_c denotes the constant money-capital advanced for means of production (MOP), buys back a portion of the overall commodity-product C'. M_v represents the variable capital used to purchase labor power for next year's production. Workers can thus spend their money on means of subsistence (MOS), buying back a second portion of the available commodity-product

C'. Finally, capitalists buy a certain amount of goods for personal consumption. The inner area of the diagram 1 indicates the money flows between different departments.

Diagram 1

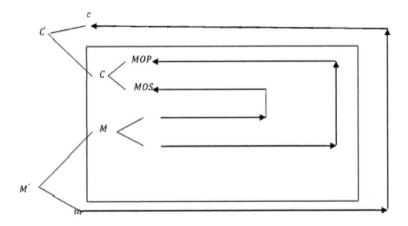

The circuit of capital M-C encompasses two processes: direct exchange M_c-MOP and indirect purchases in the circuit M_v-LP-MOS. It follows that any transfer of value arising from price-value differences remain internal to the circuit of capital: what one capitalist loses as the seller of MOP and MOS, another gains as the buyer of MOP and LP.

The remaining circulation to consider is that of the capitalists' own circuit of revenue $m - c$. Here too, what the sellers of commodity-capital lose in value through a price below the direct price is gained by the capitalists in the form of a lower price for their articles of consumption. But now a crucial difference arises (Shaikh 1984, 84). What the capitalists lose as sellers will show up in business accounts as the amount by which actual profit is below direct profit (profit proportional to surplus value). Shaikh thus ignored the possibility we considered in the dynamic transformation model, that is, the balance between surplus value and profit generated by may also be lost.

Shaikh pointed out that in most cases, the analysis of social reproduction does not deal with the circuit of capitalist revenue. It would be mysterious if the prices of a given surplus product deviated from the values in such a way

213

that a given mass of surplus value could manifest itself as a variable mass of profit. However, once social circulation as a whole was analyzed, the mystery disappeared. Shaikh further pointed out that value and surplus value were created in production, and expressed as money magnitudes in circulation. Since the latter were more concrete and more complex, they were more necessarily determined than value magnitudes. As such, the relative autonomy of the sphere of circulation expressed itself as the relative autonomy of price from value. This independence, however, was strictly limited.

Therefore, Shaikh argued, the overall deviation of actual profits from direct profits depends on two factors. First, the difference between the price and value of articles of capitalist consumption depends on how surplus value is distributed between capitalists and the pattern of individual price-value deviations. The second factor is the division of surplus value between investment and consumption . If all surplus value is consumed, then the difference between actual and direct profits would be greatest. But if all surplus value was to be re-invested, total actual profits would equal total direct profits, regardless of individual price-value deviations.

Shaikh concluded that if accumulation was maximized so the capitalists consumed nothing, under balanced growth total profits would not significantly deviate from total surplus value. He elaborated on the equations at length including a study of the impact of withdrawing articles of capitalist consumption from social reproduction. However, he made obvious mistakes.

Firstly, his understanding of the equality between total profit and total surplus value was wrong. Average profit is the result of the proportional distribution of total surplus value in accordance with the capital advanced. Regrettably, Shaikh did not make it clear that the research goal is the distribution of the whole social product. But as long as this is done, his premise will always be valid.

Next, if our research goal is the total social product, then the existence of unbalanced growth exerts little or no influence on the equality of total profit with total surplus value in any given period. However, it may impact the deviation of the price of production of the whole social product from the value of this product.

Generally speaking, Shaikh's understanding of the theoretical foundation and essence of transformation is correct. This is rare among Western scholars. However, his methodology is not without problems. To analyze the two equalities , we argue that Shaikh should adopt a combination of static and dynamic analytic methods as suggested by the dynamic model in Chapter four.

DFL Model

In 1980, Duménil (1980, 1983) produced what he termed the 'New Interpretation' of the transformation problem. He believed that the total production price of the society's gross output did not equal total values. This equality should be expressed in terms of net output. Moreover, variable capital and surplus value should not be measured in labor time, but in their money value on the market. Marx's two equalities then became a tautology.

Foley (1982, 1986) and Lipietz (1982) independently reached similar conclusions, but their method and mode of thinking differed from that of Duménil. We will refer to the model of all three thinkers generically as the DFL model, and will elaborate on Duménil's exposition.

Duménil's 'New Interpretation'

Duménil argued that a concept of value was a necessary theoretical tool for any economist, whether recognized as such or not, and there were profound reasons to consider labor the substance of this value. Value could only be obtained from production, and in the last analysis, the means of production could only be created by labor, either directly or indirectly. Neither machines nor land can create value (Duménil 1983, 434).

Duménil maintained that the concept of price of production gave the labor theory of value significant explanatory power. He noted that according to Sraffa, these could be calculated by means of mathematical instruments, dispensing with value. If the prices of necessary material inputs were added to wages and the aggregate was multiplied by the general rate of profit, this yielded total profit, whilst production price was sum of cost price and profit. However, this calculation concerned only the quantity and price of material goods, commodity values being irrelevant. In contrast, Duménil (1983, 434) asserted, the explanatory power of the law of value did not just lie in predicting the evolution of quantity even though it could so.

> *The explanatory power of the labor theory of value can be located at the same level of cognition as that of gravity. It provides an appropriate answer to the deeper question of the nature of a given reality, and never functions as a substitute for a model of the reality. Within the limits of relevance of the prices of production model, e.g., the analysis of the competitive process of capitalist society, the labor theory of value by no means appears superfluous; it allows us to interpret the price system as a reallocation of social labor according to strictly defined rules consistent with the capitalist character of society. The act of pricing does not create the social substance, but merely distributes it. The real act of production takes place when any productive process is activated. This activity results in the increase of the social substance termed value. This price system can only arrange the distribution between individuals and among class. If the price of a set of inputs is multiplied by (1 + r), nothing is augmented or created. This was the core of Marx's theory.*

He hence made Marx's theory the theoretical basis of his new interpretation. He commented on these approvingly and then pointed out that the transformation problem could be solved only by clearing away misunderstandings. His starting point was his criticism of these misunderstandings.

The first was value and price. Many Marxist economists, he argued, had confused the law of value and the law of exchange. Volume III of Capital was presented as a transformation from values to prices of production in which the basis of the exchange relationship — prices of production — ceased to be consistent with value. Economists contended there was no logical foundation for such a transformation because no relevant connection could be established between the two autonomous spheres of value and price. Duménil however argued that price fluctuations were still confined within the limits of the articulation between value and production price.

There was only one law of value, while there were two laws of exchange in Marx's Capital: exchange based on commodity value and exchange based on prices of production. Labor time was the value standard. However, there was no parallelism between the two laws of exchange and Duménil did not distinguish between them.

The second misunderstanding was net and gross product, the core of his New Interpretation, and more generally of the DFL model. Duménil pointed out that for decades, the transformation controversy had hinged on the satisfaction of the two equalities. However, Duménil claimed, this was possible only in a regime of proportional growth where all surplus value was accumulated. On this he sympathized with Shaikh. It could not be maintained, he argued, that Marx regarded this specific case as the normal path of capitalist development.

Instead, the equality between the price and value of social production must be established on the basis of the net product, not the gross product of a given period. In any given period, all national accounting and economic calculation addressed the yearly net product. The foundation of the labor theory of value was the link between total labor expended and the production associated with it — the net product. Its price equaled the total income of the period, being the sum of wages and profit. Marx, however, strongly argued that inputs inherited from a previous period did not merely transmit their values or prices of production to the object of production but that these inputs were revalued. Duménil thought the expression of values in prices expresses the re-allotment of the social labor of the period according to a unique set of prices applicable both to commodities produced during the period and to those inherited from the previous one. As a result, the equality between total income and total labor can be used to express the equality between total prices and total values.

Duménil adopted what has become known as the MELT (see the discussion of TSSI later in this chapter) to calculate constant capital and surplus value. Foley gave a conceptually clear definition of the underlying idea which was to calculate the ratio between the net product in money and the living labor consumed in production. Duménil believed that on this basis, the two equalities became tautological. Variable capital and surplus value were completely determined by the price of labor and profit, so there was no problem as regards the transformation of variable capital.

The third misunderstanding concerned exploitation and exchange, and the equality between total profit and total surplus value. Surplus value was not only the result of the production process but also the share of values on which the workers' pay was based, which was in turn related to the normal exchange. So the correct sequence of the law of value, the law of surplus value and the law of exchange was:

Law of value →
Law of exchange under capitalism →
Law of surplus value

where 'capitalism' could signify either a simple commodity economy or a capitalist economy. This contrasted with what was generally believed:

Law of value →
Law of surplus value →
Law of capitalist exchange

Or

Law of value →
Law of simple commodity economy →
Law of surplus value →
Law of capitalist exchange

Analysis of the new interpretation

During the 1970s, through the effort of Meek, Dobb, Morishima and Steedman, the Sraffa system, which was designed to solve the transformation problem, was widely accepted by transformation scholars. The DFL model was widely believed to a strong criticism of the Sraffa system. Duménil's New Interpretation successfully defended the scientific nature of the labor theory of value.

First, the DFL model maintained that Marx's labor theory of value and production price theory be made the theoretical foundation of transformation. Moreover, the DFL model employed the MELT to interpret the labor theory of value. All were significant in helping perfect the labor theory of value and solving the transformation problem scientifically.

Second (He and Liu 2002, 33-36), using the MELT to examine the consistency between value and production price was highly significant and may help study how value lies beneath the surface of market price and capital at a macro level. The MELT offered new thinking in the conflicts in Marx's dual system.

It was significant that the protagonists of the DFL model insisted that scientific theories be the basis of their study. However, their treatment of transformation theory gave rise to confusion and contained some weaknesses, incurring criticism from Shaikh (1984), Ajit Sinha (1991), E. Ahmet Tonak (1994), Fred Moseley (1999) and others.

Duménil first gave conflicting definitions to the terms of constant capital, variable capital and surplus value, a sign of a lack of understanding of the implications of value. He measured constant capital in terms of labor time and variable capital and surplus value in accordance with the MELT.

This was a return to Adam Smith's second definition of value according to which variable capital and hence surplus value change when the price of labor and hence money profit change. The uniform rate of surplus value then ceases to be a reasonable assumption. What factors then determine the price of labor and profit? Actually both variable capital and surplus value are independent of the price of commodities. These are determined only by labor time. the DFL model thus failed to throw off the shackles of the Sraffa system.

Second, Duménil's elaboration on the laws of value, exchange and surplus value was mistaken. According to Marx, the law of surplus was deduced from the law of value based on a simple commodity economy rather from the law of exchange of capitalism. Seen from another perspective, what could be deduced from the law of exchange of capitalism was profit instead of surplus value. But actually the law of surplus value and exchange were all deduced from the law of value. The point is that the conditions under which the law of surplus value and the law of exchange developed differed from those under which the law of exchange of simple commodity economy and capitalism developed.

Thirdly, the DFL model was unable to discover the source of variable capital and surplus value. It studied transformation within the framework of distribution rather than that of Marx's reproduction diagram. Within Marx's perspective transformation arose from competition among capitalists rather from between capital and labor. The DFL model's treatment thus failed to use the historical method. Worse, the logical method contained some faults.

Fourthly, the MELT, as the theoretical foundation of the DFL model, lacked originality. In *Capital*, the definitions of capital, constant capital and surplus value were all expressed in monetary units. Marx calculated value in monetary units. The definitions of variable capital and surplus value given by Duménil and others stated that variable capital and surplus value could be deduced from money price, which were the diametric opposite to Marx's thesis. Duménil *et al.* argued that their way of treating the transformation problem made the labor theory of value more operable. But in fact, it was impossible. Production price and price are concepts on different levels, it is impossible to measure value using market money price. This was a logical error.

Finally, the DFL model inappropriately excluded constant capital from transformation. But constant capital is indispensable to social reproduction. If it is excluded from transformation, its relationship to production price cannot be properly clarified. Worse, the relationship between total production price and total values cannot be determined, and the reason for the conflict between them cannot be clarified. At the same time, by relying on the MELT to calculate variable capital and surplus value, the DFL model made the verification and validity of the two equalities a natural conclusion. However, the DFL model never directly addressed the issue of whether or not these can be verified. Instead, model avoided the debate on the equalities, which Duménil acknowledged this point.

The DFL model was constructed and proposed by Duménil, Foley and Lipietz and then developed by Glick and Ehrbar (1989), Devine (1990), Mohun (1994) and Campbell (1997). As it had serious flaws, it paled in comparison to the WCR model and the TSSI school.

The WCR Model

Richard D. Wolff, Antonino Callari and Bruce Roberts (1982, 1984) proposed a solution to the transformation problem which we term the WCR model, within the analytical framework of static equilibrium. Their paper *A Marxian Alternative to the Traditional "Transformation Problem"*, published in 1984, made a comparative study of Ricardo and Marx's value theory and then articulated this theory.

220

They suggested that distinguishing Ricardo and Marx's theories was the key to understanding and solving the transformation problem. It was widely believed that there was some degree of continuity in value theory between Marx and Ricardo, since as the theories of both stood in contrast to neo-classical economic theories. However, Wolff, Callari and Roberts argued, Ricardo did not distinguish capitalism as a specific system of social production. Marx distanced his theory of alternative economic systems from that of the classical economists, introducing the concept of labor power as a commodity, and arguing (Wolff *et al.* 1984, 118) that value could be transformed into production price in capitalist societies:

> *Ricardo is known for the attempt to reduce commodity value to a magnitude of physically embodied labor time. For Marx also, value was to be a labor time magnitude, but for Marx the magnitude of labor time expressing a commodity's value was explicitly grounded in the capitalist social conditions of its production, while for Ricardo this magnitude was, in effect, determined by only the technical conditions of production. For Ricardo, commodity value was determined by the quantity of labor time-both living and embodied in the used-up means of production-technically required to produce it (making the usual classical allowances for skilled differentials among the workers). This Ricardian theory of value we call the physical quantity labor theory of value.*

They further pointed out that for Ricardo, the determination of value was purely technological with no further social determination. Ricardo's production theory thus abstracted from the conditions of circulation and distribution.

Marx's approach to determination took into account social processes which is why the starting point of his theory was the creation of surplus value, not use-value. this was different from the classical economists including Ricardo. In studying value and the form of value, Marx argued that production and circulation mutually impacted each other. Unlike Ricardo, he thus took historical conditions into consideration.

Wolff, Callari and Roberts then approached transformation from a logical-mathematical perspective, starting from a unique understanding of constant capital.

They pointed out that in Volume III of Capital circulation conditions had no effect on the living labor component of commodity value, which was, as before, solely determined within the sphere of production. "The question is", they wrote (Wolff *et al.* 1984, 126), "given the processes of production and circulation, what quantity of social labor time associated with the consumed means of production represents the amount socially necessary to reproduce the commodity output as the product of capital" They believed that the magnitude of value was equal to the prices of production of the means of production consumed. This allowed social reproduction to proceed on a normal path. In other words (*ibid*):

> *Under specifically capitalist exchange as well as production conditions, value-form is no longer quantitatively equal to value; to signify this transformation of value-form, 'price of production supplants exchange value as the relevant category....Where commodity exchange-values are transformed into production prices via market exchange of equivalents, this transformation must include those commodities purchased as elements of constant capital. Their prices of production are then incorporated into the value of newly produced output, since those production prices express the labor time now socially necessary to produce that output.*

They recognized that their value theory was significantly different from that of Marx, but, nevertheless sought proof within Marx's theory. Marx pointed out that for the commodity itself, as the result of production process, the gap between its cost-price and value could be filled by considering how constant capital entered the commodity in production. Variable capital, no matter how its value deviated from the cost-price, always contributed a definite amount of labor power to the produce, independent of its compensation. It thus did not affect whether the value of a new commodity was be greater or smaller than its price, it was not that important. In contrast, if a commodity whose value differed from its price was an input to the production process of a new commodity, then the gap between cost-price and value would be transferred to the value of new commodity. Marx's statement illustrated the different ways in which constant and variable capital entered the formation of the values of new commodities. Wolff, Callari and Roberts defended their arguments based on this statement. However, they misinterpreted Marx's original purpose and their viewpoint on the equality between the value of constant capital and price of production was therefore untenable.

First of all, they believed that the value transferred to the new commodity by constant capital is equal to the magnitude of its production price, because social reproduction cannot otherwise proceed, but did not further elaborate on this point. This non-empirical research method was inappropriate here. When value has been transformed into production price, which differs quantitatively from value, can be used to buy back the original magnitude of value and so realize simple social reproduction. We find Wolff, Callari and Roberts's statements ambiguous in this respect.

Secondly, if the value transferred from constant capital is quantitatively equal to prices of production even though commodity values are not equal to prices of production, this implies that constant capital *per se* can have the potential to create value. This would contradict both the labor theory of value and their own understanding of it.

After reinterpreting the value transformation of constant capital, Wolff, Callari and Roberts formally proposed their model.

Assume n single-product industries with no fixed capital. Marx's production prices differ from money prices in their *numéraire*, and the price ratios depend on the n prices of production, each being a definite quantity of social (abstract) labor time per unit of commodity. If we therefore take the kth commodity as *numéraire* we can write:

$$P_j = \rho_j / \rho_k \tag{1}$$

where ρ_k is the *numéraire* and P_j the production price of department j. *Numéraire* prices were clearly not expressed in the labor time units.

We can then write

$A = [a_{ij}]$ for the matrix of physical commodity inputs per unit output;

$L = [L_j]$ for the row vector of direct (living) labor inputs per unit output;

$b = [b_j]$ for the column vector of commodities advanced per unit of direct labor (the 'real wage bundle');

$X = [X_j]$ for the column vector of gross output levels in physical units;

$Y = [Y_j]$ for the column vector of net output levels in physical units, such that ;

$V = [V_j]$ for the row vector of commodity values (value per unit commodity);

$p = [p_j]$ for the row vector of production prices per unit commodity;

$P = [P_j]$ for the row vector of numeraire prices according to Equation 1, with $P_k = 1$;

r for the general rate of profit.

$A, L, b,\ X$ and Y are historically determined and given—the result of capitalists' choices, accumulation, class struggle, and so on. P, p, V and r are endogenous variables. The basic transformation system can be expressed as follows:

$$p = (pA + pbL)\,(1+r) \qquad (2)$$

$$V = pA + L \qquad (3)$$

$$r = (LX - pbLX)\,/\,(pAX + pbLX) \qquad (4)$$

Equation 3 suggests that the value of each commodity should be understood as sum of the prices of production of its means of production and living labor. This is the conclusion of the authors' interpretation of Marx; (4) expresses the general rate of profit, a pure number. The denominator of this equation is the total capital advanced in labor time terms and the numerator is surplus value. Thus the general rate of profit is the ratio of the surplus value to the capital advanced. Clearly, (4) meets the requirement of total profit being equal to total surplus values. If we add 1 to both sides we can obtain:

$$(pAX + pbLX)\,(1+r) = LX + pAX \qquad (5)$$

Applying equations (2) and (3) yields:

$$pX = Vx \qquad (6)$$

Equation 6 shows that total price of production of outputs equals their total value. Therefore, the two equalities are both valid.

Based on our previous comments, we find the following weaknesses:

First, equation 3 is wrong. As we know, the value transferred from constant capital is based on prices of production. This point has been clarified in previous sections.

Next, the general rate of profit in (4) is also wrong. $pbLX$ is the production price of labor-power rather than the value of labor-power. The capitalists demand that workers should reproduce variable capital in accordance with the value of their labor-power rather than its production price. We analyzed this point in our discussion of the dynamic transformation model.

Because of these wrong conclusions, WCR also deduced that the production price of inputs is equal to their total value. This suggests that the magnitude of the value of constant and variable capital is equal to their price of production. So, the total production price of commodities must equal total values. In addition, the calculation of the general rate of profit by equation (4) is correct in form, but wrong in the way it divides living labor into necessary labor and surplus value.

Third, according to equations (2) (3) and(4), when A, L, and X are determined, if b changes, V and ρ will also change. Therefore, according to WCR model, the conclusion could be drawn that commodity value will change as a result of a change in the wage. This is not true. As the wage b changes, production prices may also change. Since the WCR model insists that the magnitude of value transferred by constant capital is equal to its price of production, the change in commodity value should coincide with the change in the production price of the commodity and wage, according to equation (3).

Wolff, Callari and Roberts correctly pointed out the differences between Marx's value theory and neoclassical theory, as well as Ricardo's value theory. At the same time they also articulated important implications of Marx's theory of production price. However, they set as their goal the verification of the two invariant equations from the outset. Moreover, they misanalyzed the problems arising from the fact that constant capital transfers value while variable capital creates it, their conclusions being based on shaky foundations. They thus lacked a deeper understanding of the concept of value and the fact that living labor is the only source of value. Consequently, they failed to grasp the essence of the transformation problem, nor did they integrate historical, logical analysis with static and dynamic analysis.

The TSS school and transformation theory

The solutions to the transformation problem proposed by TSS scholars [1]have captured wide attention in academia. However, the TSS school has not clarified the transformation problem from a logical perspective because, according to TSS scholars, a proper understanding of the implications of value theory, the cornerstone of Marxist philosophy, should precede any solution to the transformation problem. Therefore, a unique point raised by TSS school was to provide new interpretations for the theory of value. Ernst (1982), Carchedi (1986), Kliman & McGlone (1988，1999), Giussani (1991), Freeman (1995, 2010), Maldonado Filho (1994), Ramos (1995), Freeman, Kliman and Wells (2001)[2] are widely recognized to have made a valuable contribution to the development of the thought of the TSS school. Among these, Freeman and Kliman were two key actors.

Revision of the concept of value by TSS school

The TSS school argued that value and price should be defined in accordance with the following the first order difference equation:

$$\lambda_{t+1} = P_t A + L \tag{7}$$

$$P_{t+1} = P_t A + L + g_t \tag{8}$$

In this equation, λ, P, A and L denote vectors of values, price, the input-output matrix and labor input respectively. The subscript t denotes period of

---

1   The term 'Temporal Single System' or 'TSS' was first suggested to Andrew Kliman by Gil Skillman and adopted by Kliman in 1995 and after that by all TSS scholars. Freeman previously called it Sequential Non-dualism. However, the two terminologies conveyed the same idea. Kliman (2007) also explained that the approach should be termed TSSI rather than TSS, standing for 'Temporal Single System Interpretation' to clarify that it was an interpretation of Marx, not an attempt to define a new theory. This has passed into general usage.
2   Editor's note: most early TSSI works are available at the IWGVT website www.copejournal.com. Kliman and Potts (2015) have reprinted some of the key debates.

time (a discrete variable) and g denotes the vector of value-price deviations. Thus the centerpiece of the TSS school's philosophy is as follows:

a. The value of the capital advanced at an earlier time depends on the prices, not the values, of the inputs. This is exactly what the term 'single-system' implies. Kliman (1996) argued that from the perspective of Marx, value and price were determined interdependently. On the one hand, the prices of inputs play a role in determining the values of outputs; on the other hand, the value profit rate may also play a role in determining the prices of outputs.

b. Price and value magnitudes were determined in historical time rather than simultaneously. The value of a commodity can be decreased to zero by being consumed. Inputs and values and prices (including prices of production) of outputs are different. This is the meaning of the concept of 'temporal' system.

c. All Marx's contested conclusions can be deduced from (1) and (2). For example, the two equations can both hold, and the rate of profit continues to fall.

The TSS school argued that their interpretations can be best understood as a 'reclaiming' of Marx's theory rather than a completely new theory. However, the definition of value given by the TSS school is significantly different from Marx's labor theory of value. Not surprisingly, the reinvention of the concept of value by the TSS school provoked disapproval from Fred Moseley (1993), Gerard Duménil & Dominique Levy (2001), and others.

Important weak points inherent in the definition of value can be found, based on the three hypotheses proposed by the TSS school.

First and foremost, the TSS school simplified the concept of value, failing to distinguish value from price. According to them, the value of capital advanced at an earlier time determines the price of inputs. This argument negates the objectivity of value and also the fact that labor is the source of value. The TSS school thus did not develop a correct understanding of value, nor did it distinguish it from prices of production and prices. In sum, the TSS school shows less adherence to Marx's concept of value than it claims.

Secondly, it is meaningless to discuss value magnitudes at different points of time in history. Value can only be defined used for comparative purpose under given social conditions. At times in history, the S & T level and labor productivity are different.

Thirdly, the TSS analysis of the value of capital is contradictory. On the one hand, they believed that changes in value magnitudes are independent of technological advance and increases in labor productivity. But on the other hand, they believe that the value of capital advanced is determined by the spot prices of inputs. However, at different points of time in history, price are different. Their variation depends on the supply and demand of inputs. the TSS dynamic analytical method therefore failed to provide any convincing points, nor level effective criticism at the WCR model and the static analysis of neo-Ricardian school.

Next, will analyze the key points outlined by the TSS school from different perspectives.

Value and price determination and concept of time

The validity of the 'single-system' approach is based on the value equation (9):

$$\lambda = PA + L \tag{9}$$

This defines the value of constant capital as its price. Value and price are thus placed in a single equation. Obviously, TSS borrowed the implications of the MELT. The DFL model in contrast applies the MELT only to variable capital. Like the WCR model, the single-system analysis applies it to constant capital.

However, Marx never believed that the value of a commodity equaled its price of production. To support Marx's argument, we offer two points for consideration. The first is that the organic compositions of the units producing constant capital equal the socially average organic compositions, and the second is that the value of constant value is determined by prices. Obviously, the first point is not in general a requirement, but the second concerns the definition of the concept of value, which can be viewed as a subversion of the centerpiece of labor theory of value.

The TSS school further argue that the gap between prices of production and value arising from the gap between profits and surplus value, raised by Marx, can be answered by the single-system approach. Marx's argument rests

228

on the assumption that the prices of production of inputs are unchanged, just as the static transformation model states. In this case, the gap between the price of production and the value of a single commodity is the gap between profit and surplus value. They argue that if inputs are included in prices of production, then the gap between prices of production and values of inputs will impact the gap between the prices of production and values of outputs. However, TSS bases its defense of Marx's arguments on the validity of equations (7) and (8). Paradoxically, the validity of these two equations is based on the revision of Marx's concept of value and prices of production.

The TSS scholars believed that the single-system was insufficient to prove all of Marx's arguments, particularly that about the tendency of the profit rate to fall. To correct this deficiency, the temporal system should be adopted. they thus defined the concept of value by referring to (7) and (8). To validate the two equalities, they defined the concept of value in historical time. As this value is created by living labor in previous periods of time, it makes the two equations appear somewhat contradictory.

To elaborate on this issue, we assume that a certain economy only produces a certain type of commodity X under the following technological conditions:

1 unit of commodity + 1 unit of labor ≥ 1 unit of commodity

Equation (7) then becomes

$$\lambda_{t+1} = aP_t + l = a\lambda_t + l \qquad (7')$$

Let us assume the initial value $P_0 = \lambda_0$. The value of period is then

$$\lambda_t = [P_0 - l / (1 - a)] \, a^t + l / (1 - a) \qquad (10)$$
$$P_0 a^t + (1 - a^t) / (1 - a)$$

In this 'single' system, the productivity requirement is that $a<1$, or $\lambda<1$ could be meaningless. However, the temporal system proposed by the TSS school did not require this productivity factor since $\lambda_t = P_{t-1}A + L$, and λ_t is always positive as long as $P_{t-1}>0$. This can be viewed as a strong point of the TSS school (Kliman & McGlone, 1999). However although the joint system boasts this strong point, it fails to solve another issue raised by Marx which was when the labor input decreased, the value magnitude of a commodity falls. Based on equation (10), we find that when $a>1$, the value magnitude of a commodity tends to infinity. This is a mistaken hypothesis. As we have noted earlier, it is essentially meaningless to examine the value magnitudes of the same commodity in different point of time in history under different social production conditions.

Freeman (1999) argued that the validity of the concept of time formulated by TSS was dependent on a correct understanding of 'spot costs' rather than the revision of the concept of value. But the real fact is not so.

Matrix A denoted that the inputs of constant capital were purchased during the end of period t (or during the early period $t+1$) at the price of P_t. However, during the end of the period $t+1$, constant capital could not be purchased at the price of P_t on one condition which is $P_t = P_{t+1}$. In other words, P_t is no longer an actual price but a price in the accounting sense. Therefore, the 'spot costs' must be calculated based on $(1+\rho) P_t$ rather than P_t. Among these, ρ denoted the time factor determined by the rate of price increase and the rate of labor productivity. Therefore, equation (7) can be changed into the following equation:

$$\lambda_{t+1} = (1+\rho) P_t A + L \tag{7''}$$

equation (7) and(7'') we find that very clearly TSS hypothesized $\rho = 0$.

From this perspective, the temporal system and the single system proposed by the TSS school are mutually contradictory.

The TSS school emerged as an antithesis of the redundant labor theory of value formulated by Samuelson and Steedman. However, the TSS school failed to give strong criticism to Samuelson and Steedman's hypothesis as suggested by Equation 7:

$$\lambda_{t+1} - \lambda_t = (P_t - P_{t-1}) A \tag{11}$$

As suggested by equation (11) the evolution of value magnitudes from period t to period was only determined by the technological factors and the prices of inputs. It clearly contradicts the TSS hypothesis that the determination of value was a prerequisite for the determination of price.

Conclusion

The TSS school argued that in accordance with the temporal and single-system approach, all Marx's arguments could be tested and finally proved. From this perspective, the approach is more acceptable than other transformation theories since Bortkiewicz's solution. However, it may not be appropriate for TSS school to modify the conceptualization of value. In practice, TSS theory was an application of the MELT. The difference was that MELT was applied to define the value of constant capital. The application of MELT was different than DFL model but was more or less similar to WCR model.

Based on our previous analysis, we argue that the reconceptualization of value by TSS school is inappropriate and it a fundamental deviation from Marx's labor theory of value. At the same time the temporal system and single system aspects of the approach contradict each other. As a result, the criticisms leveled by the TSS school appeared less powerful.

References

Note: the authors of this book cited many Chinese translations of Western titles. The convention that we have tried to follow is to cite the original Western versions where they are the source of quotes or where they are standard works, especially Marxist works, but to cite the Chinese versions where it is important to recognize that the authors consulted these in translation. In some cases, these two requirements conflict. Therefore, whilst we have taken every precaution, on some occasions the page numbers cited in the text may not correspond to those in the English editions.

Aglietta, M. (1979), *A Theory of Capitalist Regulation: The US Experience.* London: New Left Books.

Arthur C.J. 2008. 'Systematic Dialectic: Against the Logical-Historical Method: Dialectical Derivation versus Linear Logic'. In Ollman B., Smith T. (eds) *Dialectics for the New Century.* Palgrave Macmillan, London

Bai, B. 1999. *Value and Price Theory.* [In Chinese.] Beijing: China Economic Press.

Bai, B. 2002. *Hot Topics in Value of Labor.* [In Chinese.] Beijing: Economic Science Press.

Barkai, Haim. 1965. Ricardo's Static Equilibrium, *Economica* 32, no. 125,15-31.

Barkai, Haim. 1967. A Note on Ricardo's Notions of Demand, *Economica* 34, no. 133,75-79.

Baumol, W. 1974. "The transformation of value: what Marx 'really' meant – an interpretation." *Journal of Economic Literature*, vol. 12, no. 1, pp. 51–62.

Blaug, M. 1979. *Economic Theory in Retrospect*, 3rd edn. Cambridge: Cambridge University Press.

Bortkiewicz, L. von (1906[1952]), 'Value and Price in the Marxian System'(part I), in *International Economic Papers,* 1952(2), 5-60. Originally published in two parts in German as 'Wertrechnung und Preisrechnung im Marxschen System'(part I), *Archiv für Sozialwissenschaft und Sozialpolitik,* Band XXIII (I), July 1906; (parts II and III) *Archiv für Sozialwissenschaft und Sozialpolitik,* Band XXV, July and September 1907.

Bortkiewicz, L. von (1907[1984]), 'On the Correction of Marx's Fundamental Theoretical Construction in the Third Volume of *Capital',* in Sweezy (1949), German edition 'Zur Berichtigung der grundlengenden theoretischen Konstruktion von Marx im dritten Band des *Kapital',* *Jahrbücher für Nationalökonomie und Statistik,* Serie 3, Band XXIV, July 1907.

Brewer, A. 1995. 'A Minor Post-Ricardian? Marx as an Economist'. *History of Political Economy* 27:1 (1995), pp 112-115

Campbell, A. 1997. 'The transformation problem: a simple presentation of the "new solution"'. *Review of Radical Political Economics,* vol. 29, no. 3.

Copernicus, Nicolaus. 1543 [1995] *On the Revolutions of Heavenly Spheres.* (*De Revolutionibus Orbium Coelestium*). Amherst, N.Y: Prometheus Books.

Desai, M. 1974. *Marxian Economic Theory.* London: Gray-Mills.

Desai, Radhika. 2013. *Geopolitical Economy: After US Hegemony, Globalization and Empire.* London: Pluto Press.

Devine, J. 1990. 'The Utility of Value: the "New Solution", Unequal Exchange, and Crisis. *Research in Political Economy.* Volume 12, pp 21-39.

Dickinson, H. D. 1956. A comment on Meek's 'Note on the transformation problem.' *Economic Journal,* Dec, pp. 740–1.

Ding, Baojun. 1995. 'Was Marx only halfway?' [In Chinese.] *Beijing Social Sciences,* no. 1, pp. 35–48.

Ding, Baojun. 1999 'Studies on the transformation problem.' [In Chinese.] *Social Science in China,* no. 5, pp. 21–36.

Ding, Baojun. 2001. 'A review of Sraffa's price theory.' [In Chinese.] *Contemporary Economic Studies,* no. 1, pp. 19–22.

Dmitriev, V.K. (1898) 'The theory of value of David Ricardo', in Dmitriev (1974).

Dmitriev, V.K. (1968), *Economiceski ocerki*. Moscow 1898. Published in French in 1904 as *Essais économiques: Esquisse de synthèse organique de la théorie de la valeur-travail et de la théorie de l'utilité marginale*, republished 1968. Paris: Éditions du Centre de la Recherche Scientifique.

Dmitriev, V.K. (1974), *Economic Essays on Value, Competition and Utility* (ed. D. M. Nuti) Cambridge: Cambridge University Press.

Dobb, M. 1955. 'A note on the transformation problem,' in *Economic Theory and Socialism*. London: Routledge & Kegan Paul.

Dobb, M. 1973. *Theories of Value and Distribution Since Adam Smith*. London: Cambridge University Press.

Dobb, M. 2014 [1937] *Political Economy and Capitalism: Some Essays in Economic Tradition*. London: Routledge.

Dow, Sheila C. *Macroeconomic Thought: A Methodological Approach*. New edition. Oxford: Blackwell Pub, 1987.

Dumenil, G. 1980. *Valeur aux Prix de Production*. Paris: Economica.

Duménil, G. 1983. 'Beyond the transformation riddle: a labor theory of value.' *Science and Society*, vol. 4, pp. 427–34.

Dzarasov, Ruslan. 2013. *The Conundrum of Russian Capitalism: The Post-Soviet Economy in the World System*. London: Pluto Press.

Earle, Joe, Cahal Moran, Zach Ward-Perkins, and Mick Moran. 2016. *The Econocracy: The Perils of Leaving Economics to the Experts*. Manchester: Manchester University Press.

Foley, D. 1982. 'The value of money, the value of labor power and the Marxian transformation problem'. *Review of Radical Political Economics*, vol. 4, no. 2.

Freeman, A. 1995. "Marx without equilibrium." *Capital and Class*, vol. 19, issue 2.

Freeman, A. 2000. 'Marxian Debates on the Falling Rate of Profit - a primer'. https://www.academia.edu/6997022/Marxian_Debates_on_the_Falling_Rate_of_Profit_-_a_primer. Accessed June 29, 2019.

Freeman, A.2006. 'An Invasive Metaphor: the Concept of Centre of Gravity in Economics'. www.academia.edu/11692549/

An_Invasive_Metaphor_the_Concept_of_Centre_of_Gravity_in_ Economics. Accessed July 5, 2019.

Freeman, A. 2007. [2007b]'Heavens Above: What Equilibrium Means for Economics' in Mosini, V. (ed) (2007) *Equilibrium in Economics: Scope and Limits*, London: Routledge.

Freeman, A. 2009. 'Why does the US Profit Rate Fall? A response to Brenner.' https://www.academia.edu/175987/What_makes_the_US_profit_ rate_fall. Accessed 29 June 2019

Freeman, A. 2010. 'Marxism Without Marx: notes towards a critique'. *Capital and Class* 34, vol 1. pp84-97, December 2010.

Freeman, A. 2010. [2010e]'Trends in Value Theory since 1881'. *World Review of Political Economy*. Vol 1., No. 4. December 2010.

Freeman, A. 2019a. 'The sixty-year downward trend of economic growth in the industrialised countries of the world'. Geopolitical Economy Research Group Data Project Working Paper #2, January 2019. https://www.academia. edu/38192121/The_sixty-year_downward_trend_of_economic_growth_in_ the_industrialised_countries_of_the_world. Accessed 29 June 2019

Freeman, A. 2019b. 'Divergence, Bigger Time: The unexplained persistence, growth, and scale of postwar international inequality'. Geopolitical Economy Research Group Data Project Working Paper #2, March 2019. https://www.academia.edu/39074969/Divergence_Bigger_ Time_The_unexplained_persistence_growth_and_scale_of_postwar_ international_inequality. Accessed 29 June 2019.

Freeman, A. and Carchedi, G. (eds) 1996. *Marx and Non-Equilibrium Economics*. Cheltenham: Edward Elgar.

Freeman, A. Kliman and J. Wells. 2001. *The New Value Controversy in Economics*. Cheltenham: Edward Elgar, 2001.

Freeman, A., A. Kliman and J. Wells 2007.*The New Value Controversy in Economics.* Aldershot and London: Edward Elgar

Fullbrook, Edward, Peter Earl, Jeroen van Bouwel, Yanis Varoufakis, J. E. King, Mohamed Aslam Haneef, Thomas Mayer, et al. *Pluralist Economics*. 1 edition. Zed Books, 2013.

Giussani, P. 1991. 'The Determination of Prices of Production', *International Journal of Political Economy*, Vol 21, Winter (1991-1992), pp67-87.

Glick, M. and H.Ehrbar. 1987. 'The Transformation Problem: An Obituary'. *Australian Economic Papers*. 1987, December,, pp294-317.

He, Y., and Liu, L. 2002. "Evaluating time of labor by money: elaboration and comment." [In Chinese.] *Teaching and Research*, no. 5, pp. 33–36.

Heath, Thomas Little, and Aristarchus of Samos. 1913 [2014]. *Aristarchus of Samos, the Ancient Copernicus ; a History of Greek Astronomy to Aristarchus, Together with Aristarchus's Treatise on the Sizes and Distances of the Sun and Moon : A New Greek Text with Translation and Notes*. Oxford : Clarendon Press. Reprinted free online by Cambridge University Press in 2014

Heinrich, Michael. 2013. 'Crisis Theory, the Law of the Tendency of the Profit Rate to Fall, and Marx's Studies in the 1870s'. *Monthly Review* 64:11, April.

Hicks, .J. R. 'Mr. Keynes and the "Classics"; A Suggested Interpretation'. *Econometrica* Vol. 5, No. 2 (Apr., 1937), pp. 147-159 (13 pages)

Howard, M. C. and Ian Bradley (eds). 1982. *Classical and Marxian Political Economy: Essays in Honour of Ronald L. Meek*. Basingstoke, UK: Macmillan.

Howard, M. C., and King, J. 1985. *The Political Economy of Marx*. London: Longman.

Hu, Daiguang. (ed.). 1990. *Studies on Marx's Capital Theory by Contemporary Western Scholars*. [In Chinese.] Beijing: China Economic Press.

Hu, Daiguang. 1988. *Review of Western Economic Theories and Econometrics*. [In Chinese.] Beijing: Economic Science Press.

Hunt, E.K. and Jesse G. Schwartz (eds). 1972. *Critique of Economic Theory*. Harmondsworth, UK: Penguin Books

Junankar, P. N. 1982. *Marx's Economics*. Oxford: Philip Allan.

King, S. 2018. 'Lenin's theory of imperialism: a defence of its relevance in the 21st century'. https://www.academia.edu/17135368/Lenin_s_theory_of_imperialism_a_defence_of_its_relevance_in_the_21st_century. Accessed 29 June 2019.

Kliman, A. 2007. *Reclaiming Marx's Capital: A Refutation of the Myth of Inconsistency.* Lanham, MD: Lexington Books.

[2013q]Kliman, A. Alan Freeman, Nick Potts, Brendan Cooney and Alexei Gusev. 2017.'The Unmaking of Marx's Capital: Heinrich's Attempt to Eliminate Marx's Crisis Theory'. https://www.academia.edu/4106981/The_Unmaking_of_Marxs_Capital_Heinrichs_Attempt_to_Eliminate_Marxs_Crisis_Theory. Accessed 27 June 2019.

Kliman, A. and McGlone, T. 1988. 'The Transformation nonProblem and the nonTransformation Problem', *Capital and Class*, 35, Summer, pp5683.

Kliman, A. and N. Potts. (eds) 2015. *Is Marx's Theory of Profit Right? The Simultaneist–Temporalist Debate.* Lanham, MD: Rowman and Littlefield.

Kliman, A. and T McGlone. 1996. 'One system or two? The transformation of values into prices of production versus the transformation problem'. In Freeman, A. and G. Carchedi (eds.) 1996, pp 29-48

Kliman, A., and McGlone, T. 1999. 'A temporal single-system interpretation of Marx's value theory'. *Review of Political Economy*, vol. 11, no. 1.

Kotz, D., and Fred Weir. 1997. *Revolution From Above: The Demise of the Soviet System.* London and New York: Routledge

Kuhn, Thomas S. 1966. *The Structure of Scientific Revolutions.* (1st ed.) University Of Chicago Press.

Kuhne, K. 1979. *Economics and Marxism.* Basingstoke, UK: Macmillan.

Laibman, D. 1973. 'Values and Prices of Production: The political economy of the transformation problem' *Science and Society* 37:4

Laibman, D. 1983. cited in *The Japanese Data Compiler Center of the Chinese Research Association.*

Lipietz, A. 1982. 'The so-called 'transformation problem' revisited.' *Journal of Economic Theory*, vol. 26, no. 1, pp. 59–88.

Maldonado-Filho, E (1994), 'Release and Tying up of Productive Capital and the "Transformation Problem"', URPE conference at the ASSA, fall 1994. http://copejournal.com/release-and-tying-up-of-productive-capital-and-the-transformation-problem-eduardo-maldonado-filho/. Accessed June 20, 2019.

Mandel, E. 1974. *An Introduction to Marxist Economic Theory*, 2nd edn. London: Pathfinder.

Mandel, E. 1979. *An Introduction to Marxist Economic Theory*. [In Chinese.] Beijing: Commercial Press.

Marx, K. 1857 [1964]. *A Contribution to the Critique of Political Economy*. Moscow: Progress Publishers.

Marx, K. 1867 [1965]. *Capital*, vol. 1. Moscow: Progress Publishers.

Marx, K. 1875 [1971] *Critique of the Gotha Programme*. Moscow: Progress Publishers.

Marx, K. 1894 [1965]. *Capital*, vol. 3. Moscow: Progress Publishers

Marx, K. 1962. *Poverty of Philosophy*. [In Chinese.] People's Publishing House.

Marx, K., and Engels, F. 1972a. *Selection of Karl Marx and Frederick Engels*, vol. 2. [In Chinese.] People's Publishing House.

Marx, K., and Engels, F. 1974. *Karl Marx and Frederick Engels*, vol. 26(Ⅲ). [In Chinese.] People's Publishing House.

Marx, K., and Engels, F. 1979b. *Karl Marx and Frederick Engels*, vol. 46(I). [In Chinese.] People's Publishing House.

Marx, K., and Engels, F. 1996. *Karl Marx and Frederick Engels*, vol. 35. New York: International Publishers.

May, K. 1948. 'Value and production price: a note on Winternitz' solution.' *Economic Journal*, vol. 58, no. 232, pp. 596–9.

Meek, R. 1956a. 'Some notes on the transformation problem'. *Economic Journal*, vol. 66 (March), p96.

Meek, R. 1956b. *Studies in the Labor Theory of Value*. New York: Monthly Review Press.

Meek, R. 1975. *Studies in the Labor Theory of Value (second edition)*. New York: Monthly Review Press.

Meek, R. 1977. *Smith, Marx and After*. London: Chapman & Hall.

Meek, R. 1982. 'From values to prices: was Marx's journey really necessary?' In *Smith, Marx, and After: Ten essays in the development of economic thought*. New York: Springer, pp. 12-33.

Mirowski, Philip. 1991. *More Heat than Light: Economics as Social Physics, Physics as Nature's Economics*. Reprint edition. Cambridge: Cambridge University Press, 1991.

Mohun, S. (1994). 'A re(in)statement of the labor theory of value'. *Cambridge Journal of Economics, 18*, 391–412.

Morishima, M. 1973. '*Marx's Economics: A dual theory of value and growth*.' Cambridge: Cambridge University Press.

Morishima, M., and George C. Catephores. 1978. *Value Exploitation and Growth*. New York: McGraw-Hill.

Moseley, Fred. 2017. *Money and Totality: A Macro-Monetary Interpretation of Marx's Logic in Capital and the End of the "Transformation Problem."* Reprint edition. Chicago, Ill: Haymarket Books.

Okishio, Nobuo. 1961. 'Technical Changes and the Rate of Profit', *Kobe University Economic Review* 7. pp 86-99.

Okishio, Nobuo. 1974. 'Value and Production Price', *Kobe University Economic Review* (in English)

Parijs, Phillipe van. 1980. 'The Falling-Rate-of-Profit Theory of Crisis: A Rational Reconstruction by Way of Obituary'. *Review of Radical Political Economy* 12.

Ramos, A. (1995) 'The Monetary Expression of Labour: Marx's Twofold Measure of Value'. Mini-conference of the International Working Group on Value Theory (IWGVT) at the Eastern Economic Association. http://copejournal.com/wp-content/uploads/2017/02/Ramos-The-Monetary-Expression-of-Labour-Marxs-Twofold-Measure-of-Value.pdf. Accessed June 29, 2019.

Ramos, A. and A. Rodriguez. (1996) 'Money, the postulates of invariance and the transformation of Marx into Ricardo'. In Freeman and Carchedi (1996)

Ramos-Martinez, A. 1995. 'The Monetary Expression of Labour: Marx's Twofold Measure of Value'. http://copejournal.com/wp-content/uploads/2017/02/Ramos-The-Monetary-Expression-of-Labour-Marxs-Twofold-Measure-of-Value.pdf

Ramos-Martínez, A. and Rodríguez-Herrera, A. 1996. 'The Transformation of Values into Prices of Production: A different reading of Marx's text', in Freeman and Carchedi (1996)

Robinson, J. 1960. *Essay on Marxian Economics*. London: McMillan.

Rosdolsky, R. 1982. Marxist-Leninist Institute of Chinese Academy of Social Sciences

Ross, J. (n.d.) *Learning from China* website. https://www.learningfromchina.net/

Samuelson, P. 1957. 'Wages and interest: a modern dissection of Marxian economic models.' *American Economic Review*, vol. 47, no. 6, pp. 884–912.

Samuelson, P. 1971. 'Evaluation of the research of the contemporary western scholars on *Das Kapital*.' *Journal of Economic Literature*. Issue 6.

Seton, F. 1957. 'The transformation Problem.' *Review of Economic Studies*, vol. 24, pp. 149–60.

Shaikh, A. 1977. 'Marx's Theory of Value and the 'Transformation Problem'', in J. Schwartz, *The Subtle Anatomy of Capitalism*. Santa Monica, CA: Goodyear).

Shaikh, A. 1984. 'Transformation from Marx to Sraffa, in E. Mandel and A. Freeman (eds.), *Ricardo, Marx, Sraffa*. New York: Verso.

Shaikh, A., 1990. 'The Poverty of Algebra', *the Debate on Value*. Beijing: The Commercial Press

Sraffa, P. 1960. *Production of Commodities by Means of Commodities: Prelude to a critique of economic theory*. Cambridge: Cambridge University Press.

Steedman, I. (ed.) 1981. *The Value Controversy*. London: Verso.

Steedman, I. 1977. *Marx after Sraffa*. London: NLB and Verso.

Stigler, George J. 1965. Textual Exegesis as a Scientific Problem, *Economica* 32, no.128,447-50.

Sweezy, P. (ed.) 1949. *Karl Marx and the Close of His System by Eugen von Böhm-Bawerk and Böhm-Bawerk's Criticism of Marx by Rudolf Hilferding*. New York: Augustus M. Kelly.

Sweezy, P. 1993[1942]. *The Theory of Capitalist Development: Principles of Marxian political economy*. New York: Monthly Review Press.

Winternitz, J. 1948. 'Value and prices: a solution of the so-called transformation problem.' *Economics Journal*, vol. 58, no. 230, pp. 276–80.

Wolff, R., Roberts, B. and Callari, A. 1982. 'Marx's (not Ricardo's) "Transformation Problem": A Radical Reconceptualization'. *History of Political Economy*, Vol 14 No. 4., pp 564-582.

Wolff, R., Roberts, B. and Callari, A. 1984. 'A Marxian Alternative to the Traditional "Transformation Problem"' in *Review of Radical Political Economics*, Vol 16(2/3) 115-135 (1984).

Yan. Z. 2001. 'Revisiting Marx's labor theory of value.' [In Chinese.] *Developments of Economics*, no. 3, pp. 18–22.

Yue, Hongzhi. 2002. 'A restudy of the transformation issue'. [In Chinese.] *Contemporary Economic Studies*, no. 10, pp. 41–5.

Zhang, L. 1988. *The General Theories on Political Economics*. [In Chinese.] Sichuan Social Science Press.

Zhu, Z. 1991. *Studies in Marxist Economic Theories by Western Scholars*. [In Chinese.] Shanghai: Shanghai People's Press.

Further reading

Bai, B. 2001. "The duality of the category of labor and production in Marxist philosophy and its unification." [In Chinese.] *Contemporary Economic Studies*, no. 5, pp. 5–11.

Bai, B. 2003. *Labor and Value of Wealth*. [In Chinese.] Beijing: China Economic Press.

Cheng, E., and L. Hu (eds). 2002. *Methodology in Economics*. [In Chinese.] Shanghai Finance and Economics University Press.

Ding, Baojun. 2000. 'Defending Marx's labor theory of value, ' pp. 238–49 in J. Hu and J. Fan (eds), *Deepening Understanding of Labor Theory of Value*. [In Chinese.] Beijing: Economic Science Press.

Ding, Baojun. 2002. 'On broadening the scope of application of the labor theory of value,' in J. Hu. and J. Fan (eds.), *Issues in Deepening the Cognition of the Labor Theory of Value*. [In Chinese.] Publishing House of Economic Science.

Hu, D. 1988. *Review of Western Economic Theories and Econometrics*. [In Chinese.] Beijing: Economic Science Press.

Hu, J. 2001. 'Understanding Marx's labor theory of value.' [In Chinese.] *Internal Circulation*, no. 9, pp. 5–7.

Hu, J., and Fan, J. (eds.). 2001. *Deepening the Understanding of Labor and Theory of Labor and Value*. [In Chinese.] Beijing: Economic Science Press.

Hu, J., and Fan, J. (eds.). 2002. *Some Key Issues during the Process in Deepening the Understanding of Labor Theory of Value*. [In Chinese.] Beijing: Economic Science Press.

Meek, R. 1967. *Economics and Ideology and Other Essays: Studies in the development of economic thought*. London: Chapman & Hall.

Meek, R. 1979. *Smith, Marx, and After: Ten essays in the development of economic thought*. New York: Springer.

Samuelson, P. 1987. *Economics*, 2nd edn. New York: McGraw-Hill.

Samuelson. 1957. 'Wage and Interest: A Modern Analysis of Marxian Economic Model.' [In Chinese.] *The American Economic Review*, no. 12: 888.

Yan, P. 2002. 'A review and reflections on the debate about labor theory of value,' In *Deepening Understanding of Labor Theory of Value*, edited by J. Hu., and J. Fan.

Yan, P. 2002. 'How to understand labor and the labor theory of value: pros, cons and reconstruction,' in H. Jun and F. Jianxin (eds), *Deepening Understanding of the Labor Theory of Value*. [In Chinese.] Beijing: Economic Science Press.

Zhang, L. 2001. "Labor creating value cannot be the basis of creating an income distribution system." *Introduction to Teaching Thoughts and Theory*, issue 7, pp. 34–6.

Zhang, L. 2002. "Understanding and developing labor theory of value," in H. Jun and F. Jianxin (eds.), *Deepening Understanding of the Labor Theory of Value*. [In Chinese.] Beijing: Economic Science Press.

Zhu, F. 2001. 'A paradox in the labor theory of value and its explanations.' [In Chinese.] *Jiangsu Social Sciences*, no. 4, pp. 1–6.

Zhu, S. 2000. *Classic Economics and Modern Economics*. [In Chinese.] Beijing: Beijing University Press.